WALK

WALKING AWAY

A FILM-MAKER'S AFRICAN JOURNAL

Charlotte Metcalf

Edited by Gordon Medcalf

published by Eye Books

Walking Away
1st Edition
October 2003

Published by Eye Books Ltd
51a Boscombe Rd
London
W12 9HT
Tel/fax: +44 (0) 20 8743 3276
website: www.eye-books.com

Set in Frutiger and Garamond
ISBN: 1903070201

British Library Cataloguing in Publication Data
A catalogue record for this book is available from the British Library

Cover photograph with kind permission of Michael Keating
Author photograph by Matt Holyoak

In loving memory of
Peter Parker
who was the first to encourage me to write this book

Acknowledgements

Thanks to:

Michael Keating for showing me Africa in the first place; Robert Lamb and Jenny Richards for sending me on all those African assignments that make up much of this book; Hugh Phillimore for his patience, support and faith in the book; Roly Williams for introducing me to Eye Books; Gordon Medcalf, my saintly and inspired editor; Dan Hiscocks, my publisher whose enthusiasm and patience are limitless; finally to all the Africans who so generously allowed me into their lives and whose stories form the heart of this book.

Contents

Foreword by Lenny Henry

One of the downsides of being an 'International Megastar' is the constant begging and demands on my time. I thought once I had started doing Comic Relief people would leave me alone thinking ... "That Lenny - he's a good chap doing his bit."

Eye Books chased me hard in order to get me to write this foreword. They kept on saying how the book gets away from clichés and gets under the skin of Africa's real problems, away from the perceived ones. How it highlights the seriousness of the problems whilst being an antidote to cynicism because it shows how the people are clearly so capable if given the chance.

They also banged on about how in the same way that I appeal to many millions to do something, however small, that will make a massive difference to the receiver, I should take some of my own medicine and realise that me supporting this book was doing what I asked of others on Red Nose Day. A small something that could make a BIG difference.

Having now read Charlotte's book I realise they were right and offer my wholehearted support. *Walking Away* vividly brings to life some of the real issues facing Africa. It also celebrates the amazing spirit of the African people.

This is an important book. Hopefully it will show people why we do what we do and inspire some who read it to go out and make a difference, to do something positive to help this beautiful continent. Too many just walk away.

"The best part of the job is when you feel you may have made a difference.
The hardest part is when you have to walk away".

Charlotte Metcalf
London, 2002

RELEVANT COUNTRIES WITHIN THE AFRICAN CONTINENT

PRELUDE TO ADVENTURE

Drums throb and the crowd coils round a group of dancing women, shaking their shoulders and hips in a sensuous frenzy. Those closest to the dancers clap with rhythmic intensity, echoing the insistent beat of the drums. The women pant and sweat, though it is cool and a grey sky hangs low over the plain like a damp dishcloth.

Bill, the cameraman, and I work our way through the throng, pushing into a breathing, pulsating wall of flesh. We reach the dancers in the centre. Someone has gone to fetch the bride. The drumming and the dancing become more frantic.

The father of the bride is a tall, skeletal man in a ragged jacket. He grins proudly, showing a mouthful of rotten teeth glinting with metal. He stands with his daughter in front of him, his hands protectively on her shoulders. The bride wears an exquisitely embroidered white, woven dress and heavy silver jewellery with custard-coloured amber beads. Black kohl is smudged round her eyes.

She looks at the dancers, then at us and spots the camera. Her father pushes her towards us. Her mouth quivers and she begins to cry. She opens her mouth and bawls. Tears pour down her face in inky streams. The weeping bride is just four years old.

I am appalled. What are we doing here, with our intrusive camera, prying into another alien culture we barely understand and adding to the misery of this frightened child? How has my erratic path led me inexorably to this throbbing clearing in the Ethiopian uplands?

The trail begins twelve years before, the day I first arrive in Kenya...

The plane doors open, and in surges the fire-hot smell of Africa

– woodsmoke, charred meat, rancid butter, leather, sweat and dung. I breathe it in and step out into the glare, the heat and a chapter of my life that is to change me in more ways than I can imagine.

It begins inauspiciously. I eat Brown Windsor soup, boiled fish with overcooked vegetables and tapioca pudding in the panelled dining car of the night train to Mombasa. At Watamu Beach on the Indian Ocean I slather myself in locally produced suntan oil and spend three days in bed with acute sunburn. Thus I learn the first important lesson about Africa, that the sun is vicious and malignantly potent.

Things improve rapidly. I fly in a tiny plane to Lamu, a somnolent, golden island off the north Swahili coast, fragrant with spice, jasmine and charcoal. There I lie in a hammock and watch wooden sailing dhows glide past on a lacquer-smooth sea luminous as mother-of-pearl in the setting sun, while the cry of the *muezzin* mingles with the early evening woodsmoke as it drifts up to my rooftop from the mosque below.

I plunge deep into the bush to stay at George Adamson's camp, where each night lions gather to be fed. George looks like a Biblical prophet. Long white hair and beard frame a narrow El Greco face from which blazes a pair of shrewd blue eyes. He wears nothing but a loin cloth on a sagging, leathery torso, and his toenails are mustard-coloured talons, strong as horn, so long that they curl over each other.

Every dusk George goes to the perimeter fence with a bucket of meat. It seems wholly implausible that this boney, withered Elijah can summon the Lords of the Bush with a simple bucket, but some nights we end up with nine or ten lions just a few feet away, purring and frolicking about like kittens.

From there I drive a Landrover through the bush to the camp of 'the leopard man', Tony Fitzjohn, who is dedicated to saving the elusive Kenyan leopard. With his mane of bleached hair and muscular torso, Fitzjohn so resembles Tarzan that he once played the role in a locally produced B movie.

One morning he suddenly yells to me to run for cover. A female leopard, jealous of Fitzjohn's Australian air hostess girlfriend, has leapt the high wire fence and now crouches in the compound, flicking her tail in readiness for confrontation. Cowering behind a door, I hear snarls, grunts and growls – from both Fitzjohn and the leopard – thumps, more grunts and breaking glass.

When it grows quieter I peek out. They are rolling around on the ground, entwined. One of Fitzjohn's arms is bleeding, but the leopard is now purring throatily, eyes narrow with pleasure. Wooed and placated, the leopard goes. The air-hostess stays.

Back in Nairobi I swig beer with white cowboys on the terrace of the Norfolk Hotel, and sip gin and tonic amidst the floral chintz and cut glass accents of the Muthaiga Club's drawing room. Here I encounter Surrey golf club etiquette in the wilds of sub-Saharan Africa. I lounge on elegant verandahs surrounding heavily guarded colonial mansions in the lush white suburbs of Karen and Langata. I listen to Karen Blixen's Kikuyu manservant, Kamante – immortalised in *Out of Africa* and now old and grizzled – sing at a party.

Italian photographer Mirella Ricciardi takes me under her wing and together we visit the artist Peter Beard in his sumptuous, cedar-scented tent. Lounging against cushions on his teak deck, I think this is about as glamorous as life gets.

I travel north to Isiolo to help out with famine relief. It is my initiation – compared with what I will meet later almost a gentle one – into the massive range and extent of Africa's problems. I am deeply perturbed by the Giacometti silhouettes of the Masai mothers and the stick limbs of their babies, and also hideously conscious of my meaty white thighs in shorts and my juicy bare arms.

After a while the brisk British matrons stop weighing babies and distributing sacks of grain. I am shocked when they open tupperware boxes and picnic on hefty sandwiches in front of the starving Masai. When I feel unable to join in I am quickly reprimanded:

'If you don't keep your strength up how on earth will you do your job properly?' tuts a stern woman with an iron grey perm.

Meekly I eat a ham bap.

In Maralel I meet Wilfred Thesiger, who lives in a compound surrounded by his African 'family'. In the thudding heat he emerges from his thatched earth hut wearing a three-piece tweed suit and polished, lace-up brogues. Manipulatively, but gratefully, he purloins all my paperbacks.

I sit in companionable silence with an ochre-painted, beaded Samburu warrior on an escarpment overlooking the vast Rift Valley. I drink milk and blood in a Masai *boma*. I chew the mild narcotic *mirar* on an all-night bus. I water-ski amongst crocodiles on Lake Baringo.

By the time I arrive back in London I am hopelessly, and as it turns out permanently, under Africa's spell. Later, when I am offered a job in Nairobi working as production assistant on a documentary film, I do not hesitate.

1 DOGSBODY BEWITCHED
Kenya

'No-one else wants to do it,' says my agent. 'It sounds a bit dodgy.'

I don't care. I can't wait to get back to Africa. I set out to meet Uru, the son of my prospective employer, Sharad Patel.

Uru is just over five feet tall. His face is child-like and almost beautiful, but spoilt by a sullen, exhausted expression and the marks of a dissolute lifestyle – puffy eyes and a wan complexion. I brace myself to be grilled. Instead he looks me up and down appraisingly and asks if I've ever been to Kenya before.

'Yes,' I say, 'I loved it.'

This seems to have the desired effect. He stands up and grabs a very big bunch of keys.

'Let's go,' he barks.

He drives me to buy my air ticket in a white Mercedes that dwarfs him. It is hard to believe this pint-sized playboy is really in a position to hire me, but fifteen minutes later I am outside the British Airways office in Regent Street, a ticket to Nairobi in one hand and a wedge of cash in the other.

'Ciao,' says Uru, 'Have a good time!'

His Rolex glints as he waves goodbye. I still have no idea what the job entails.

Three days later I am at the New Stanley Hotel in Nairobi where Graham, my director, is waiting for me. We sit in the Thorn Tree café, in the shade of the famous tree which has messages for travellers pinned optimistically to its trunk. Waiters in green uniforms, trays held high, weave around groups of khaki-clad Americans studying their guide books between safaris. I need a cup of coffee, but Graham looks as if he needs something stronger. His eyes are red and his hand trembles as it strokes his straggly grey beard.

Graham is a cameraman who has not directed before, nor has he been to Africa. He landed the job because he has made in-house corporate films for an airline. He asked the Patels for a British production assistant and here I am.

'Am I glad to see you!' he says. He smiles ingratiatingly, showing stained teeth.

'It's been chaos here,' he goes on, 'Working with these blacks is like trying to deal with a bag of monkeys.' My heart sinks.

Later that day we are sitting in front of Sharad Patel's substantial desk. Though small, Sharad is stocky and upright with a head of thick grey hair. A pair of spectacles lends his round face an owlish air. He treats Graham with deference. Towards me he is polite but dismissive.

Along with all the other Asians, Sharad and his family were thrown out of Uganda by Idi Amin. They fled to Kenya. Sharad is a formidable wheeler-dealer and networker who thrives on social contacts and government connections. Within just a few years his company, the Film Corporation of Kenya, has made two feature films and a horde of commercials, documentaries and educational films.

The offices are in Mama Ngina Street above the Red Bull, a rather dreary Spanish restaurant which – despite excellent tortilla and Rioja – is often forlornly empty. Sharad is inordinately proud of the movie he made about Idi Amin and the promotional posters for it are framed and displayed on the office walls. They show a crude, coloured drawing of Amin, eyes bulging and mouth foaming, with an Indian wriggling on the end of a bloody bayonet.

There is also a poster for *Bachelor Party* starring Tom Hanks, with which Sharad's eldest son Raju had something to do. He is apparently big in Hollywood. Raju is expected in Nairobi any day, and meanwhile the middle son Viju is to look after Graham and me.

While Uru is living it up in London's casinos and the Patel mansion on the North Circular, and Raju is mixing with the stars in Los Angeles, Viju is stuck at home working for Daddy. Sharad also has a daughter, aptly named Pretty, who is somewhat over-protected, and kept at home with her mother while Sharad seeks a husband for her.

Meanwhile it is rumoured that Sharad gallivants with Iba, the office accountant, a cheery, roly poly woman with a squeaky voice. She has a London flat in Oxford Street of which she frequently boasts. She sits in a pokey back room from which she dispenses petty cash from metal boxes which she unlocks with a substantial bunch of keys she keeps on a chain under her sari.

The Film Corporation owns several mobile cinemas. They travel all over Kenya, setting up screens in remote villages and attracting huge rural audiences. This ability to 'spread the message' gives Sharad leverage when money raising. Now the Kenyan post office has stumped up a large budget to make a series of films – some television commercials and a long documentary to explain how the post office works. One of the most common problems is that people send letters addressed, for example, to 'Mr. Mkwori, Nairobi' and expect them to arrive. The Lost Letter Room is overwhelmed.

The films are also to encourage and teach people how to use pay phones and faxes. Graham is to shoot the films, with Viju overseeing him. When available, Sharad or Raju will direct. The rest of the crew is Kenyan, apart from James, a nineteen-year-old British public schoolboy on his gap year who acts as a technical assistant.

Despite my title of production assistant I resign myself to being a decorative dogsbody. I am so happy to be back in Africa that I don't really care. I tolerate Viju shouting at me when I spell Technicolor with a 'u', English style, on the camera report sheets. Later I don't even protest when I get the lowest and humblest credit they can give me: 'Runner'.

Two days after my arrival I turn twenty-nine. Graham invites me to dinner. I need to be on good terms with him if we are to work together successfully, so I accept. Graham arrives for our date wearing a white three-piece suit with a kipper tie. He has combed his long grey hair, but he still looks like a rumpled Bee Gee.

The Film Corporation only pays our per diems if we eat in the hotel so rather than spend his own money on a restaurant, Graham opts for the New Stanley Dining Room. It is gloomy and oppressive. The carpet is dark brown, the floor-length curtains orange and violently patterned.The waiter scurries forward and ushers us to a corner table amongst dusty pot plants. He lights candles with a flourish and smiling wishes us a pleasant evening. Graham asks for the wine list.

'I'm not paying that for a bottle of French plonk,' he says, 'It's extortionate!'

He orders palm wine instead. It is filthy.

We attempt conversation. He tells me about his wife and children and runs me through his CV. There's more moaning about blacks being incompetent. The dingy lighting is giving me a headache. The over-decorated cod is tasteless and soggy. I am depressed. I drink the palm wine.

Next day work begins in earnest. The team gathers at Mama Ngina Street. George Githu, the production manager, wears a tartan tam o'shanter with a red pom pom. On top of a very thin, six foot four Kikuyu it looks hilarious. I like him immediately. I also meet Mohammed, the handsome focus puller, Gibril, the grip, and various other electricians and camera assistants. It is immediately obvious that the Africans are on very low wages and that they are to be treated very differently from us whites.

'It's always the way,' says George cackling, 'Old man Patel is notorious.'

The Patels are very hospitable to Graham, James and me, and we frequently lunch at their mansion. It is a glitzy affair, full of shiny gilt, gold-plated taps, cut crystal and marble. While the Kenyan crew eat basic African food on the stoep outside, we are treated to fragrant, delicately spiced curries in the airy, marbled dining room. Sharad's wife and the exquisite Pretty wait on us. I learn to eat Indian-style, scooping up the curry and rice with a deft twist of fingers and thumb. It seems to taste better that way. Graham persists in asking for a fork.

Towards the end of the first week, the long-awaited Raju arrives from Los Angeles. He is sleek behind designer sunglasses, sweating slightly into an olive green silk shirt. His teeth gleam when he smiles. His accent is American. When he directs, he likes us all to behave as if we are on a big movie set.

Raju directs a scene in a metal foundry. The African workers look bemused to be treated like Hollywood extras, but take it in good spirits. It isn't every day that an Indian man in gold jewellery turns up with lights, cameras and a crew including three whites, just for a couple of shots of them smelting whatever they are smelting in their furnace. As Raju repeatedly shouts 'Action!' they become more amused and are soon acting their socks off, hurling irons into the fire with exaggerated vigour. Raju is thrilled with the results and takes us all for a drink afterwards to celebrate.

I am becoming friendly with our technical assistant James. To begin with I am wary of his public schoolboy swagger. He tends to show off his Swahili or his superior knowledge of Kenya. I am infuriated by the way he comments daily on what I am wearing. He takes a particular fancy to my denim jacket. However, I do not have a car, and I'm stuck in the hotel every night because of the per diems arrangement. When James suggests taking Graham and me out for the day one weekend, I accept gratefully.

We go to the Nairobi Game Park and then to a country club for lunch and a swim. After the dusty bustle of Nairobi I am glad to be lounging in the dappled shade of a jacaranda tree. I can hear James splashing around in the pool and I can smell jasmine, and also the barbecued meat we will eat for lunch. I am surprised that Graham allows James to pay. His frugality is starting to irritate me. I am frosty with Graham but he seems not to notice, and back at the hotel that night he invites me to his room.

'How about a perfect ending to a perfect day?' he suggests as we stand together in the lift. I flee.

Next day I go to Iba and beg to be allowed a car. I also ask to have my per diems paid in cash so I can eat out. Iba is a tough negotiator and dislikes parting with money but I persist. By mid-morning she is reluctantly counting out a wad of Kenyan shillings and by lunchtime she is telling Viju to give me a set of car keys. I am free at last.

My own battle over per diems alerts me further to how little the African crew are being paid compared with us expats. Rashly and naively I decide to talk to Sharad. He is livid. His success is based on shrewd, frugal management and he doesn't need the dogsbody telling him he is not paying people enough.

The upside of the very public dressing down which follows is that it endears me to the crew. Shortly after this, Jibril, the grip, asks to borrow $100 because his wife is in hospital. I am reluctant to dip into my funds – by British standards I am being paid very little – yet I have no concept of how to refuse him. On the one hand it is racist not to trust him to repay me. Equally, it is racist to feel obliged to lend him the money for fear of being politically incorrect. In the end, I lend him the $100. Viju finds out and shouts at me. He tells me I am stupid and deserve never to see the money again.

Two nights later Jibril comes to the New Stanley, pays me back and invites me home so his wife can thank me. In a shanty town on the outskirts of the city he leads me through a warren of narrow streets. Ragged little boys kick footballs around in the dirt, their bare feet grey with dust. Women lope home chattering with each other, carrying plastic jerrycans of water on their heads. Skeletal cats crouch over mounds of evil-smelling garbage, and a dog with a broken leg and sores round its eyes barks at us as we pass.

Jibril lives with his entire family in one small room that smells of sour milk and urine. Dressed in a pristine white blouse Jibril's wife makes tea on the communal stove outside and then perches on an upturned crate to watch me drink it. I sit on the bed amongst the children, who gaze at me solemnly as we chat. It is all rather formal. Then one of the little boys gives my hair a curious, experimental tug. It breaks the ice and we all laugh. I am glad I lent Jibril the money.

Encouraged by the friendly atmosphere on the set, Mohammed the focus puller declares he is in love with me. Every day he stands with his head bowed, his posture forlorn, begging me to pity him. Whenever I am within earshot he pleads with me.

'Just one date. Please Charlotte, I am hurting inside, please help me,' he whispers. Eventually I capitulate, partly because he wears me down, partly because I am keen to spend more time with Africans away from work. Besides, Mohammed is undeniably handsome.

He takes me to a darts match in one of Nairobi's cheaper hotels. I am the only white person there. He spends almost his entire week's salary on beer and lines up the brown bottles on the table in front of us. Though I do not like beer very much, it's a lot better than Graham's palm wine, and I drink as much as I have to to be polite. Mohammed says very little but sits proudly with his arm round me and surveys the room. I feign an interest in darts.

The evening ends fairly disastrously. I have tried chatting to Mohammed about everything from darts to his ambition to be a cameraman. He interprets this as a come-on and when I resist his unexpectedly forceful advances, he attributes my rejection to the fact that he is black. I am furious.

The next day he is sullen and angry and my attempts to mollify him fail. Later, avoiding my eye, he asks to borrow money. I lend it to him without question and tell no-one. He never pays me back. The incident dents my confidence. I feel a fool, tricked and belittled by cultural codes I am unable to decipher.

Nine months later Mohammed will die of AIDS. Three months after him four others on the crew will also be dead – the great epidemic has started and none of us realise how closely it will touch our lives.

James has followed Mohammed's interest in me with amusement, and teases me about it. I find his light-hearted attitude a relief after the intensity of Mohammed's attentions. One night we go to the cinema together, and afterwards James asks if he can crash out in my room because he has no transport to go back out to Langata. I do wonder how he normally returns home, but think it would be prissy to refuse him.

We talk all night, and two days later he moves into my hotel room. No-one is as surprised as I am by this turn of events. The last thing I expected was to fall for a boy just out of school, but there is something delightful about abandoning the responsibilities of being a woman nearing thirty and becoming a lovestruck teenager again. And I am in Africa – miles away from the cares of my real life in London. I have the rest of my life to be sensible.

We try to keep our relationship secret, but it is difficult with Graham in the same hotel. He is angry when he finds out. He resorts to drink and the moral high ground in swift rotation. His temper becomes worse, as does the reek of alcohol that hangs around him like an oily veil.

A week later we are filming in a big open-air market which specialises in cheap metalware. As far as the eye can see there are piles of metal pots, pans and braziers for burning charcoal. The constant din of beating and clashing metal jars my nerves. Viju stands on the roof rack of our truck, bellowing at the crowd through a megaphone. I am standing clutching my clipboard when a huge man looms up and jabs me in the chest with his forefinger:

'You! You *muzungu*! Even me, I do not like your face!'

People snigger and the crowd starts to swell around us. Faces turn hostile. Viju jumps down from the truck and begins to shout and push people away. Someone throws a stone. I am hemmed in against the truck. People are so close that I can smell the scraps of meat between their teeth.

Without warning Graham turns and runs. He looks old, tired and frightened as he clumsily hurries away. This simple unheroic act breaks the tension. The children start to laugh, and soon everyone is jeering at Graham and hooting with mirth. For Graham this is the last straw. He announces he has had enough and it is time for him to go home.

The night before he leaves Graham takes James and me out to a Chinese restaurant and presents me with a silver elephant hair bracelet and ring in a green silk pouch. I am overwhelmed, mainly with feelings of guilt. I have recoiled from his racism and have been neither supportive nor sympathetic. Now he is being gracious and generous in defeat, and I feel truly sorry.

Any thoughts I had of returning home have evaporated. I have earned just enough money from the shoot to survive a couple of months, and as soon as filming ends James and I take a plane to the coast. As we land in Mombasa, I have no idea where we are going or for how long.

We rent a motorbike and take a hut on Diani beach close to some of James's teen-age friends. The days pass in a sun-drenched blur. At night we burn money at elegant beach bars, go to parties or dance with prostitutes and Masai tribesmen in a sleazy nightclub called Bush Babies. It's like a golden dream, but occasionally I find myself yearning for the greyer reality of adulthood.

I am relieved when we go back to Nairobi. I should call it a day and go back to London but I am still paralysed by Kenya's potent spell. We move in with Joss Kent. Heir to the Abercrombie and Kent fortune, Joss is also blessed with charm and looks. In the lush suburb of Karen his father has a house called Bahati, nestling amongst avocado trees behind high, white walls swathed in bougainvillea. In his father's absence Bahati is Joss's palace.

We spend our days by the pool at the Muthaiga Club, picnicking in the Ngong Hills or lounging in the Bahati sauna, which we enliven by pouring vodka onto the hot coals. Nightly, regular as clockwork, the golden girls and boys of Nairobi arrive to party. We usually drift on to dance at Bubbles nightclub or play blackjack at the Casino. It is a decadent lifestyle based on money and idleness. I don't care. It is a delicious novelty and I am making up for my own lost teenage summers, spent in dreary typing jobs to pay my way through university.

Eventually I am seriously broke, but before facing London again I badly want to go on safari, so James and I set off for the Masai Mara with his friend Paddy. At this time the game reserves are full of well-heeled American tourists and going on safari is prohibitively expensive.

We plan on camping, but arrive after dark when it is forbidden to drive around the reserve. We have no choice but to head for one of the lodges. We cannot afford the luxury tents or cabins at $70 or $80 a head, but having driven so far we are determined not to turn back. We decide we will split the cost of a single cabin. I will pose as a lone woman and James and Paddy will sneak in later.

The first part of the plan works, and I move into the hut alone. Alone that is unless you count the tarantula with whom I share the tiny lavatory for an hour or so, me sitting on the loo and the tarantula's hairy legs curled round the inside doorhandle. Eventually I manage to scramble carefully over the partition, but it takes me a long time to recover.

Finally the boys find their way to my hut and we settle down, three to the bed, for an uncomfortable night. At dawn we are woken by a screeching, tearing noise followed by thumps and hysterical shouting. A bull elephant has blundered into the camp and is crashing around, knocking down flimsy walls and causing havoc. The management evacuates us all, so we are discovered, given a dressing down by the hotel manager and told to leave.

We set off into the bush and look for somewhere to camp. We meet some rangers who, for a small bribe, show us a place by the river where we can pitch our tent. I haven't camped since I was at school and have forgotten how much I used to enjoy it. We sit round a fire under the stars, sipping icy cold beer from the coolbox as sausages split and sizzle on the griddle. A family of hippopotamus snorts comfortingly in the river and watches us, eyes red as embers in the dark. I fall even more hopelessly in love with Africa.

Two nights later James and I have a fight. Later I will not even remember what it is about, but he slams his hand down so hard on the car bonnet that he dents the metal. I run tearfully into the bush. It isn't till I stop that I realise I have no way of finding my way out again. I listen for the sound of voices. Nothing. I daren't sit down, for fear of snakes and insects. I was born without a sense of direction so I do not even consider retracing my steps. I stand there for what must be about an hour, acutely conscious of every rustle. I imagine a lion behind every bush, a leopard in every tree. It isn't until nearly dawn that they finally find me.

When I climb into the car, it is all over between James and me. A few days later I am on the plane home to my parents, who are very worried as I am long overdue. I feel irresponsible, selfish and contrite. Not before time. As for James, I am sure I will never see him again. I am wrong – but that's another story.

Back in London I felt dislocated and depressed. I was not ready to settle back into the comfortable but muffling security of my home city. I went back to work as a freelance pop promo producer, but day-dreamed about Africa. I became a Kenyan Ancient Mariner. I had what the French in Nairobi refer to as 'le virus'. I was still bewitched and nothing but another dose of Africa would make me feel better again.

Just a year later I am back in Nairobi, having persuaded the managing director of Island Records that the British reggae band, Aswad, will benefit enormously from a video shot in Kenya. So here I am, a producer no less, at the airport to meet the three main members of the band – Brinsley, Tony and Drummie. I can see their tall hats stuffed with dreadlocks bobbing above the crowd. Children cluster around, mouths slack with curiosity – Rastafarians are an unusual sight, especially ones like these in flamboyant boots and expensive leather coats.

We film first at the Carnivore, an enormous Brazilian-style restaurant and nightclub, just off the main highway out of Nairobi. It is strikingly laid out in a series of open-sided thatched huts, where every conceivable animal is grilled over open fires and served at the table from swords. You can refuse what you like but the waiters keep coming, brandishing blades heavy with chunks of cow, giraffe, zebra, impala, wildebeest, crocodile tail, buffalo, ostrich, kudu and many more.

American and British voices drift through the charcoal smoke, 'Giraffe – how gross!' or 'Crocodile? You've got to be kidding!' but there are always chicken wings or fish and a stab at salad for the squeamish. True vegetarians are best advised to stay at home.

Aswad play a set and go down a storm. The crowd swells round the stage, singing along and waving their arms. Afterwards Aswad disappear into a sea of surging, gorgeous girls.

After our initial success at the Carnivore we leave Nairobi to film at Lake Magadi. As we drive out of the city the great red mountains rise ahead of us, shimmering in their glistening coat of heat and dust. Kenya reclaims me as I feel the landscape pulse with an

15

insinuating, hypnotic, primeval beat.

Lake Magadi is like a furnace. The salt flats reflect bright white light. Within minutes pale faces are red, noses already blistering. Aswad sweat into their heavy locks. The British crew tie *kikois* round their heads like handkerchiefs which make them look like exotic versions of Blighty Boys at the Seaside on an Edwardian postcard.

We film Aswad performing with a troupe of local dancers wearing leopard skins and headdresses, under acacia trees that throw their bony arms towards the sun in graceful silhouette. Long, white clouds scud across the sky and the lake shimmers pink in the ferocious heat. I am truly, madly, deeply in love with Africa again.

Back in Nairobi the band wants a night out so I take them to the Casino. A mountainous bouncer blocks our entry.

'No hats,' he says, folding his arms across his body. He has no neck above his bow tie, and his dinner jacket strains at the seams.

'Don't be ridiculous,' say I, trying to sound like a woman in charge.

'Why not?'

'Regulations'.

The bouncer stares over my head impassively. Admittedly, the Aswad headwear is particularly lavish. Tony's hat is in crocheted wool, the colours of the Ethiopian flag. Drummie wears a patchwork suede peaked cap in purple and navy with blanket stitching, and Brinsley a two tone leather affair.

'But they're Rastafarians, their hats are part of their religion. You wouldn't throw a Sikh out for wearing a turban would you?'

No reaction.

A small crowd has gathered on the stairs up to the Casino Entrance. People are asking for autographs, or staring and making comments to each other about Aswad's hats.

'We'll take our hats off then,' says Tony.

The bouncer's eyes bulge as he braces up for a fight.

'You cannot come in.'

We try invoking Princess Diana and Aswad's Buckingham Palace gig, to no avail.

'What's the problem, brother?' Brinsley persists, stepping forward. The bouncer makes a sudden movement and we back off fast. The bouncer has the last word.

'If you're my brother,' he shouts, then points at me: 'What you doing hanging out with that white trash?'

Next morning we are up early to go to Amboseli Game Park to film another scene. After the night before we aren't too sorry to be leaving Nairobi, but it is raining and no-one is in a good mood. We drive along in grumpy silence under sagging black clouds.

We plan to do some filming and return to Nairobi, but our journey takes us far longer than we anticipated because the rain has made the roads muddy and treacherous. By the time we realise we are lost, it is dark.

We drive on. The road crosses a seemingly endless plain of waist-high grass, till a small Masai boy with a herd of goats materialises in the headlights. He raises his spear and shows us a big, toothy smile. We stop to ask him the way – anywhere. He jumps happily into the back of the minivan and directs us through the bush for about five miles till we reach a small lodge. Then he scampers off into the dark again to find his goats.

In the lodge a sullen young man behind a makeshift reception counter tells us there are only three rooms available. We will all have to share. Aswad start grumbling again. They lay the blame squarely on me – this is a hopeless production, they want to go back to Nairobi immediately, they are fed up with this. I stand my ground, albeit shakily, and say that I will happily share with the camera crew and director, four or five to a hut. Surely they can at least share one, or even two, huts between the three of them?

As we argue, a woman slinks from the shadows behind us. She wears a stretch satin, flowered dress that clings to her sumptuous curves. She reeks of hair oil and gardenias. She smiles and leans languidly against the door frame.

'Hello boys,' she drawls, ' My name is Lydia. Do you want to play with me?'

She holds up a dart and thrusts it at them suggestively. Then she laughs mischievously, showing gold teeth. It is a throaty laugh, thick with sexuality. Brinsley, Drummie and Tony look like rabbits caught in headlights.

Tony clears his throat:

'I don't mind sharing a room,' he says. Then they all start talking at once. Thanks to one small prostitute they agree to move into a hut together.

We regroup in the shabby little bar where Lydia is playing darts. The wooden tables are rickety, sticky and stained. A few other men are sitting around but they soon leave. At nine o'clock the power fails. Lydia chuckles and comes to sit with us. We wait in the dark till a boy brings oil lamps and candles. When they are lit the bar looks less seedy and rather cosy. Steaming bowls of goat stew arrive. We realise how hungry we are. There is nothing to drink but a dusty bottle of Grand Marnier, but its syrupy golden liquid tastes like nectar.

Just after Tony and Drummie have gone to bed a very old Masai man hobbles in, leaning on his spear. He stops and stares at Brinsley. He has seen plenty of white people before but never a black man with dreadlocks and leather trousers. He shuffles across the room and sits huddled in his red check blanket, looking at us with such earnest curiosity that it is impossible to be offended.

Brinsley is in an expansive mood after his fourth Grand Marnier. He greets the old man and in return receives a wonderful, ear-splitting, virtually toothless smile. Brinsley has a CD walkman with him. The old man points, indicating he wants to look at it.

'Wait!' says Brinsley, jumping up, 'I've got an idea!'

He rushes out to the minivan and comes back with a Bob Marley CD. Like a scientist setting up an experiment he carefully puts the cushioned headphones over the old man's head then adjusts the volume. When Brinsley is sure the old man is ready he presses the play button and Bob Marley's *Jammin* thunders into the old man's ears.

He freezes, eyes wide with shock. After about a minute, he raises a gnarled hand to the headphones and touches them gingerly, as if to check that he is not imagining them. He closes his eyes. He starts to sway. The swaying becomes more rhythmic as a smile spreads across his face. Strange noises emerge from his throat. Soon, his whole body is moving in time to Marley's beat and the old man is singing along. I am moved by the extent of his delight. Momentarily, the greasy little bar becomes magical.

Meanwhile, Lydia has decided that John, the director, is the man for her. John is a strong, silent type from Birmingham with a down-to-earth approach to life but, like all of us, he has drunk too much Grand Marnier. He soon has his arm round her and is offering her a cigarette.

'John, oh John!' pants Lydia, as she snuggles into his armpit, 'You know how it is when you split a chicken?' She makes an alarming snapping movement with her hands.

'This is how I am wanting to do with you tonight.'

She licks her lips and her eyes gleam in the lamplight.

She nearly has her way. She hunts John down to the pit latrines. He manages to eschew her embraces there, but about four in the morning I hear squeaks outside the hut I'm sharing with the crew. At first I think it's an animal but it is Lydia.

'John, John!' she is whispering, '*Wataka wewe* – I want you!'

I go to the door and open it. Lydia's smile disappears. She spits, says something obscene, then turns and stumbles off into the bush.

Next morning Brinsley, Tony and Drummie are all big eyes and drama.

'Did you hear that big animal?'

'Yeah, definitely some kind of wild beast.'

'I couldn't sleep at all,'

'Must have been a lion,'

They are shivering with lack of sleep. The men we hired to help carry the equipment are very amused.

'*Simba?*' they snort, '*Majingo kweli kweli!* A lion? The bloody fool!' They fall about chortling.

'They think there was a lion.'

'Maybe it was a rat!' More laughter.

'What are they saying?' asks Tony. I never tell him.

Back in London Aswad's song was not a great hit, though the video was much admired. The world of pop videos was unlikely to take me back to Africa. Little did I know it would take me six years, and a career change via Pakistan and Afghanistan, to find my way back there again.

2   THE TRANSPORT OFFICERS
Zambia

I went to Zambia to direct a film about cholera for the World Health Organisation. The object was to draw attention to the escalating crisis and teach people how to defeat cholera. Since it is one of the simplest illnesses to cure, thousands of people were dying quite unnecessarily. I was excited about the project, believing it could educate people and put pressure on the government to act. Back then I still had a passionate belief in the efficacy of both film and the United Nations.

I arrive in Zambia with big ideas and a small budget. I expect it to look like Kenya, and I am disappointed. As my taxi drives into Lusaka there are no mountains, no monumental sculptural clouds hanging in an eternal sky, no giraffe lumbering across the road, no veil of rust-coloured dust blurring the horizons, not even a whiff of woodsmoke. We drive past shabby concrete housing and huge billboards saying 'AIDS is everywhere,' or 'Stay alive – stay faithful'. People pick their way listlessly home along the railways lines. Goats root around in the sewage along the side of the road.

I book into the Pamodzi, an ugly, multi-storey hotel set in a walled garden. Thanks to my UN status I get 'diplomatic' rates, but it is a difficult place in which to be a lone woman. By the pool waiters hover insistently. There is a plague of mangy cats, some blind, others with limps, one with a bleeding mutilated ear. They whine pitifully and rub against me whenever I so much as contemplate a sandwich.

In the bar men wait for women tensely in the shadows, while couples canoodle in dark corners. The music is tinned and smoochy, the cocktails syrupy, expensive and served with little parasols and pineapple garnish. In the Jacaranda coffee shop trelliswork and dusty plastic ivy struggle to create a 'patio' atmosphere.

Despite the efforts of the smiling chef who presides over the hot plates, the food is uninspiring and over-priced – the ubiquitous Nile perch, soggy potatoes, limp salads, okra mush, stale bread rolls. The other white people, mainly aid workers or businessmen, eat hurriedly with bowed heads. They study reports or read books and then scuttle off with their briefcases. Zambians arrive in groups and stick together. I want to explore but feel marooned, not knowing how to negotiate my way downtown alone.

Unlike the empty evenings my days are frantic, organising locations and permissions, tracking down the right people to interview and trying to ascertain the full extent of the cholera crisis. Hiring a driver is beyond my budget and self-drive is not available, so I rely on taxis and choose a grizzled old man to drive me around. His taxi boasts a fringed, brown carpeted dashboard, fairy lights and a selection of beads, feathers and carved amulets dangling from his rearview mirror.

Every day I battle with bureacracy. I have to account for myself to endless hospital committees or representatives from the Ministry of Health. Daily I slog up the six flights of concrete, urine-spattered stairs in the United Nations building to obtain further written permissions or to justify myself yet again to another committee. One Zambian doctor, whose role I never quite ascertain, presents me with an enormous budget for his services, including a hefty per diem allowance. I despair of ever delivering the film on budget.

I am relieved when the crew arrives from Zimbabwe. I have to hire from Zimbabwe because there are neither equipment nor crews available in Zambia. The cameraman, Tzvika Rozen, is Israeli but has lived in Harare for over a decade. He has spiked hair and a pony tail and wears pink shorts. The sound recordist, Peter Maringisanwa, wears pristine, ironed Wranglers and a complicated camera assistant's waistcoat full of pockets and flaps like an angler's.

We start filming in George Compound, one of Lusaka's overcrowded shanty towns with limited water and virtually no sanitation. A primary school has been turned into a makeshift cholera centre. It is a long, low building set in a parched garden. A guard in a white coat and wellingtons and wielding a gun stops us at the gate. When we say we want to go inside he laughs.

'Aren't you afraid? Don't you know how infectious cholera is?' he asks. As I wipe my feet on the disinfected rags at the entrance to the wards he looks at me with amused contempt, as if I were very, very stupid.

Inside the scene is grim. In the first ward men are lying on blankets on every available inch of floor, many attached to drips. Most are too exhausted to object to the camera. They gaze into the lens with eerie intensity. I can see Tzvika and Peter are shaken, but they do their job doggedly.

The women's ward is worse. One woman is having violent diarrhoea into a red plastic bucket. Mothers lie weary and weak, cradling their stinking, dehydrated children. To identify them nurses have stuck plasters on the children's heads with their names on them. The stench of disinfectant and excrement is sickening. Nurses in wellingtons lumber amongst the drips that festoon the room. In a corner, someone pulls a grey blanket up over the head of a woman who hasn't made it. Once this was a classroom.

Because cholera is so dehydrating, people's skins wither, particularly round the eyes and mouth and on the backs of the hands. Young women look seventy, their eyes sunk into pouches of puckered skin. The children are unusually quiet, lending the rooms a ghostly atmosphere.

Half way through the morning a delegation of South African businessmen from a pharmaceutical company arrives. They wear aviator sunglasses, crisp, short-sleeved shirts and pressed flannel trousers with shiny shoes. They insist on being sprayed with disinfectant. They even hold up their briefcases to be protected from contamination. Once in the wards they stand round the edges and will not go within six feet of any patient. Their caution is totally unnecessary. Well fed, well watered, healthy men like these will not catch cholera. Cholera goes for the malnourished, with weak immune systems. It preys on the poor.

When the South Africans have gone Hope, the chief nurse, offers us refreshment. She has been twinkling at Peter since we arrived. She regards him slyly out of the corner of her eye as she pours tea on the little stone terrace which surrounds the building. Tzvika grins conspiratorially at me. Peter never seems to grasp the effect he has on women.

Peter is chatting to Hope about her home village when a new patient arrives. Hope puts down her cup reluctantly and goes back to work. Just inside the gate a group of boys surrounds a wheelbarrow containing a heap of filthy rags. They have wheeled it ten miles. The rags materialise into a woman. Her name is Catherine. Critically ill and too weak to walk, she is carried into the ward by four nurses.

I want to follow a cholera patient's story from arrival at the ward, and Catherine would be the perfect focus for our story but there now arises a familiar tension. For the good of the film I need to shove our camera in Catherine's face, but my instincts tell me to leave her to suffer privately. The film-maker wins and Tzvika moves in. Happily, after a few days of treatment with oral rehydration salts, Catherine has recovered. We find her sitting up in bed, smiling, ready to go home.

As we drive back to the hotel we see a dilapidated car driving slowly towards us, a megaphone thrust out of the window. Children run alongside it shrieking with delight. Our driver translates the message blaring from the loud-hailer:

'Beware of the faeces! The secret of cholera lies in the faeces – oh, yes my friends. I am telling you, never defecate under the mango tree and then eat the mangoes – this way you will contract the cholera.'

'Overtake that car,' I say at once. When you are filming a depressing topic, lively characters who can reinforce the message with a light touch are like gold dust. The man behind the megaphone is Kennedy Mbau, who has been a bodybuilder and once held the title of Zambia's Mr. Universe.

'I was unspeakably strong, oh yes,' he says. Today he is a stooped middle-aged man with a ragged scar down one side of his face. After a member of his family died of cholera, he decided to dedicate his services to combating the disease. He speaks in stilted but passionate English:

'My message to the people is as follows: I tell them to guard against any habit that can make them drink or eat faeces. Above all, they must retreat from those flies. Those flies are very bad. Flies are the transport officers of cholera. Oh yes, my friends!'

Flies are indeed transport officers and cholera spreads quickly in unhygienic conditions. The toilets at George Compound are disgusting and they serve hundreds of people. I want Peter and Tzvika to film them.

'You're joking,' says Tzvika.

'I don't think so,' laughs Peter.

Tvzika asks:

'But how will people watching ever begin to imagine the stench?'

We cover our noses and brave the toilets. The concrete floor is slimed with urine. Cockroaches feast on coils of excrement and rustle amongst discarded twists of shit-smeared paper.

The meat market is another gruesome sight. Sheep's stomachs fester in the sun. Cows' feet, complete with hooves and fur, lie jumbled up in crates. Flies swarm round the oozing eye sockets of goats' heads. Yards of slimy, yellow tripe, dripping scraps of gut lining and bladder hang from hooks. Stallholders wave pieces of cardboard lethargically above the stinking offal but the battle is lost and the victors are the flies, shiny, plump, hyper-active and buzzing about spreading cholera like wildfire.

The local bar, or 'bottle store', is equally hazardous. Outside a squat concrete shack an old woman in a woolly hat is stirring cassava beer in a rusty tin drum with a wooden pole. She laughs like a witch, which I assume is a sign of intoxication. Over her eyes is a milky film. Inside men are drinking vomit-coloured beer out of filthy plastic containers. A whoop of excitement goes up as I walk in. One man tries to stand and falls over. Others stand, staring and swaying. I doubt if they have seen a white woman in their bottle store before. One man, sweating profusely, the flies of his stained shorts undone, staggers up to me.

'Madam,' he shouts. 'Give me one kwacha for beer!'

A roar of approval goes up from the crowd and then a woman in the corner starts screaming something incomprehensible. The crowd laughs obscenely as the man comes closer. I can smell the sour beer on his breath.

'Madam,' he insists, 'Even I am thirsty. Give me beer.'

I am eager to escape, but out of the corner of my eye I see that Tzvika and Peter are filming away. I am creating a handy diversion.

'Madam,' says the man, angry and desperate now, 'I am telling you!' He grabs my arm.

'Let's go,' says Peter, taking hold of my other arm.

There is a brief tussle and then we are outside again, surrounded by children excited by the commotion and noise.

The markets are full of traditional healers or witch doctors, taking advantage of the crisis to tout their wares. I had imagined chanting, sweating, feathered voodoo-men with rolling eyes. Instead they tend to be canny merchants in suits, with alluring smiles and reassuring blurb about their products.

At one stall a cardboard sign reads: 'Get your cholera cure here' in English. There are bowls full of feathers and little pieces of unidentifiable bone, chicken's feet, powders, dried plants, leaves and roots neatly laid out on a blanket. On a stool in front of it sits a man in a brown suit. Our translator poses as a cholera patient.

'I can assist you' says the witch doctor in excellent English. He holds up a gnarled root that looks like a cross between a piece of ginger and a finger.

'This is very good medicine for the cholera if you are purging and vomiting.'

'How much are you charging?' asks our translator. The witch doctor eyes our expensive camera equipment shrewdly.

'Just 500 kwacha for one root,' he says.

The vastly inflated price genuinely takes our translator by surprise. He tips back on his little stool.

'500 kwacha? For only that one root?'

The witchdoctor shrugs.

'Perhaps you prefer to die than spend the money.'

While traditional medicine can be beneficial, in the treatment of cholera it is of course an expensive waste of time. Immediate rehydration is the only cure. A mixture of water, salt and sugar is usually sufficient. We are still to discover why this simple message is failing to circulate round Zambia.

We fly up to the Copper Belt where Kitwe, the capital of the North, has been the worst hit area in the country. During the rains of November 1992 over five hundred people died. A driver meets us at Ndola airport and takes us straight to the Ministry of Health's local representative, Patrick Mubiana. Mubi, as we nickname him, apologises for not coming to the airport himself. He is also a pastor and has been preaching his Sunday sermon. He is a plump little man with a high-pitched giggle that makes his body wobble like a jelly. He is passionate about 'this terrible cholera business' and is prepared to do all he can to help us film.

The road to Kitwe is straight, the landscape flat and dull. We see no animals except a couple of vultures picking at the entrails of a dog's corpse on the road. Tribal dress has been abandoned in favour of Western clothes – brown slacks and anoraks for the men, skirts and nylon patterned sweaters for the women. Kitwe is a dismal frontier town. There are half-finished concrete buildings everywhere and it rains relentlessly, churning the roads and pavements to mud.

Mubi has booked us into the Edinburgh Hotel. The decor is a monument to the worst of the sixties. Tube lights are suspended from the ceiling. A swirling staircase leads up to the dining room. It has once been a ballroom and we eat lunch under an elderly glitter ball, next to a round stage framed by blue velvet curtains, now rotten.

My bedroom has a hole in the ceiling, a dripping pipe, broken air conditioning and a view of Kitwe's sad main street. In the bathroom the ancient blue linoleum is peeling. My bed is soft and soggy. This is the best hotel in town.

Next morning we order fried eggs for breakfast. Half an hour later nothing has happened. Peter and Tzvika shout at the waiters and there is much scurrying but no eggs. Finally, an old man hurries out of the kitchen, bearing three plates proudly. He is sweating and apologetic. The plates are piled with bacon, sausages, tomatoes and beans.

'There are no eggs,' says Tzvika. The old man looks bewildered.

'Where are the eggs?' asks Peter.

Light from the glitter ball falls on the old man's crumpled face. He offers to cook the eggs himself, but nearly an hour has passed and we have to go. Once this was a grand hotel. Now it is dirty, crumbling and sad, a metaphor for modern Zambia.

We go to Kitwe's main water plant. The water is choked with dead flies, moths and lumps of excrement. There are no chemicals or chlorine to rid the water of suspended solids. Machinery used to add the chemicals is broken anyway. Pipes and filters are clogged with filth and rusting. All the windows are smashed. Chemicals for a plant of this size supplying an entire town cost up to sixteen thousand dollars a week. Kitwe has simply run out of money.

After filming so much decay and filth we are tired and hungry. Mubi senses the mood and takes us to the Pink Squirrel for lunch. The restaurant is the highlight of Kitwe. Through an archway hung with crimson velvet curtains is a seedy little basement upholstered in velveteen. There are lamps with pink fringed shades and fading photographs of Alpine scenery on the panelled walls.

We settle down in a dim corner and a waitress emerges from behind a bead curtain. She eyes Peter lasciviously as she takes our order. She wears a see-through white, nylon shirt and a very short skirt revealing thick thighs. She writes nothing down and brings us the wrong food.

I eat fish with whorls of mashed potato and the crew eat steaks in brandy sauce. Mubi hacks at a rubbery, bloody chicken thigh. We wash everything down with warm Coca Cola. Mubi beams at us, his chin greasy with gravy and a napkin tucked in over his suit.

We squeeze into Mubi's little jeep to set off for the Copper Belt's next biggest town, Ndola. I sit between Mubi and the driver. After his lavish lunch Mubi falls asleep with his head on my shoulder, meaty breath and snores emerging from his open mouth. Every time we hit a pothole he wakes with a jerk and giggles with embarrassment.

The New Savoy in Ndola is charging outrageous prices for dank rooms done up in sleazy brown velveteen. I wave every official paper I can find at the receptionist and eventually persuade them to lower the rates, but it is still ridiculously expensive.

We have dinner in the hotel's attempt at an American diner, a dismal room with dirty windows looking out onto cars parked in the rain. We eat defrosted hamburgers with sachets of ketchup and we drink Fanta. There are chips with everything and no other vegetables.

It rains for days on end. I am trying to track down a Dr. Manasseh Piri who has made a name for himself during the cholera crisis by appearing nightly on state television. His role is to tell the public the latest news about the epidemic and to inform them how to avoid the disease. His fame has spread as far as the World Health Organisation in Geneva, where I was given his name with a request that I interview him. Since arriving I have left several messages for him, so far without response.

With nothing else to do while we wait for Dr. Piri to telephone, we go for a walk round Ndola. It is a decrepit and desultory town. We shelter from the rain in the Copper Belt Museum. Inside are display cases containing rock, copper slime, slabs of malachite, strange pieces of old equipment and some rotting stuffed animals. As we return to the hotel through the rain a funeral procession passes, a great cluster of black umbrellas like monstrous, wet bats moving down the street towards the cemetery.

A crisply dressed man is waiting for us. Dr. Piri has surfaced at last. He has broad features and a neatly trimmed beard, which give his face a square, authoritative look. Though he is small he gives off a sense of caged energy which makes the room seem cramped for him. His smile is as white as his trousers which, despite the mud and the relentless rain, are pristine.

I ask him why cholera is still so rampant in Zambia. Dr. Piri's eyes narrow and the smile retreats into his beard.

'Haven't you seen for yourselves? Our water treatment plants in

29

all our cities are broken down. It's a disgrace. Of course we have cholera.' He refuses a Fanta impatiently, warming to his theme:

'If it means razing these townships down and building for people decent housing with running water and proper sewage systems, then this must be done because otherwise every single rainy season we will have cholera,' he continues.

He dismisses contemptuously the idea that the government is doing good by setting up clinics:

'What is implied in establishing clinics is: "Let people get the diarrhoea first and then we'll treat them." Why don't we address instead the causes of the problem by giving people decent housing, decent food, decent water and sewage facilities and decent health education? Then people won't get diarrhoea and we won't need to have these clinics.'

To prove his point Dr. Piri drives us round the Copper Belt. We film new, raw graves in cemeteries where women keen and wail. We see more filthy markets and disgusting toilets under veils of feasting flies. We film people drinking brown, stagnant water from infected wells and children walking home from school across broken pipes, leaking sewers and ditches slimy with excrement.

Meanwhile, the Ministry of Health is claiming that cholera is under control. We hear rumours that the government is giving out antibiotics in an attempt to win votes. The World Health Organisation deplores the use of antibiotics because they are useless. The cure is rehydration and the government is better off spending money on sanitation, clean water and some basic nationwide education about hygiene.

I hope our film will help to educate people but Dr. Piri is gloomy about its chances of distribution. There are not enough video players or televisions in the country for people to watch it. I am mystified by the government's inability to take control of the situation, and I decide to interview the Minister of Health himself, Dr Boniface Kawimbe. 'Good luck,' mutters Dr. Piri cynically.

Back in Lusaka, Dr. Kawimbe keeps us waiting an hour. We sit in a stuffy anteroom with a dozen other supplicants. When he finally arrives Dr. Kawimbe is unapologetic. He takes his place behind a big desk under the Zambian flag, his chunky cufflinks and gold-rimmed glasses glinting in the light. He smiles patronisingly as he answers my questions.

'May I add at this point the fact that our view of health is that the individual, the individual Zambian, the individual citizen should have responsibility for his or her health,' he says, speaking slowly so I will not miss a word.

I suggest that this is abdicating responsibility.

'I personally have supervised the cleaning up of the water plants,' he retaliates. I tell him we have been to the plant at Kitwe and witnessed the disgraceful state of neglect. He says dismissively:

'Clearly you have not been there recently.'

Before I can contradict he adjusts his face so that he looks suitably tragic, and tells us the cost of the lives lost in Kitwe and Lusaka is 'incalculable'. He is a consummate politician, and cholera is just one more political issue. He looks at his expensive watch to indicate our interview is drawing to a close. He smiles for the camera as he delivers a last election promise:

'I should say that by 1996, by the time we go for the next general elections, we should have no cases of cholera anywhere in Zambia.'

The interview is over.

The crew leaves for Harare and I fly to Livingstone to see Victoria Falls. I cross the bridge across the falls connecting Zambia with Zimbabwe and it is like changing continents. Suddenly there are sparkling hotels with glitzy souvenir shops, gaming arcades and art galleries. Men in red tailcoats with shiny brass buttons and top hats open doors into cool, marble lobbies. Tourists wear gold jewellery and bright, designer clothes. Chunky jeeps disgorge laughing, bronzed teenagers to play tennis. It is a shock to see such health, wealth and conspicuous consumption after Zambia, and I am not at all sure I like it.

I meet Bill, a burly, ruddy-faced, very cheerful British-born market researcher now living in Johannesburg, who cheers me up. We drive round a game park looking at impala, wildebeest, warthog, baboon and zebra, buffalo and giraffe. I am thrilled and restored to be in the African wild again.

Back in Lusaka on my last night in Zambia, Bill takes me to Bandidos, a Tex Mex restaurant serving decent chips and passable steaks camouflaged by a comprehensive array of sauces, in a cheap and cheerful bistro atmosphere. It is particularly popular with airline crews.

Bill is known here and Leo, its Russian-Italian owner, joins us. Leo is rather lugubrious, an effect heightened by a droopy moustache and hair that flops round his face like a curtain. A group of brawny Afrikaans men sit down at our table. They are drinking at a furious pace. Bill begins to talk about 'wogs'. The more sour I become, the more Bill laughs.

'Don't mind her,' he says, 'She's a liberal. I picked her up at Vic Falls.'

I think about walking out, but this blatant, unrestrained racism and sexism fascinates me. I am intrigued to see where the evening will end and if I can keep my temper. Leo suggests we go on somewhere, so Bill and I pile into a car with two of the Afrikaaners. We head for the Pamodzi Casino and on the way the Afrikaaners chide me for having no sense of humour. One of them even pinches my cheek.

Leo manages to talk our way into the casino without paying. A waiter brings us a tray of Scotch, vodka and beer. The Afrikaaners jeer at him and say he looks as if he has AIDS. I tell them I think their jokes are in poor taste. They bellow with mirth and call me an 'ignorant liberal'. A very drunk, shabby-looking Welshman lurches up, sits down beside me and tries to kiss me. There is nearly a fight as Leo sees him off.

Again, instead of leaving I stay, fascinated by what they have to say. After all, offensive as it is, this is as true a side of Zambia as a cholera centre or a game park. I have numbed my anger with vodka. When we are finally thrown out of the casino, one of the Afrikaaners bows, kisses my hand and says I am a 'fine and true lady'.

My hangover the next morning is atrocious. I can't even face a cup of tea. I resort to Andrews Liver Salts for the first time in my life. Once on the plane back to London I finally sleep. I dream that the Afrikaaners have cholera and I have to insert their drips.

I showed my cholera film to the World Health Organisation in Geneva a few weeks later. I was told to tone it down and take out several shots of excrement: the film might cause offence to the Zambian government. I had rather hoped it would do exactly that, but I was ordered to make it blander, and to delete any defamatory references to the Zambian Minister for Health.

I was disillusioned, but later encouraged when the film was used during the cholera outbreak that followed the Bangladesh floods. It was also shown on Zambian television, and an edited version was broadcast on ITN's 'Roving Report'. But despite all the WHO's attempts at education, cholera is still perceived in the developing world as a merciless and uncheckable killer.

Immediately I had finished with the cholera film I returned to Zambia, this time drawn by a far deadlier killer which is to ravage and change Africa forever.

3 CONSENTING ADULTS
Zambia

I was asked by Television Trust for the Environment, a London-based charity, if I would make a film about AIDS. I had already had an unforgettable experience which made me realise that I had no real understanding of the nature and scale of the AIDS epidemic, and that if I ever got the chance I wanted to do something to help.

I first see the book over tea and cakes with Dr. Karuicki at UNICEF in Lusaka. It lies innocuously on the table between us. It is A4 sized and has a pale blue cover like any standard academic publication. The title is *A Colour Atlas of AIDS in the Tropics*.

Dr. Karuicki meticulously dabs crumbs from the corners of his mouth with a napkin as we chat about the weather. We sip tea from flowered cups. I am absolutely unprepared for what I am about to see.

Anyone who is in any doubt about the ravaging physical impact of AIDS needs to look at this book. But it is not for the squeamish – it makes me physically sick. But it also makes me furious that in the West we are so ignorant and care so little. It gives me a real sense of mission and further cements my relationship with Africa.

Inside the book are medical photographs showing various parts of the body distorted into unimaginable shapes, sizes and textures. In the section on Karposi's Sarcoma, a kind of skin cancer, the flesh of grotesquely bloated feet and hands bursts through blackened, gangrenous skin. In the chapter on sexually transmitted diseases, swollen penises blister and bleed. There are brightly-lit close-ups of vaginas swarming with warts, sores and evil-looking growths.

Then there is a section in which people no longer have skin, reduced to shapeless lumps of rotting flesh. Babies' tiny bodies erupt with pustules. Poisonous rashes crawl over children's skin. Tongues ulcerate and form crusts of scab, eyes ooze with yellow mucous, lymph glands thrust from neck and groin, ripe and hard as melons. Scaling breasts are cancerous and tumid, gums a riot of scarlet sores, mouths frothy with fungus. The putrid gashes in the black skin are lurid in the camera's merciless flashlight, the brilliance of the colours accentuating this torrid violence against the body. The people portrayed in the book – at least, those who have not been blinded by the disease – gaze balefully and hopelessly at the camera.

The book gives me nightmares. I cannot erase its images from my mind. When I set out to make the AIDS film I learn that the United Nations Development Programme (UNDP) has donated some funds, but not enough. I am determined to find the rest of the money myself – right here in Lusaka. So I start trudging round the aid community.

The Zambian agencies have no spare money. USAID boast about their free distribution of condoms and their substantial funding but can give me no cash for the film. Norwegian NORAD and Swedish SIDA voice concern but fail to help after numerous meetings in their serene, blond wood consulates. Finally, a harassed-looking man at the British Consulate agrees to give me £5,000. It is still not enough.

Someone suggests I try the international banks and so I go to meet Nicholas Brentnall, a tall Englishman in a very well-cut suit, who runs Barclays in Lusaka. He has fierce eyebrows at odds with the friendly warmth of his bird-bright eyes. He has worked for Barclays all over the world but has a particular love for Africa. He agrees with me wholeheartedly that not enough is being done to make people aware of the severity of the crisis.

At first I think he is just being polite, but then he tells me about Barclays company policy. He has instigated HIV and AIDS awareness training for all his staff, he does not sack anyone who is HIV+ and he employs a full-time counsellor to look after sick employees. For a country like Zambia, in denial about the appalling severity of the epidemic, this is a futuristic, enlightened approach. Brentnall then agrees to pay all my local costs like food, transport, internal flights and hotels. With his contribution I can just about make the film.

Just as I have raised the necessary money, word comes from London that perhaps I should put the film on hold. There is a wave of opinion in Britain, headed by Andrew Neil and a campaign in the Sunday Times, that AIDS in Africa is wildly exaggerated. But I have seen that book and talked to enough Zambians not to doubt that the situation is critical and cries out for media attention. I am determined to prove Andrew Neil and his collaborators wrong.

A couple of weeks later the Zambian Government informs me that I have all the necessary permits. I go to see Dr. Kawanda at the Ministry of Health to confirm dates for filming. Dr. Kawanda sifts through a pile of papers very slowly with fat, stubby fingers till he finds my permit.

'Ah yes!' he says. He smiles at me, stroking his lush silk tie.

'You are permitted to film,' he says, then smoothly with barely a pause: 'providing you do not interview any person or persons who are HIV+ or any of their relatives.'

I am stunned.

'I can't possibly make the film without talking to people who are HIV+,' I say.

'This is for their own protection,' he replies. He leans back in his seat and concentrates on flicking a speck of dust from his lapel.

'But what if they agree to cooperate?' I ask.

He frowns and looks at his watch.

'This is a government decision,' he says. 'It's final.'

There is virtually no-one in Zambia who does not have a relative with AIDS. The government has effectively written a clause into my permit that forbids me to interview most of the population. The crew is arriving from Zimbabwe in a few days and there is no time for delays like this. I contemplate going ahead without permission, but I know I won't be able to tackle such a sensitive subject without full government approval.

I blunder out onto the street, unsure what to do. I decide to visit Father Michael Kelly, an Irish Jesuit priest and clinical psychologist who has set up Hope House, a refuge for HIV+ people. I like him enormously. He is a clumsy, untidy man with smeared spectacles, scraps of hair plastered to a flaking scalp and a big tummy tumbling over crumpled trousers.

I arrive at Hope House and I can hear Father Michael from the front door. I find him very red in the face and shouting angrily at a young Zambian man about petrol and petty cash. The Zambian on the receiving end of this tirade is HIV+ and clearly very ill. His eyes are hectic in a gaunt face and there is sweat on his upper lip. He sidles out of the room, rigid with resentment.

'I hate it when they lie,' says Father Michael, brushing aside a heap of papers from a sagging, beige sofa. He sits down heavily, like a big sack, and a little cloud of dust rises around him.

'Sit down,' he says with a welcoming smile, patting the cushion beside him.

Father Michael insists on treating HIV+ people as equals and makes scant allowance for their illness. According to him being ill does not exempt people from social rules or acceptable codes of behaviour. Stealing and lying are out of order and Father Michael takes such misdemeanours personally. He blows his nose noisily into an oversized handkerchief.

'Those boys. What am I to do with them? They make me so furious.' he says.

'And you've got one hell of a temper,' I suggest. He roars with laughter.

'Oh indeed I have! I have indeed, there's no arguing with that. But you know when you see death every day, and you know they're going to die for sure, you get so frustrated. I know I have a tendency to pick a fight but when I come up against death and sickness I tend to get angry – it's much easier to fight than to cry.'

He takes off his glasses and rubs them frantically with his handkerchief. Specs back on and handkerchief dispatched to the inner reaches of his voluminous trousers, he is ready to face me again, composure regained.

'Now, tell me all about Dr. Kawanda,' he says.

I tell him about my frustrating meeting.

'The man's an idiot,' says Father Michael. 'Let's see what Wingstone has to say about this.' He lumbers over to the door, hitching up his trousers as he goes, and yells down the corridor. Moments later Wingstone Zulu hobbles into the room.

Wingstone has sharp cheekbones and a wide, radiant smile. His eyes portray intelligence, cunning, sexual curiousity and vulnerability in equal measures – a potent combination. His body is stick thin and one of his legs is withered by polio, so he walks with a lurching limp. His physical frailty only serves to accentuate his confident charm. I am spellbound.

Wingstone was the first person in Zambia to go public about having AIDS. It was a courageous move in a country in which HIV+ people were shunned, even by their families. Since then he has given numerous interviews to radio and television and become a national celebrity. Still he is treated with suspicion and, while people admire his bravery, most continue to keep their distance. Wingstone trusts Father Michael precisely because he is over-emotional and has a hot Irish temper.

'It makes me feel I'm still alive,' he tells me, 'The attitude of counsellors is usually very pitying and I don't like that. Michael treats me like anyone else – he shouts at everyone, including me!'

Wingstone has agreed to take part in the film and now I tell him about Dr. Kawanda's impossible restrictions.

'Those stupid government people,' he says, 'This is supposed to be a democracy. Who's to stop me talking to you? I'm a free citizen.'

I know it isn't that easy, but decide not to voice my doubts.

'Everyone will talk to you,' Wingstone assures me. 'Come and meet the others.'

Hope House is a series of bright, airy rooms which open out onto a scruffy garden. It was set up as a safe house for people who have been sacked from their jobs or thrown out of their homes for being HIV+. About thirty people live here. They are given counselling, and taught skills like candle-making, basket-weaving, soapstone sculpture and batik. In exchange for this, the residents join an outreach programme as AIDS educators. Wingstone has named them the PALS, or the Positive and Living Squad.

In the kitchen Wingstone introduces me to Simon, who is cooking dried fish and rice. His face bears the traces of herpes zoster, a vicious virus that manifests itself in a hectic rash. We stand and talk in a haze of pungent, fishy smoke as the pan hisses angrily. When

Simon hears about the Minister he smiles kindly at me.

'Oh dear. That's very bad. I'm sorry,' he says, 'But he cannot stop us talking to you.'

Out in the yard, people are weaving baskets and sculpting. Clement, who was sacked as soon as his employers found out he was HIV+, is squatting amongst his sculptures, chiselling away at a soapstone female form. He is sweating from the exertion in the dusty heat. I am surprised that his creations are so beautiful. Then I feel ashamed of my surprise. I am always coming up against my own preconceived ideas.

Wingstone tells Clement what is going on. He lays down his chisel and looks up at me with a slow, sweet smile.

'Now they are even denying us the right to speak. What else is the government going to deny us? Our right to die? Don't worry, we'll talk to you.'

I feel a surge of warmth for these people and fury against the government. I doubt if Dr. Kawanda has even been here.

I go to see Ibrahim Koroma, the local representative for UNDP, in his bland office off an institutional corridor. An elegant blazer and scarlet tie mask Ibrahim's anxiety.

'I can't believe the Ministry's done this,' he says from behind his spick and span desk under a whirring fan.

'They assured me we would have the permit, and that meeting you was just a formality.' He knows that if we do not have all the right film permits, then his job is on the line with headquarters in New York.

We decide to appeal to the World Health Organisation' representative in Zambia, Dr. Boyaue, a Liberian who appeared in and helped me with the cholera film.

'Please!' I implore Dr. Boyaue's secretary, 'We won't take up more than a minute of his time.'

She regards me over her manual typewriter doubtfully.

'Please!' I repeat.

She shrugs and glances down at her long, crimson nails.

'Just one minute, I promise,' I say. 'I'll be in and out so fast you won't notice me.'

'He's busy,' she says.

'I've flown thousands of miles just to see him.'

She laughs,

'OK, OK, but I'm warning you – just a few minutes.'

I am dithering from foot to foot and biting my lip.

'You're in such a hurry,' she says.

With a rustle of pleated skirt and a waft of Dior's *Poison*, she steps elegantly into Dr. Boyaue's office.

Ibrahim raises an eyebrow. We wait. Once the secretary's potent perfume has evaporated, the smell of urine mixed with dried fish being violently fried in cheap oil drifts in from the staircase. Just as I am wondering who to ask for the key to the lavatory, the door opens.

'He is ready now,' says the secretary.

Dr. Boyaue's calm, avuncular manner reassures me. He waves us towards a brown sofa.

'I'm glad I didn't break your camera on the cholera film,' he says, chuckling.

'Oh no, you were brilliant,' I say, a little over-eagerly.

'Really?' he asks, with a hint of irony. 'So, what can I do for you?'

I tell him what has been going on.

'The situation is very serious,' he says, 'And you have gone about it the wrong way. But Zambia needs a film about AIDS and besides, we know you now.'

I could kiss him. Instead I shake his hand warmly.

'Thank you, thank you!' I say.

Dr. Boyaue shakes his head like an exasperated parent.

'OK, OK, I'll see what I can do.'

After lunch my spirits sag. I cannot start filming till that permit is firmly in my hand. I sit anxiously in Ibrahim's office by his telephone, waiting to hear from Dr. Boyaue. At about five o'clock people start to go home. When I phone the World Health Organisation again no-one answers. I decide the best thing to do is to leave Dr Boyaue to do what he can behind the scenes, and carry on as if the film is going to be made.

The first thing I need to do is fly up to the Copper Belt, where

AIDS is having an impact on the mining communities. It will be my last chance to find the people I need to set up the shoot before the crew arrive. If I hurry I have just enough time to catch a plane up north.

I arrive in Ndola late that night and check into the foetid local hotel, all damp brown carpet and fake wood. There's a TV set so ancient it may have been JM Baird's prototype, and I flop gratefully in front of a trashy pirated film called *Consenting Adults*. Every few seconds an announcement rolls up on the screen indicating that this is an illegal copy and anyone watching it should alert the authorities immediately. It is typical of most of the hotels I stay at in Africa – no-one pays the slightest attention to pirating. I abandon the ridiculous plot and sleep fitfully on my sagging mattress.

Next morning my old friend Mubi arrives, the local Ministry of Health representative who helped me on the cholera film. He gives me a hug and thanks me for the dress I sent his wife from England. When I tell him what has been going on he looks grave.

'This government of ours,' he says, shaking his head, 'Sometimes I wonder. But, with God's grace, we will make this film. It is very necessary. Come on let's go.'

We set off in his bumpy little jeep, driven by a very old man in a crumpled blue suit.

Copper accounts for three quarters of Zambia's exports and now the miners are dying faster than replacements can be trained. The mines have slowed to a virtual standstill. Mubi has already identified some miners who are HIV+ and who might talk on camera.

He takes me to meet Godfrey, a twenty-nine year old man, already suffering from an AIDS related illness. His wife of twenty-three is also HIV+. We find Godfrey alone at home, too sick to work. He lives in a hut with a corrugated iron roof under a budding jacaranda tree. In the background the great mine chimneys loom, a dismal, industrial backdrop to Godfrey's little yard, with its chickens and orange marigolds perky in paint tins.

Godfrey invites us in to a dark room hung with paperchains, and Mubi and I squeeze onto a tiny sofa draped in a pink cloth. The conversation takes place in Bemba but I can see from the glances

Godfrey darts my way that he is assessing me, and I trust Mubi to convince him that I am OK. Half an hour later he agrees to take part in the film.

We return to Mubi's office to call Dr. Boyaue. He has made progress and talked to Dr. Kawanda. He has persuaded the Minister to let me interview Wingstone Zulu but no-one else. Dr. Kawanda is leaving for Livingstone on Monday and will not authorise any filming till he has seen me again in person. Today is Friday. I only have the weekend.

I rush back to the hotel and start calling the Ministry of Health. Dr. Kawanda is out so I leave a message. I sit by the phone. At last it rings but it is just reception telling me to move room because of a leak in my ceiling. I ring the Ministry again but Dr. Kawanda is still unavailable. If only I could go round there and wait for him but I have missed the last flight back to Lusaka. Unless...

I call Zambian Airlines. The 4.30 flight to Lusaka has been delayed. If I leave now I might catch it at 5.30. Sometimes I love the inefficiency and unreliability of Africa – it can provide room for manoeuvre. I throw my clothes into my case, in my hurry leaving behind a treasured travelling alarm clock my mother gave me.

'You are very fortunate,' says the airline official, looking at me sternly over half-moon spectacles, 'There is one seat left.'

'Thank you,' I say, checking my watch. At this rate I am going to have to seek out Dr. Kawanda at home.

'But you are very late,' chides the official. 'In future, please be on time. You are lucky that the plane has been delayed another twenty minutes.'

I sit amongst the other passengers on an uncomfortable plastic bucket seat. I watch a fat Zambian woman in peach-coloured robes and a hat blooming with artificial flowers as she argues with an official about her luggage, a series of cardboard boxes tied up with string. She waves her blue diplomatic passport as if it were a magic wand. The baggage handlers regard her sullenly while the official examines her passport reverentially, turning it over and over in his hands. The woman stamps her foot. It is quite entertaining, but each minute seems an hour.

I worry about finding Dr. Kawanda on a Saturday if I miss him tonight. The plane is on the tarmac, the luggage ranged in rows alongside it to be identified as we board. Finally we start to shuffle towards the exit.

I am standing in the queue to board when an armed policeman taps me on the elbow. I am led to a telephone but can hardly hear above the scream of the plane engine. I identify the voice of Dr. Kawanda:

'You have been filming up there without permission,' he accuses me furiously.

I point out that the crew and camera are still in Zimbabwe.

'You have been talking to people with HIV,' he says, 'You were expressly forbidden to do so.'

I wonder how he knows. I am even more curious to know how he has tracked me down to the airport. I begin to feel paranoid about spies.

'Dr. Kawanda, let me explain,' I shout above the deafening roar of the engines.

'You will interview Wingstone Zulu and no-one else!' he cuts in.

A man from Zambian Airways hovers.

'Madam, you must board now please.'

It is now or never. I start to grovel. I tell the Minister I am desperately sorry to have messed up the protocol. Perhaps I can come and see him at home on Saturday to explain? That tips the balance. He does not want his weekend interrupted.

'All right. You can make your film,' he barks.

I start to thank him.

'But only if you have written permission from everyone involved,' he interrupts.

With that he rings off. I have won. I grin at the official. He is stern.

'Madam, you have delayed the plane,' he says. 'Hurry. Please.'

As I board I am walking on air and oblivious to the hostile glances around me. I say hello with a friendly smile to the man next to me. He scowls and turns back to his magazine, but I don't care. We have our permit.

4 BLIND LOVER
Zambia

After ten lonely, stressful days, I was thoroughly fed up. I felt an urgent need for some human companionship in a relaxing environment. Bandidos was the only restaurant I knew in Lusaka, so I went back there. Being a Friday night it was packed. I joined Leo, the owner, at his regular table, and it soon became clear that once again I had not fallen amongst kindred spirits.

'The whores in Jo'burg are hot, man,' says Leo, nudging me.

He is already several Irish coffees down and his speech is beginning to slur. He dominates the conversation, to the evident approval of his equally macho cronies, and his next topic is pornography, on which it seems he is also an authority. After that he lurches into an unprovoked diatribe against homosexuals.

Leo is not only a homophobe he is a deluded one, because he really believes homosexuality does not exist in his country. Just as I am about to become embroiled in a stand-up fight with him someone else suggests we go on to a club. I am mighty relieved to escape from Leo and his crew.

We go to Marco Polo's, an open-air restaurant and discotheque attached to Lusaka's polo club, with soothing views over lawn and paddock. It is run by a young blond Englishman called Paul, and the week-end dance nights are popular with expats and Zambians alike.

I meet Erik, a sad-looking Finn. He is doing conjuring tricks and making pretty shadows with his fingers while drinking copious amounts of neat vodka. An engineer, he has a lonely job maintaining electricity plants around the countryside. He is polite, gentle and shy – a marked improvement on my recent foul-mouthed company – so when he invites me to have lunch with him tomorrow I accept readily.

Next day, after canelloni at the Intercontinental Erik accompanies me to a service at St. Ignatius Church in memory of those who have died from AIDS. Father Michael preaches and reads from the Bible. His cassock flatters him and he has managed to paste down most of his hair. He speaks with authority and passion. Wingstone recites a poem and his friend Simon gives a moving account of living with AIDS. A woman from Hope House sings a song about being HIV+. Her thin, clear voice fills the church:

> *AIDS virus is a monster,*
> *It goes into the families, killing its members,*
> *Widows and orphans, it's a homebreaker,*
> *No-one is too strong.*
>
> *AIDS virus is a monster,*
> *It tramples our economy, stealing manpower,*
> *People the world over, moaning and wailing,*
> *There's no colour, no status,*
> *It's a blind lover,*
> *No-one is too strong.*

As she sings pink, yellow and blue paper stars are handed out as a sign we are close to someone who is HIV+. We light candles and walk round the church. There are not many people here but I feel close to tears. Father Michael is gruff, hiding his emotion, but Wingstone is full of mischief, winking and gesturing in Erik's direction.

'Stop it!' I say crossly, 'I've only just met him.'

'What did I say?' he asks disingenuously, and hobbles off chuckling.

Erik takes me to Munda Wanga Gardens and we sit on a bench next to an ornamental pond and share a bottle of wine. Erik becomes mournful as he watches Zambian children playing amongst the flowers. He confesses a desire to marry.

'My life has been empty, but now you have walked into it,' he says.

He turns and looks at me with pale eyes the colour of sea, and asks me to join him for a weekend at Victoria Falls. I tell him, truthfully, that once the crew arrive I will have no time to spend with him.

'Can I see you tomorrow?' he persists.

'No, I'm sorry,' I say as gently as possible, 'and now I have to get back.'

The next day the price of breakfast has doubled. Taxi prices have also soared because the cost of petrol has doubled overnight. Gloomily, worrying more about my film budget than Zambia's tottering economy, I take my expensive taxi into town and run around doing errands, booking crew tickets up to the Copper Belt, finalising their customs clearances and making various courtesy visits to the UN and the Ministry.

Back at my hotel I go for a swim, and when I emerge from the pool I find Erik stalking around furiously. He has bought tickets to Victoria Falls, ignoring the fact I have told him I cannot go. He is not to be put off.

'I'll be here tomorrow,' he says.

Irritated by Erik's persistence, I perversely accept an invitation to go out to dinner with Ali, a Scot over a decade younger than me. He comes from North Uist and knows my uncle there. It is his first time in Africa and I like his relentless enthusiasm for it. He arrives close-shaven and pink-faced and takes me back to Marco Polo's where we eat crocodile tail for dinner and then dance until four.

In the course of the evening Paul, the English manager of Marco Polo's, is particularly attentive to Ali and me and I rather like him. His visits to our table become more frequent and later, while Ali is drunkenly performing Scottish reels on the dance floor, Paul takes my hand and leads me to see the polo ponies. My social life is definitely looking up. They are very handsome ponies.

I finally fall into bed at five only to be woken an hour later by the telephone. Now Paul is downstairs in the lobby, inviting me to breakfast. I am confused and blurry with lack of sleep.

'Come on,' he says, 'It's Africa Freedom Day – it's a public holiday. There's going to be an all-day party.'

He drives me back to Marco Polo's as the sun comes up. The disco is only just coming to an end and there are at least twenty hungry revellers ready for breakfast. Paul has laid a long table out on the lawn and produces coffee and platters of steak and eggs. A Greek girl with pock-marked skin and a totally see-through miniskirt sits on her Zambian boyfriend's lap. A girl with enormous breasts in a tiny dress announces she is a non-practising Muslim from Pakistan but then confesses she hails from Madras. With that she falls over.

'You're just an ordinary Zambian, my dear,' says a very camp Somali who is trying to chat to me about London Fashion Week.

A Zambian man, swigging from a bottle of vodka, is cracking jokes about President Chilube's sex life which have the entire company doubled up with laughter. Two young men lurk behind dark glasses and sit grinning but silent, with their arms slung round each other's shoulders. The non-practising Muslim girl suddenly bursts into tears. The Somali strokes her hair:

'It's all right my dear, you can tell me.' Over the top of her weeping head he winks lasciviously at the boys in sunglasses. I wonder what Leo would make of the scene, given he firmly believes there are no gays in Zambia.

Everyone eventually staggers away to start their holiday. Paul takes me out for lunch at the Intercontinental and then back to his house, a haven cloaked with bouganvillea where we sit, laze around and talk. I could have stayed all day. Sadly, I need to organise myself before the crew arrives.

Back at the hotel I find Erik pacing up and down the lobby. He is wearing a particularly unflattering shell suit with mauve stripes. I reiterate that the crew is arriving the next day and I do not have time to see him.

'I'm prepared to wait,' he says. 'I want to take you to Europe. Let's go to Salzburg and listen to some music.'

I feel his homesickness and loneliness.

'I left you a rose,' he says.

He comes with me to pick it up from reception. The girls behind the desk are giggling.

'These came for you too,' they say.

Paul has sent me a dozen red roses wrapped in cellophane and tied with ribbon. Erik takes one look at them and walks out of the hotel.

Peter and Tzvika arrive and I am very glad to start filming. We are to shoot our first scene at Hope House. As we walk in Simon, Clement and the others hold their hands out with eager friendliness. Peter and Tzvika linger, arms at their side. I gesture to them to shake hands but they just stand there. Later I find out they have been given all kinds of false information in Zimbabwe. They think HIV can be transmitted via a handshake.

'Come off it!' I say, 'You know better than that.'

'But that's just the point,' says Peter, 'No-one knows anything about this illness. Isn't it better to be safe than sorry?'

'Absolutely,' agrees Tzvika.

I want to knock their heads together.

In the evening as part of the PALS outreach programme, Simon is giving a talk on AIDS to the staff of the Pamodzi Hotel. Since we are staying there, I decide to film it. Simon sits and waits for chairs to fill up in one of the hotel's brightly lit but depressing function rooms. Staff sidle in and sit at the back. Apart from two nurses the front four rows are empty. There seems to be an acre of carpet between the audience and Simon, who sits quietly behind a desk, sipping from a glass of water. I try to make people move forward but they won't.

Simon tells his story simply and honestly, speaking without self-pity. Only his slender hands, which he wrings constantly, betray his emotion. The audience is very quiet. Faces are tense, arms crossed defensively across chests.

'I know you have all heard about AIDS,' says Simon. 'That explains why so many chairs are empty. You don't want to hear about AIDS. You shun the talk.'

People shift uneasily. Women snigger coyly behind their hands.

'But the thing most people want to know is, how does a person look who has AIDS? I'm sure when I arrived most of you didn't realise I was HIV+.'

Simon scans the room.

'Well, let me tell you, the person with AIDS looks normal, just like the person sitting next to you. That person next to you is the one who's going to infect you.'

A man in the audience looks at the woman next to him and prods her to move over. She stands up and changes her seat. The audience laughs nervously. Simon smiles patiently and waits for the laughter to subside.

Over dinner the crew are thoughtful.

'That Simon, he's a hell of a guy' says Tzvika, 'This AIDS thing is radical. It's hectic,'

'Oh it's hectic all right,' I say, thinking of the photographs in the blue book.

Next day I am very glad to see Peter and Tzvika shaking people's hands at Hope House.

We interview Clement surrounded by his sculpture:

'In the early days I wanted to commit suicide. But since I came to Hope House I've learned to value my life. There's no other place like it in the country. The way AIDS is presented in the posters and on the electronic media – well, it's a fairytale. Here HIV and AIDS have a human face,' he says, and grins.

I glance at the tortured faces of his carvings.

'We all die one time or another,' he goes on, 'So why should I make a big fuss about it? After all, death is not going to catch me unawares. I'll be ready for it.' He chuckles.

We accompany David, another Hope House resident, to Kasisi Girls' Boarding School where he is giving a talk to the pupils. Before he was diagnosed HIV+ David planned to be a Catholic priest. He is just twenty-two.

At the school three hundred girls in yellow shirts wait in the dining hall. At first there is a lot of nervous giggling as they eye the open sores on David's face. David takes control:

'During the session you might find me humorous but we're talking about something very serious,' he says, pacing the stage and looking sternly at the girls.

'The Ministry of Health says one person in four is infected. That's a quarter of everyone in this room. Everybody, including the teachers and the crew here, could be infected.'

There is a surge of hubbub as the girls exclaim in disbelief. David waits before continuing. By now the girls are mesmerised. They question him slyly and provocatively about sexual positions and then ask downright silly questions about the number of condoms their boyfriends can wear. There are questions about kissing and tongues that provoke shrill little giggles and wriggling, so the room appears to be full of fluttering birds.

David takes all this in his stride and answers with self-possession. I can see some of the girls admiring him. Sores apart, he is handsome and in another life would have made someone a fine husband.

After the session the girls swarm round him, eager to look at him more closely and to seek his approval and attention. I wonder if David's talk has really done any good, but talking to the girls afterwards most say they have learned a lot.

'David's courage was really something,' a girl says. 'It really teaches us that even if you've got the disease you don't have to die just like that.'

We spend the next day filming with Father Michael and Wingstone. Father Michael wants to show off his new venture and takes us to a construction site that is to be a resource centre providing information, a research library, seminar rooms and training in counselling and management. Father Michael hopes that someone will see the film and donate some funds. He is wearing a very silly blue cap and arrives with a dachshund puppy called Hopey, after Hope House. Hopey finds Father Michael's trousers wildly exciting and spends most of the day hurling himself in a frenzy of lust at the Father's thighs.

Wingstone's extended interview makes me weep. When he was twenty-six he received a scholarship from the ruling party to study in the Soviet Union, along with seven others. They had to have a medical before they left and five of them, including Wingstone, tested HIV+. He met a Born Again Christian who told him that prayer would cure him.

Prepared to try anything Wingstone prayed fervently and regularly for three months and then had another test. While he waited for the results he prayed even harder. When he heard he was still HIV+ Wingstone was so disappointed he fell ill. He asked the Christian why he had filled him with false hope.

'You didn't pray hard enough,' said the Christian, 'You are obviously a sinner.'

Wingstone tells this sorry story to illustrate a prevailing attitude in Zambia. People believe that people with AIDS 'deserve it' and have had unsavoury and sinful lifestyles. The Zambian public regard sufferers with fear and loathing. It was after this that Wingstone made the decision to go public.

'AIDS is terrible,' says Wingstone, 'You can't compare it with anything else. I'm in a predicament. On the one hand I'm going round saying that HIV is normal, look at me, see how you can live with it, but on the other hand I know it's the most abnormal thing which can happen to anyone. I think AIDS is the biggest global problem since the world war.'

During the interview Wingstone asks for a break. He says he is distracted looking into my eyes. I am embarassed. I know I am communicating more than a professional interest. I am enthralled by him – more by his courage and serenity than by his beauty. I readjust my face into a neutral mask but as his story continues it is hard to hide my feelings.

'He should come to Zimbabwe,' says Peter afterwards, 'They should hear this guy. We've got no-one like him in Zimbabwe.'

Nor anywhere else, I think sadly.

I'm glad to be leaving for the Copper Belt next day. Mubi meets us at Ndola airport. He has booked us into a new hotel, a bizarre, motel-style place adorned with macabre, rather mangy, stuffed heads of buck and eland. The rooms lead off stone corridors and open onto bare flower beds. The restaurant plays four Elvis Presley songs on a loop. My room stinks and is full of mosquitoes. I cannot turn the radio off.

We drive out to the mining district to interview Godfrey and his wife. Godfrey is wearing a white shirt which makes filming difficult, because Tzvika cannot balance the contrast between the brightness of the shirt and his face. I take off my denim shirt and lend it to him. It sags on his thin frame.

'I don't know if I'll live till next year. When it starts to hurt, deep down inside here,' says Godfrey, indicating his heart, 'I feel life is escaping me.'

Godfrey's wife starts to cry.

'I try to tell him stories to try and stop him being eaten up by his condition, but it's all in the hands of God now,' she says. She bends her head and wipes her eyes furiously with the hem of her apron.

We want a shot of Godfrey walking towards us with the mines in the background, but his lungs are so weak from advanced TB that he has to rest after every few steps. Godfrey personifies the impact of AIDS on industry. Unlike most illnesses which target the infirm, the old or the very young, AIDS preys on the backbone of the workforce. If the miners aren't dying themselves they are off work coping with sick families or attending funerals. The mines are grinding to a halt for lack of manpower.

We go on to Wasikili Hospital where a pretty but exhausted doctor shows us wards full of AIDS patients waiting to die. There is no longer space for people with treatable illnesses. There are not enough doctors or nurses to cope with the AIDS crisis, let alone treat those not in dire and immediate need. There are no more beds, and medicines are quite simply running out.

'Home based care is the only solution,' says the doctor, 'The health service is on the brink of collapse.'

We drive thirty miles out of Ndola to look at the impact of HIV and AIDS on agriculture. In a village of thatched huts, ducks and chickens scratch around in clean, yellow soil, the sun shines and people run out to smile at us. I almost feel cheerful. Then we interview Sam, a young farmer, and his grandfather. Sam used to grow maize and sorghum on his grandparents' land but since contracting HIV has become too ill to work. There is no machinery to help him.

Sam and his grandfather take us out into the fields and show us an area rampant with weeds and grass.

'All this used to be maize,' says Sam, gesturing as far as the horizon.

His grandfather stands, straight and proud, listening to his grandson. He has no shoes but he puts on a threadworn white jacket especially for the camera. This dignified gesture makes me want to cry.

'Now there is only grass in the field. I do not have the strength to plough,' says Sam.

If AIDS continues spreading there are not going to be enough people to grow the food that Zambia so desperately needs. This seems to me to be apocalyptic news, and I want to shout it from the mountain tops to the Andrew Neils of this world to shake them out of their ill-informed and dangerous complacency.

After the Copper Belt it is back to Lusaka where we begin filming with Barclays Bank, as an example of the impact of AIDS on business. A Mr. Bright Nyerende invites us to attend one of his training sessions. Bright sports big square spectacles and long sideburns. He picks up a wooden penis and a condom. He does not mince his words:

'Now for the purposes of understanding, I will talk about the human anatomy freely. Today we are going to break down taboos.'

His audience holds its breath. Such explicit talk and action are rare. While practical and grave about the risks of non-protected sex, Bright manages to be both entertaining and witty. Every so often he stops in mid-sentence and, with pencil or piece of chalk (and once the wooden penis) poised in mid-air, he asks:

'Are we together?'

The class nods eagerly. At the end there is a huge round of applause. Bright is Barclays' secret weapon.

'Now I am going to visit one of our employees who is sick. You might want to come,' Bright says to the crew and me, still clutching the wooden penis.

'Are we together?'

'Yes,' the three of us chorus, and without hesitation we pile into his car with the camera. On the way to the suburbs Bright talks about the effect of HIV on business.

'A man who is HIV+ can work for five, six, maybe ten years. But it's the stigma which kills. Once these people are rejected they just give up and die – they are outcasts. If we learn to treat people properly and with respect there's no reason why their usefulness to the company can't extend by a decade or even more. Home visits keep morale and performance levels high,' he explains.

Burns Lubinda is one of Barclays' top men in foreign exchange but is now severely ill with TB. Though it is obvious that Burns is probably in an advanced state of AIDS, he has refused to be tested. Bright respects his choice and wants him to feel he is emotionally supported by his colleagues and bosses.

We arrive at Burns's compound and go into a spotless living room dominated by a huge television draped in white lace. We sit on a sofa festooned with pink doilies. Burns's wife emerges smiling and shy from behind a beaded curtain with a tray of Fantas. She wears a pleated skirt, shoes with bows on them and a flowered sweater. She introduces us to their son, a good-looking twelve-year-old in new trainers.

Burns's skin is pallid and his eyes are livid and feverish in dark hollows. He is skeletal, and when he coughs into his handkerchief there are globules of blood in his phlegm. Burns's son winces each time his father coughs. He listens intently to Bright as if the answers to his father's problems lie with this kind, bespectacled man.

'First we will all take Fanta, then we will have some chatting and then I believe it will be good to pray. Are we together?' Bright asks, opening his bottle with a loud hiss.

Bright starts to pray. I look at his bowed head and at Burns's son who has screwed his eyes up tight as if to implore God to help. The presence of AIDS hangs over the pin-neat little room like a monstrously toxic vapour. Seeing the ever-practical Bright resorting to prayer makes me realise how useless we all are in the face of this remorseless killer. As we are leaving Burns's wife holds onto my hand and thanks me as though I have personally brought a cure. I feel humble and helpless, and snap at Tzvika and Peter all the way back to town.

Later we go to film Wingstone addressing a group of industrial workers. In a bare, whitewashed room some tin chairs have been arranged in rows. Men in orange overalls drift in. One man comes up to me.

'So, how long will it be before we have the cure for this AIDS?' he asks. He waits for my answer with a bright, expectant smile.

I plump for the truth:

'I'm afraid I simply don't know, but then nor does anyone else.'

The man's face closes down.

'Thank you madam,' he says stiffly as he backs away.

Wingstone arrives with Joseph, another Hope House resident. Joseph has herpes zoster which has ravaged his skin. A terrible, angry scar runs down one side of his face. The workers regard him with fear and hostility, alienated by his physical appearance. Wingstone sits down quickly behind the desk so few will notice his withered leg. He begins to talk, but his audience is not an easy one.

'Can you ever sleep with a woman again?' asks a man.

There are sniggers and snorts of laughter. Wingstone takes it in his stride. I wish I had Bright's faith in prayer. I'd do anything to be able to believe that a cure is on the way.

Following the success of his nightly television and radio broadcasts during the cholera crisis, Dr. Manasseh Piri has been offered a new post by President Chilube. He is now Director General of ZBC, the Zambian Broadcasting Corporation. If his interview in the cholera film is anything to go by he will have a lot to say on the subject of AIDS.

ZBC is deserted except for a man mopping the floor. We lug the equipment up several flights of stairs. We find the Director General's office, but it is locked. Tzvika shrugs.

'He's not going to come, I'm telling you,' he says.

'That's what you said last time,' I retort. He ignores me and lights a cigarette.

'What now?' asks Peter.

'We wait,' I snap.

Half an hour later Dr. Piri appears. The beard has gone and his face is wreathed in smiles above an immaculate suit and tie. He gives me a big hug.

'The cholera film was great!' he says. 'I've already broadcast it twice on Zambian Television.'

He shakes hands warmly with the crew.

'Nice to see you guys again,' he says. 'Congratulations on the cholera film – really. It was excellent.' Tzvika is mollified.

Dr. Piri gives a brilliant, articulate interview in which his searing intellect and complete grasp of the situation makes his image jump out of the screen and take the audience by the throat:

'AIDS is not just a health problem. It's an economic problem, a social problem, a political problem. Above all, it's an individual problem. Every single individual in Zambia has got to think in individual terms. Recently a delegation of Indian doctors came to visit me and asked if I had one piece of advice to India, what would it be?'

Dr. Piri leans forward intently into the camera.

'I said, if there's one single piece of advice, it's "Admit it. Admit it, recognise the problem and then start to do something about it."'

Afterwards I feel elated and emotional. I know Dr. Piri has given me the backbone of rigorous and risky straight talking my film needs. He has to rush off to supervise the evening news, but just as he is leaving he offers me a job.

'I can't pay you British prices, but it'll be a handsome salary for Zambia,' he says. 'Think about it.'

In the presence of this clever, passionate, committed man I nearly accept the offer on the spot.

The story has a sad ending. Dr. Piri knows that television is a crucial weapon in the battle against AIDS. All over the city posters advocate marital fidelity or abstinence. Dr. Piri also knows enough about human nature to know these are unrealistic messages, especially amongst the young. People are not going to stop having sex. Condoms are the only sensible and affordable barrier between life and death.

Most young men we have talked to regard condoms with contempt as threats to their virility and masculinity, but Dr. Piri comes up with a brainwave. He gathers the Zambian football team together. Zambian footballers have heroic status because the former team died tragically in an air crash. If the footballers will testify to the importance of condoms on television every young Zambian male is guaranteed to rush to the chemist in imitation of his heroes.

President Chilube hears about the campaign. He is outraged. As a Born Again leader of a Christian country he thinks Dr. Piri has taken leave of his senses and is using television to degrade and disgust his countrymen. Dr. Piri is removed from his post immediately. Since then AIDS has continued to ravage Zambia. Current estimates claim that as many as one person in two is affected.

To me Dr Piri's dismissal sums up much that is wrong with Africa. Brilliant visionaries who are simultaneously grounded in reality are few and far between. Dr. Piri is such a visionary. He should be speaking out, not just to his own country but to Africa as a whole and to the United Nations. I have rarely heard anyone talk such sense. Yet he has been prevented from doing what he does best – analysing the causes of and finding solutions to the crises confronting modern Africa.

The interview with Dr. Piri completes our filming, and to celebrate I take the crew out to dinner. After I've paid the bill and the crew has gone to bed I find Paul waiting for me in the lobby. He has procured a bottle of wine and two glasses. We sit by the pool and talk late into the night. I could have grown close to him but I am leaving for a different world in the morning and so, reluctantly, I resign myself to parting. I have not seen him since.

I edited the film and took a rough cut to UNDP in New York. A group of representatives gathered to watch. None of them liked it. They wanted more facts and figures, graphs and information. They felt the film was not enough of an 'advocacy tool'. They were not interested in what were for us, the crew, the intensely moving human stories. They would have preferred an illustrated script with wall to wall commentary.

What they did with the film, I do not know. What I do know is that AIDS continues to ravage Africa and most of what we predicted in the film has come to pass.

5 THE RED TERROR
Ethiopia

I was living in Kenya when Rags Ek telephoned me from London. Rags was a Danish academic who, though not a film maker, had landed a commission from the BBC to make a documentary about Ethiopia. She had recruited the well-known journalist George Alagiah as a presenter but they needed a director. I could not wait to take the first plane out of Nairobi. I had been living there a few months waiting on films that never happened, making dull, worthy local documentaries and cheap commercials.

What's the film about?' I ask when Rags phones.

'Mengistu,' she says.

'Who?'

I am shamefully unaware of the extent of atrocities committed against his own people by the Ethiopian Communist Dictator, Colonel Mengistu Haile Mariam. During the notorious Red Terror in the late seventies Mengistu condemned thousands to the torture chamber, death or both. While I was at Cambridge in the late seventies having the time of my life, dancing at May Balls and drinking Pimms on ancient college lawns, Mengistu was conducting his Red Terror, Pinochet was in charge in Chile and over two million people were dying in Cambodia under the Khmer Rouge.

Mengistu fled to Zimbabwe in 1991 and still lives in Harare under President Mugabe's protection. Now it is 1994 and Ethiopia is groping its way towards a working democracy. Meles, the new president elect, has initiated the long and complicated process of trying to extradite Mengistu for trial. Mengistu and thousands of his aides and supporters have been charged with crimes against humanity. People believe the impending trials will be on the scale of Nuremberg.

When I arrive in Addis Ababa to 'recce' the film, there is no-one to meet me. Rags has assured me she will be here, so I haven't established in advance where I am staying and I have no phone number for her. I am quite used to waiting around in Africa so I sit down on my bag and observe the crowd. I am immediately impressed by how exquisite the Ethiopians are, small and slender with high cheekbones, almond-shaped eyes, long, fine noses and chiselled lips.

Two hours later a man appears with a tattered piece of paper bearing the name 'Mr. Matcale' in green ink. I might have ignored it had he not also written 'Rags Productions' in small letters. I climb into the slithery plastic seat in the back of his taxi and we set off for the centre of town.

Shanty towns cling to the hillsides around Addis. In the city centre the vast, now shabby avenues and squares are testimony to the splendour of Emperor Haile Selassie's forty-four year rule till 1974. More ominous are the monuments to Mengistu's power, Soviet-style statues and bronze reliefs sculpted by North Koreans. Flags unfurl, peasants raise their fists skyward in salute, soldiers thrust their bayonets into the air and, chanting in unison, all veer towards their leader, Mengistu – portraits of an idyllic Communist state.

Even my hotel, the Ghion, reminds me of the Eastern Bloc with its grim, unforgiving façade. The less heroic aspects of Communism are evident in the hotel's decor. The place stinks of dank carpet. There are long, grimy corridors painted khaki with red rugs, now mouldy and stained, running down the middle. My bedroom is drab and decorated in beige and fading lime green. I unpack and lie down on my sagging brown bed.

Rags returns after lunch with George Alagiah. Most of his television reporting requires a solemn, even grim, demeanour so I have not seen him smile before. I am dazzled by the beauty of his grin. We go into the huge dining room where we meet Gail, a respected expert on Mengistu. Gail is passionate about the culpability of the international community during the great Ethiopian famine. I listen to her talk while I eat my chicken stew.

By the end of lunch I am convinced that in his attempt to cling to power Mengistu has commited genocide comparable with Pol Pot and Stalin. I was hired in a hurry and I was not then clear about the purpose of the film. Now I am excited. I spend the rest of the afternoon absorbing as much information as I can lay my hands on.

I am not sure what to make of Rags. She has a very direct manner, which I find disarming. Though she is in her early thirties her style is rather matronly. She dresses in long, pleated floral skirts, court shoes and jackets, often emerald silk or royal blue with boxy shoulders. Her hair is hennaed and cut into a severe bob with a precise thick fringe. This frames her round face in which glint a pair of bright blue, very alert eyes, easily her most striking feature.

She can be immensely charming and is capable of giggling child-ishly, particularly when men are around. But if there is the slightest whiff of confrontation she becomes stern and forbidding, wagging her finger and remonstrating in her clipped Danish accent.

Most nights we drink local Asmara gin in the bedroom she shares with her Canadian-Japanese assistant Vivien, to keep costs down. The sharp, clean whiff of gin mingles with Rags's scent. She wears Beverly Hills *Georgio* and it is wildly sweet and a little overpower-ing. It even permeates the curtains which otherwise smell of mud. Rags likes to talk late and after I escape to bed – leaving Vivien ashen and exhausted – Rags starts typing. She loves technology and her laptop is her latest toy.

Each morning she emerges crisply dressed, her hair impeccable and sleek. At breakfast she refuses coffee, insisting on papaya and mineral water to 'plump up the skin'. As we leave the hotel Rags orders the car to stop, so she can give a handout to two beggar girls who wait daily by the gates. As soon as they see the car the bundles of rags stand up from the gutter where they have been crouching and run up to us, eyes shining in their dirty faces.

'Aren't they cute?' says Rags. Then, her daily act of charity accomplished, she leans back and sighs with satisfaction as we sweep off into town.

Two days after I arrive news breaks that skeletons have been dug up in the grounds of the Institute of Security. During this period of investigation there are hundreds of grisly discoveries daily. Already one mass grave has been unearthed containing the remains of sixty high-ranking officials in Haile Selassie's Imperial Government. The officials were murdered as part of the first wave of executions in 1974, when Haile Selassie was deposed and replaced by a military government led by General Teferi Benti. It was the same year that Mengistu began his bloody rise to power, culminating three years later when Teferi was killed and Mengistu took over.

That mass grave yielded the bones of one prince, two prime ministers, twenty-five ministers and provincial governors, eleven lieutenant generals, four major generals, two brigadier generals, one commander of the navy, three colonels and seven officers of other rank. I wonder rather grimly what we will find in this latest grave.

A grey government Mercedes picks us up. At the gates of the Institute of Security armed guards stop us. Then follows an hour of arguing as our entrance is barred. Luckily Rags knows a colonel there who eventually allows us to proceed. Guards lead us to the grave where we find a team of forensic scientists from Argentina – young women, clean and shiny in their pressed dungarees and white T-shirts. They are dusting skulls and teasing out the grisly evidence from the mud.

I expect to be shocked by the exhumation but I am not. The shreds of clothing and the shrunken-looking skeletons do not seem real. The setting is almost beautiful. Towering cypress trees murmur in the breeze and wildflowers scent the air. Only the bunker-like building in the distance suggests the horror of the mass execution. I try to imagine the men being led out to this quiet spot and shot.

The Argentinians chatter away, sometimes laughing as they work. Their fresh, vivacious faces are almost grotesquely healthy in this filthy killing ground. Despite the banter they pay meticulous attention to each tooth or knuckle as they log details and put fragments of bone into plastic bags.

We need shots of the team gathering this evidence, so I jump down into an empty part of the grave with our Hi8 camera. The mud sticks to my shoes like toffee. Mimi, the head of the team, is brushing earth from the eye sockets of a skull. Her chestnut hair is held back by a red spotted bandana and she wears a hint of pink lipstick.

We break for lunch and Rags takes us to Fine Fine, a restaurant in an old palace. We sit on low stools under painted beams. Sunlight dribbles milkily through dirty windows. We eat the Ethiopian national dish *njira* with meat and vegetables. *Njira* is a huge pancake made from *tef*, a type of grass rich in iron. It has a grey, spongy texture which reminds me of the lining of a sheep's stomach. The pancake is flopped onto a round tin tray and dotted with piles of food. Clammy and cold to the touch, it tastes bland and is an antidote to the hot spices that camouflage the gristly meat. You eat with your right hand, tearing off pieces of *njira* with which to scoop up the food. After filming human remains all morning I am eating as though grateful to be alive.

The evidence emerging from the earth is so important that we decide to hire a cameraman - Hi8 footage is not suitable for broadcasting. Plus, the presence of a high-profile journalist like George in the city is alerting the media to the scent of a new story. We are going to have to move fast and protect all of Rags's contacts if our footage is to remain exclusive. I make a quick phone call, agree a fee and make a booking, just like that.

Sometimes the network functions well.

De Groot, a Dutch cameraman from Nairobi, arrives with his equipment the next day. He looks like the golfer Bernard Langer. We film all day at the Institute of Security but later, after dinner, de Groot informs us that he is flying back to Nairobi the following morning. We have booked him for two days but now de Groot claims that we have agreed to pay him $1,000 just for the one day. When we point out that this is way over the odds for a single day's work he becomes very shrill and defensive.

'Do you think I'm cheap?' he demands.

De Groot accuses us of cheating him. Then he justifies his hasty departure by saying he has to take the equipment back to Nairobi.

I tell him one of the reasons we hired him is because he claimed he could secure 'such a good deal on the gear.'

'Are you calling me a liar?' he shouts, red in the face.

He is now quite irrational. Rags wags her finger at him, George and Vivien look on embarassed. De Groot eventually goes to bed saying he is leaving the hotel at eight in the morning unless we pay him another $1,000. Actually I am glad to see the back of him. I have no desire to work with someone with such an attitude.

Sometimes the network lets you down.

I cannot sleep. It begins to rain and mosquitoes whine round my ear. I drag myself out of bed at half past six and join Rags for breakfast. I drink my coffee feeling rather gloomy after the fracas the night before. Rags, as usual, is drinking mineral water. Just as our papaya arrives Vivien rushes in to tell us that de Groot is leaving, but refuses to hand over the video tapes. He is convinced we have no intention of paying him. He is demanding a purchase order before he parts with the material. Rags quickly writes one out and Vivien is despatched to pacify him and bring back the tapes.

She comes back half an hour later looking troubled. De Groot has left for the airport with the tapes. His latest demand is for a first class fare. No-one working on documentaries ever travels first class. It is unheard of even to fly business class.

Rags is impressive. She telephones the airport and arranges for de Groot's passport to be withheld by the Ministry of the Interior, and then sets off instantly for the airport. She is furious. She comes back with the tapes a couple of hours later. De Groot has only agreed to part with them when he realises his passport can be held indefinitely.

After this minor drama I feel flat and uninspired, but work has to go on. We are due to start production proper in less than a month, and we are still no nearer to a coherent story.

We go to meet the Patriarch, the equivalent in Ethiopia of the Pope. At his palace we are ushered into a room and told to wait. Despite incongruously shabby, beige flowered cotton curtains, the afternoon sun streams in through a row of long windows and throws lozenges of light onto rich red carpets. Canary yellow sofas flank a scarlet velveteen high-backed throne. Behind it is a glittery representation of the Virgin and Child. In front is a table draped in a white cloth on which stand a silver vase and some baubles, winking gaudily in the sun. We are beginning to feel drowsy in the heat. As we wait our conversation is desultory.

Then a side door opens and the Patriarch walks in. He is swathed in white and festooned in jewels. Ivory beads and a huge ruby encrusted gold cross swing weightily from his neck. A white hat in the shape of an onion dome perches on his head. He looks at us with intense, glittering eyes and chuckles. He gestures us towards the sofas and takes his seat on the throne. Men in shabby coats scurry in with little tables and serve biscuits and tea in white plastic flowered cups. There is something touching about those cheap teacups in the midst of so much pomp and pageantry.

The Patriarch was arrested by Mengistu and imprisoned for seven years before being exiled to America, where he went to Princeton University.

'The world needs to know how our country suffered under Mengistu,' he says, 'I would like to encourage you to make your film.'

He gives George a penetrating and challenging glare but smiles, almost winking, at Rags and me. As a film-maker I am excited: the Patriarch and his surroundings are a visual feast.

After dinner that night we go to meet some of the key characters in the impending trial. We gather at the National Hotel in a dingy room hung with dirty net curtains, and drink Asmara gin. There's a pink-faced, balding American who is supervising the trial and a prosecutor from Atlanta who has already secured the conviction of the torturer of an Ethiopian woman. There are also a couple of researchers from Africawatch.

There is much discussion about the death penalty. Amnesty International has undertaken to support the trial so long as there is no question of execution. This is potentially an enormous problem. Ethiopian culture is steeped in Orthodox Chrisianity and favours the Old Testament style of justice, an eye for an eye and a tooth for a tooth. The population has endured years of terror under Mengistu and is now, understandably, baying for blood.

If Mengistu is tried and found guilty Ethiopian people will find it hard to accept the justice of a mere prison sentence, when most of them have personal experience of torture and murder. To-night I agree with the Amnesty standpoint and I wear my liberal hat, arguing vehemently against capital punishment under any circumstances. It is only as we begin to make the film that I start to have feelings of intense, vengeful loathing for Mengistu.

To complete our research trip we need relevant archive footage. Vivien and I go to Ethiopian Television. The forlorn, crumbling building says everything I need to know about the current state of Ethiopia. The windows are broken and the corridors deserted. Open flight cases lie abandoned and dusty. Half-assembled camera kits and broken microphones have been chucked into heaps. There are tottering piles of rusting film cans and plastic video cases, sticky with filth. A whiff of breeze from a smashed window lifts a big dustball and tumbles it down the corridor towards us.

Eventually a guard ambles up and leads us to a surprisingly efficient-looking film library, where staff show us images of their country during the Red Terror. First there are clips of President Mengistu surveying his armies as they goosestep past, following the tanks which roll through Addis's vast Constitution Square in a show of power as grandiose and ostentatious as any Stalinist display. Under Mengistu the army grew tenfold up to half a million people.

Next there is chilling footage of Mengistu ranting like Hitler to vast crowds.

'Blood will have blood,' he shrieks, his voice hoarse with venomous passion.

'We must have blood. Our enemies must bleed for the people of Ethiopia.'

As he shouts he hurls glass bottles of blood-red liquid into the square. The liquid oozes from the smashed bottles, staining the concrete and symbolising the onset of the Red Terror.

Then come gruesome shots of blackened corpses, bleeding children and wailing women, as villages in Tigray in the North are bombed in an effort to repress rebellion. It makes depressing viewing, and I am surprised that the Ethiopians who have found the footage for us can watch it so dispassionately. I try to imagine what it would be like watching similar footage of Britain only five years after the event.

'Just let the world know what happened to us,' says a young woman. She smiles and offers me another cup of tea.

Back at the hotel Rags and I sit down to try to structure the film around planned footage and possible participants. By now I am extremely concerned that we do not have any kind of shooting schedule. I am due back in Nairobi tomorrow, and Rags and George are returning to London to convince the BBC that there is potentially a strong film here. Rags seems not to grasp the importance of tying down interviewees and participants.

'Oh we'll find them nearer the time,' she says, dismissing my worries with an impatient flick of her bob.

'There are lots of people who will talk.'

'I know, but we should know who they are before we start,' I say, 'Besides, we'll need more than just talking heads. What can we shoot?'

'There'll be plenty,' Rags says confidently, turning back to her laptop.

Later we make a rare visit to Castelli's, my favourite Italian restaurant in the world. Perhaps I fall in love with the place because it represents civilisation, celebration after a hard day's work, and above all the welcome numbness as the delicious food and wine anaesthetise us against the worst effects of the harrowing stories and sights we are hearing and seeing.

A security guard runs through the rain towards our taxi with an umbrella. Yellow light spills onto the wet street from the doorway behind him. He ushers us inside and past a long buffet laid out with delicacies normally unheard of in Africa – piles of rocket and basil, gleaming black and green olives, sun dried tomatoes, aubergines and roasted peppers juicy with olive oil, soft little balls of buffalo mozzarella, wedges of parmesan, slivers of red carpaccio and bresaiola, slices of prosciutto and salami, marinated anchovies, prawns, crayfish, clams, crab and lobster.

Presiding over this splendour is an ample woman in a volumi-nous scarlet dress. She sits on a raised dais, counting money from a till in front of her. Beneath a mass of peroxide hair her lowered eyelids are turquoise and her pale skin powdered and rouged. She is the sister of the *maitre d'* who arrives swiftly and welcomes us with flamboyant charm.

Our host is silver haired and portly in a sleeveless jumper. He has lived in Addis for over thirty years and is one of the last Italian colonials. He leads us into a well-lit room with polished, wooden floors and starched white linen on the tables. Silver and glass glitter. Waiters in immaculate white jackets with brass buttons minister. After disposing of our heaped plates of antipasti from the buffet we eat spaghetti with green chillies and saffron, then succulent, spicy crab washed down with cold Pinot Grigio.

Later we drink creamy capuccino and sip home-made green grappa, an aromatic nectar and the best I have ever drunk. Relax-ing in my favourite haven after a week of hard work and eating nothing but *njira*, I feel very happy as we drink a toast to the commission of the film. Tomorrow we leave, but I am already impatient for my next visit to Addis.

Ten days later, at the beginning of April, I am back to start film-ing. Shooting is due to begin in a few days, but we still seem no nearer a firm schedule.

'Relax,' says Rags, 'Tonight we will clinch everything.'

This evening she has arranged for us to go out with Kinfe, the Deputy Minister of the Interior and Head of Security. He and his friend Beyene come to collect us. They are both wearing snazzy, disco-style shirts under smart jackets. I am surprised to see they are both in their early thirties at the most.

Kinfe's house is in a big walled compound guarded by soldiers. We walk through cavernous, beige, strip-lit rooms and arrive in a hideous parlour where we sit on velveteen flowered sofas amongst little tables covered in plastic doilies. On the tables pots of fake flowers nestle amongst photograph frames – the largest and most elaborate contains a photograph of the President's daughter.

Kinfe's mother brings us bitter barley beer, Tigrayan bread and the inevitable *njira*. Kinfe divides his attention between his mobile telephone – which rings incessantly – and two tiny, fluffy, white dogs. Occasionally he throws an apologetic smile in our direction.

A man arrives with his seven-year-old son, and the stories begin. The child drinks Coca-Cola and listens with round, solemn eyes. The man tells us about Aferworki or the 'Man in Red'. During the Red Terror Aferworki was a notorious torturer who stalked the streets of Axum, a town to the north of the country, in search of victims. He tied a red ribbon to the barrel of his gun to indicate he was on the prowl.

One victim was tortured so severely that the next time his mother took a plate of food to his prison cell he smashed the plate and used a shard of pottery to cut out his own tongue. Aferworki was so enraged by this act of defiance that he tied him to the back of his Landrover and dragged him through Axum till he died.

To my astonishment Kinfe then reveals that this monstrous Man in Red was a distant relative of his mother.

'You see,' he says, 'We are all implicated in this thing. Everyone is involved.'

I ask if Aferworki is still alive, but after he fled from Ethiopia he was torn to pieces by an angry mob in a Kenyan refugee camp.

I am to hear many more horrific stories. The following morning Jered, a gap-toothed man in a creaky black leather jacket, takes me to the Anti Red Terror Committee. Jered has very bloodshot eyes and looks exhausted. He leads me to a small, bare room that used to be a torture and detention centre. Here torture victims have gathered to talk to me.

Mathias is a grave, quietly-spoken man of 32. He lost three brothers, all under twenty, during the Red Terror. The first was dragged behind a car till he died. The second had his eyes gouged out and his hands chopped off, and was left to bleed to death. The third had his shoulder blades smashed before being fried alive in oil.

A man with very intense eyes has been watching me as I listen. The more upset I become the more closely the man observes me.

I am trying to compose myself for the next story when the man interrupts. He seems agitated and demands an answer. His eyes are hot. He speaks no English but Jered translates:

'He wants to know if you believe in the death penalty.'

I quail under the man's stare:

'I no longer know'.

The man stands up and edges towards me. He barks at Jered to continue translating.

'Imagine your eight-year-old son being tortured in front of you,' he says. He is now so close I can smell his breath.

'Then imagine he is shot through the head.

Then imagine that the murderer demands that you pay for that bullet.' He pauses and narrows his eyes.

'If you were that boy's mother, what would you want to happen to the man who ordered those atrocities?' he asks. Without hesitation I say:

'I'd want to kill him.'

He sits back satisfied and lifts his hands.

'Exactly,' he says. 'And to think we have those Amnesty people interfering with our culture and telling us what to do. Mengistu must die. There is no alternative.'

I still recall this conversation vividly. While I am glad to belong to a country which has no capital punishment, I no longer see it as a cut and dried issue. I know that had I lived through the Red Terror I too would be demanding Mengistu's blood.

At the weekend the crew arrive. I go with Abi, our Ethiopian fixer, to collect them from the airport. Abi wears navy blue blazers and van Heusen shirts with silk ties. His skin is glossy and flawless and he speaks with a lisp which gave him a slightly camp air. At the airport he seems to know everybody, and steers us through the officials with velvety smoothness.

Tzvika, the cameraman with whom I shot both the cholera and the AIDS films, has flown in from Harare, and Rags has hired Patrick from Sweden to be our sound recordist. George Alagiah is delayed in Rawanda where he is reporting on the genocide.

'How long for?' I ask. Rags shrugs.

'So what? We can do quite well without him.'

I don't agree with her, but at this stage I have more serious worries. We still have no schedule and I am desperate to finalise our interviewees. By now we should have a precise plan of exactly what we are shooting, but Rags still waves away my concerns. Tension mounts. What we desperately need are victims of the Red Terror willing to talk about personal experiences, but Rags just introduces us to a constant stream of experts and academics.

Now the crew is here with all the equipment, we are wasting money for every day we do not use them.

'Go out and shoot GV's!' says Rags.

A GV is film language for a 'general view' or local scenery. We must have filmed every monument from every possible angle all over Addis Ababa.

George has reached Nairobi, but is still delayed, so we go to interview the Patriarch without him. The Patriarch's responses to Rags' questions are long-winded and dull. The interview is dropped from the film despite the rich visual setting.

I am increasingly frustrated and on the point of abandoning the entire project. To make matters worse, Rags is determined not to spend any money she does not absolutely have to. She hires a car from a very old relative of Abi's who speaks no English. This makes negotiating our way round Addis very difficult. Besides, the car is far too small and we have to travel with the heavy metal box of lights across our knees.

George arrives at last. I find it a great tonic that straight away he shares my eagerness to lick the schedule into shape.

'What the hell has been going on here for the last month?' he asks me.

We confront Rags the very next night, pointing out that we have none of the interviews or sequences promised to the BBC.

'If we don't have a schedule by the day after tomorrow, we're going to have to tell the BBC there's no film,' says George.

We are calm but firm. Rags is not happy, but sees we mean business. Within two days we are interviewing the Prime Minister.

6 THE TORTURED

Ethiopia & Eritrea

The room in which we interview Prime Minister Meles Zenawi is vast and featureless. It is furnished with a couple of leather sofas marooned in acres of carpet, and on the walls are blown up photographs of kitsch technicolour mountain scenes. I think the Prime Minister looks very odd against an Alpine lake, so I take an Ethiopian flag from a stand and drape that behind him instead.

Prime Minister Meles is tiny and wears a double-breasted suit with enormous shouders. He sits at an awkward angle, but after I ask him to edge this way and that a couple of times he makes it clear he does not take to direction. I worry because his entire head seems to tilt away from the camera. However, as he talks and becomes passionate, he turns and looks George straight in the eye to stress a point. In the end the effect is very powerful.

'We can forgive but we can never forget,' says Meles about the Mengistu regime, reminding us that 150,000 were murdered.

400,000 more died during the great famine of 1984. Though the famine was already catastrophic, Mengistu restricted migration and stopped delivery of food to these areas on the grounds that they were rebel strongholds. When he talks about that time the Prime Minister's eyes become bloodshot and watery.

'That was the lowest point of my life,' he says.

His voice trembles and is no louder than a whisper. He turns to look intently at George:

'It was genocide on the verge of succeeding. It is very important to prove to Ethiopians that there will be some day of reckoning,' he says of the forthcoming trial. I think the interview has gone well and that George has done a fine job.

The problem facing the Ethiopian lawyers is the mass of evidence. Apart from Nazi Germany, never before has such evidence of human rights violations been amassed. There are a quarter of a million pages of documents and five thousand statements. Under Mengistu there were three hundred 'neighbourhood associations' in Addis alone, outposts of the regime making up a massive web of informants. The leaders of these associations had the power to kill, and everything was documented. Every time there was an execution all details were noted down, including the cost of the bullet.

With so much written reporting it is not surprising the evidence is overwhelming. We film rooms crammed with piles of documents tottering up to the ceiling. It would take a century to read through the mass of material just once. We find cupboards full of video cassettes – torture sessions were taped and carefully logged.

Throughout this macabre period our fixer Abi remains light-heartedly but continuously flirtatious, whispering to me about my 'overwhelming beauty'. The reality is that when working hard in this sort of heat I tend to look hot, unkempt and singularly under-whelming. Nevertheless I rather enjoy the harmless flattery and I know Abi to be a friend. He makes me laugh and when we are immersed in such a depressing story it is important to be able to lighten up. Above all, Abi is practical and efficient and understands the need for a schedule.

We have dinner with the crew at the Blue Posts restaurant, where we start talking about the film. I am still worried we have not found a torture victim to talk to us.

'I'll do the interview,' says Abi quietly. I am surprised. He does not fit my pre-conceived idea of a torture victim. In his well-cut blazer, button-down shirt and polished loafers he looks like a prosperous, preppy young man fresh out of a good university or business school. I still have a lot to learn.

'I was a student, so they arrested me,' he says. Under Mengistu students were seen as dangerous radicals because of their involve-ment in the popular revolt which had brought down Emperor Haile Selassie. Thousands were rounded up, tortured and executed. During the height of the Red Terror a quarter of a million people, some as young as twelve, were imprisoned and it is estimated that over half a million were killed.

The waiter brings a tray of drinks. We have ordered an expensive bottle of white Burgundy. The cork pops just as Abi begins to describe his ordeal.

'First they tied me up like this' he lisps.

He twists his body into a grotesque contortion. They made him kneel, then yanked his arms behind him. Then they bent his spine backwards and tied his hands to his feet. After that they hoisted him up on a big meat hook and beat him with hot irons and whips.

As Abi describes his ordeal the suave, confident gloss begins to melt and I see a small, frightened child. The noise of laughter surges around us from a nearby table. A waiter smiles and sets down a plate of food in front of me. He pours more wine. The atmosphere in Blue Posts seems far away from Abi's experience and yet torture was commonplace for thousands of innocent Ethiopians. I no longer feel hungry.

'What did they actually accuse you of?' I ask.

'They didn't need a reason. I was a student – that was enough.'

Abi shrugs, pulls himself together and then gives me one of his most charming smiles, shot through with a hint of lasciviousness.

'Really, Charlotte' he says 'I am happy to do this interview for you. My memory is still so fresh.'

Abi's cosmopolitan demeanour, and the way he wears his expensive clothes, suggest a carefree and almost pampered young man, with no hint of past trauma. My respect for him burgeons.

'Why didn't you tell me this before?' I ask.

'You know most people I work for, they want to have a nice time here. They don't want to think about all that too much, it makes them feel guilty or something,' he replies.

'More wine?'

Rags does not want Abi to do the interview. In fact it is Abi's offer that goads her to finalise a schedule. To interview Abi will suggest she is short of contacts. Within a few days we are on our way to Eritrea.

When we land in Asmara I feel I have arrived in Southern Italy.

Ochre, pink and terracotta houses with green shutters and wrought iron balconies glow in the early sunshine. Jacaranda and lilac thrust their shoots skywards and bougainvillea smothers ancient walls with papery purple flowers.

Bells toll from church towers high above steep, narrow streets. In the cemeteries stone angels crumble imperceptibly in the shadow of cypress trees. Palms and tightly-pruned trees offer shade where old men sip tiny shots of espresso, as capuccino froth foams and hisses in the nearby bars. We could be in Basilicata, except that everyone is black.

My hotel room is cool and white-washed with high ceilings. Joy of joys, there is a pristine tiled bathroom with hot water and a big window. When I throw open the shutters I look out onto a palm tree. It is extraordinary to be in an African city that feels so familiar and European. Alas, we are unable to spend time in our hotel. From the minute we arrive our prized schedule is in chaos.

The men from the Ministry, with the incriminating documents we have been promised, never materialise. Our key interviewee, Mama Abeba, arrives hours before her translator and so we sit grinning at each other in awkward silence. When the translator finally arrives Mama Abeba takes us to a dark bedroom behind a shop. This is where we have arranged to film her but there are no plugs or sources of electricity and no room for the camera. I am beginning to despair.

We want to film Mama Abeba making *njira*. We manage to drag the big, round hotplate into the shop itself where there is plenty of light, but just as we are in a position to start filming a fuse blows. By the time Patrick and Tzvika have sorted out the electrical problems Rags has disappeared. Mama Abeba looks tired, frightened and clearly unprepared. Outside it has begun to rain heavily which gives us additional sound problems.

Eventually the soothing hiss of *njira* on the hot plate and the quiet gloom of the shop reassure Mama Abeba. She sits down amongst the baskets of tomatoes and slowly begins to tell George about her experiences. She was arrested in 1978, along with twelve friends, but locked up alone in a separate cell. She never knew what she was accused of. Each night one of her friends was killed and the body thrown into her cell. She had no choice but to live and sleep amongst the corpses of her friends.

Then it was her turn. She was taken to a torture chamber and burned very badly on her stomach, neck and feet. Now she is remembering the horror of her ordeal she loses her self-consciousness.

'Look! Look at my feet!' she shouts at us.

From beneath her shabby skirt she thrusts a grotesquely swollen foot towards the camera. It is paralysed. The skin is discoloured where it has been burned.

'They molested my body and burned my belly,' she cries.

George asks her about her belly. She shrivels. She wraps her arms around herself protectively.

'What they did to me meant I could never have children,' she says. Soundlessly she begins to cry.

That night Tzvika asks to speak to me alone.

'I have to leave for Jo'burg tomorrow,' he says.

I feel sick. It is a bombshell. There is no cameraman of Tzvika's calibre for thousands of miles, and our timetable is already very tight. He tells me he has been booked to cover the South African elections. He told me this before he took the job, but promised he would sort it out with Paul, who runs Mighty Movies and fixes Tzvika's bookings. In the event Tzvika chickened out of telling Paul he would be late arriving in Jo'burg.

I am livid with Tzvika and he knows it. He shrugs. There is a pause.

'Fuck,' I say eventually.

He shrugs again. He is good at shrugging.

'Oi vey' he says, 'What can you do?'

'You can ring him up and tell him you're staying here.'

Another pause.

'I'm sorry Charlotte,' he says, 'I can't do that to him.'

'But you can do it to me?' I ask.

He shrugs once more.

'Paul can't take it. But you can. You'll be OK.'

'No, I won't,' I say.

'Give me a cigarette.'

I have not smoked for six years. We have a long talk, but Tzvika does not budge. He cannot let Paul down.

We join Rags, Patrick and George in the hotel dining room, and break the news to them.

'What's the solution?' asks Rags, glaring balefully at Tzvika. He stubs out his cigarette carefully, avoiding her eye.

'Paul will listen to Charlotte,' he says.

I book a call to Harare with no idea what I will say. When Paul comes on the line I explain I cannot let Tzvika go.

'You can't do this to me, Charlotte,' he says.

I tell him how guilty Tzvika and I feel, but I stay firm. Both of us know that there are other good cameramen in Zimbabwe. I say that unless he can find one of them to travel to Asmara overnight, Tzvika is staying with me. Half an hour later Paul capitulates.

'You owe me big time,' he says.

I am still so angry with Tzvika I cannot look at him. I smoke my fifth cigarette.

The next morning we leave for Massawa, which lies on the Red Sea looking across the gulf towards Saudi Arabia and Yemen. It is a strategic port and one of the reasons Ethiopia annexed Eritrea in 1962. Since then the Eritrean People's Liberation Front has waged an almost continual struggle for independence, capturing Massawa in 1990. To retaliate Mengistu bombed the port mercilessly for eight months.

Eritreans had to wait till 1993 for their independence to be recognised by Ethiopia. Now, just a year later, we arrive in a ghost town. It occurs to me I have never been in such a young country before.

Massawa is tragic but surreally beautiful. Marble staircases twist skywards from great mounds of rubble and end nowhere. Towers topple. Facades of buildings buckle and sag. Steel twists without function. Joists lie blackened and buckled. Glassless windows stare blankly from walls pock-marked by machine-gun fire. A crescent moon hangs at a dizzy angle from a muezzin's tower. Precarious

piles of masonry and concrete were once buildings. Broken statues lie forlorn and forgotten. Scraps of clothing flutter and wild
flowers grow amongst the devastation. Bougainvillea drapes itself
over heaps of smashed brick and plaster. Dogs limp amongst the
ruins, scavenging for skeletons.

We are so absorbed in what we are filming that we do not notice how intense the heat has become. Eventually even the dogs
lie panting in the wreckage, and we are the only people moving
through the glare amongst the shards and shreds of destruction.
Sweat trickles down my back and legs. George does a piece to
camera outside the bombed palace, his shirt wet through and his
forehead glistening.

To cool off we drive down to the Red Sea where we find a series of ugly, functional, concrete bungalows on the beach. We go
swimming in the hot, salty, sticky sea – all of us except George,
who stays firmly in the shade. In his blue button-down shirt and
khaki trousers he sips a beer, and surveys us from behind expensive
sunglasses, every inch the correct face of the BBC correspondent.
After swimming we eat fish and chips and drink warm beer at
plastic tables. I quite like the brand new, rather socialist feel of
the place.

We fly back to Addis. Abi is on the tarmac to greet us. It is a
weekend, so he has abandoned his usual blazer in favour of a
blue and purple silk shirt and ironed jeans.

'I've missed you so much,' he says as he insists on carrying my
bags. He has organised our entire schedule. I could kiss him.

We begin by visiting an old man called Omar. The Special
Prosecutor's Office has just found evidence of the execution of
Omar's son in 1978. We go with Omar and his family to see the
documentation. Sure enough, there are lengthy minutes of the son's
interrogation and then a signature against the execution order.

Omar stands up to look at the order. Slowly and carefully he
adjusts his glasses, then bends over the file with intense concentration. He fingers the cheap cardboard respectfully, as if it is a rare
and priceless document. His breath shortens as he sees his son's
name. His wife and daughter watch him closely.

Quite suddenly Omar begins to cry. A single tear runs very fast down his face. He takes off his glasses and wipes them. The women begin wailing, covering their faces with their white veils. Though Omar's face is smeared with tears, he thanks the official very politely and returns to his seat like a somnambulist.

We go back to Omar's house for coffee. Coffee is an important ritual in Ethiopian culture. It is to be lingered over and enjoyed. If you are in a hurry, never accept a cup of coffee in an Ethiopian household. First, the woman of the house changes into traditional dress and lays a carpet of grass, sage and yellow flowers. Then she lights a charcoal fire and sprinkles it liberally with granules of myrrh. The raw coffee beans are sifted then roasted.

The combination of coffee and myrrh as it wafts up from the charcoal fire is one of the most distinctive scents of Ethiopia. Once they are roasted the beans are pounded in a mortar and pestle, then brewed over the hot, scented coals in a black, pot-bellied jug with a slim neck. Finally, sometimes up to an hour later, the coffee is poured into tiny china cups and drunk strong, black and piping hot.

After we have drunk our coffee Omar tells us how his son was in an opposition group, but was betrayed by a friend. He was arrested, interrogated and tortured. His toe-nails and finger-nails were ripped out with Russian instruments till he was unable to walk. He was thrown into jail with his father. Omar tells us how his son would lie with his feet up on his father's shoulders to alleviate the excruciating pain. Then he was executed.

'I wished I'd never been born,' says Omar. He wipes away a tear.

'I will fight to the death to revenge the blood of my son,' he says, more comfortable with his anger than with his sorrow.

One morning Tzvika feels faint. We are due to leave for Tigray next day but by the evening Tzvika is so sick he cannot move. There are no visiting doctors available so Rags takes him to the hospital where food poisoning is diagnosed.

We are supposed to be conducting an interview with Meaza, another torture victim. Rather than cancel it, Patrick assures me he can film it. We arrive at the home of Meaza's mother. Now in her thirties, Meaza looks like a well-groomed professional woman. She leads us into her mother's tiny front room, crammed with furniture, and tells us her story.

At eighteen she was arrested with her little brother, both accused of being in the students' movement. They were tied up with plastic rope and suspended by their hands from the ceiling, facing each other. Meaza's brother watched her being tortured. Then Meaza was made to watch him being tortured to death.

'Can you imagine what it's like to watch your little brother like that?' she says. Her beautiful eyes brim with tears. She blows her nose elegantly.

'Sorry,' she says. It seems absurd that she is apologising to us.

'Look at my hands,' she says, holding them out to us. In contrast to her otherwise graceful slenderness, her hands are shapeless and plump. They tremble.

'After that torture they were completely paralysed for five months. Now I still cannot work. Sometimes I cannot even lift my own child.'

Suddenly Meaza smiles.

'By the way' she says 'I named my child Stephen after my little brother.'

She takes out a passport-sized black and white photograph of a serious-looking young man and holds it in the palm of her hand.

'Look at him' she says, fondly. 'As a Catholic I can forgive them. I don't want them to be killed because it won't bring back my little brother, but I want them and the world to know what they did to us.'

When we return to the hotel Tzvika is recovering but still in bed. George and I try – and fail – to persuade Rags to go up to Tigray ahead of us. She insists there is no need: everything there is well-organised, and the schedule is in the capable hands of Bridget, an Irishwoman who works for an aid organisation. So we all, including Tzvika, end up together on the little northbound plane.

In Mekele we face confusion and disorder. Bridget is a

wild-haired woman with a grumpy disposition. She has no idea what she was supposed to be organising and has done nothing. Luckily (and quite coincidentally) Tesfai, one of the interviewees she is supposed to have contacted, happens to be at the airport. He is waiting to meet a woman from Oxfam but she hasn't arrived.

'Let's grab him now,' I suggest. Bridget is justifying why she has not managed to track him down sooner.

'Let's just do it,' I snap irritably.

Tesfai drives us back to his old torture chamber, along Biblical roads which wind through wrinkled brown mountains. We arrive at a deserted spot. Brambles cluster round the entrance to the delapidated building. Inside it is surprisingly chilly. The green walls are pitted and stained and weeds thrust up through cracks in the filthy concrete floor. There are smatterings of goat shit. Light struggles to filter through the overgrown windows. Tzvika, frowns, shrugs and heaves the camera onto his shoulder.

Tesfai takes a deep breath, steps inside the torture chamber and begins his story. As a district officer he questioned one of the government's agricultural policies in 1984. He was accused of belonging to the Tigrayan People's Liberation Front, just one of seven ethnically based groups which had taken up arms against Mengistu's regime. He was arrested.

George has a report compiled by a human rights group that includes drawings by prisoners under Mengistu's regime. One shows a man bound like a fish. A rope is put through his mouth and then used to bind his feet to his hands, so that he is pulled into an arc. George shows the picture to Tesfai.

'This is how they did it,' he says, pointing to the drawing. He becomes agitated.

'This way the interrogator can really beat you,' he says. 'And of course the rope is in your mouth, so if you move your hands or feet it cuts you. And you cannot speak or scream. The only way you can communicate with the torturer is to raise one finger behind your back.'

The interview is extraordinarily powerful. Back at the hotel I want to look at the footage, so Tzvika, Patrick and I set up a monitor so we can watch our tapes.

We see Tesfai enter the building with George and then the tape goes blank. I look at Tzvika. He looks puzzled but not alarmed.

'It must be on the next tape,' he says.

'There's not another tape,' says Patrick.

I start to feel cold. I clear my throat.

'What's happened?' I squeak.

Patrick and Tzvika are hunched over the camera controls, zooming up and down the tape. It is blank.

'You can't have wiped it,' I say, very shrill. 'It's impossible.'

'I'm sorry, Charlotte,' says Tzvika.

'You can't have done,' I insist. But he has. He has wound back to check the first few frames of the interview and forgotten to spool on again. We have wiped everything but the first few words.

In a director's life there comes a moment when you think you have hit the bottom. This is my moment. My cameraman has just destroyed the most important and moving interview of the film, and the one that is hardest to repeat. Once again I am livid with Tzvika, especially as I now have to face Rags and break the bad news.

'We have no choice,' I say, 'You're going to have to ask him to do it again.' To her credit Rags is calm, forgiving and practical.

Tesfai is reluctant, but agrees to come back tomorrow. The interview is still very moving but we have lost forever that first wincing reaction, the physical response to being back in a torture chamber years later.

The next day we set off for Adigrat. It is a dusty little town dominated by a beautiful Italianate church with a brilliantly painted dome and campanile. We are here to interview Father Kevin O'Mahoney, a priest who has written a novel set during the Red Terror.

We arrive to find Father O'Mahoney is not expecting us at all; yet another interview Bridget has failed to set up. I leave George and Rags to talk to him, and go into town with Patrick, Tzvika and our Eritrean driver, Samira, to find somewhere to stay.

Temporarily (or so we are assured) the only hotel has neither electricity nor running water. There are two filthy sinks in the corridor and two stinking squatters to serve all the guests. We are shown to our rooms by candlelight and decide they are too squalid to contemplate until we absolutely have to.

We are having our first sip of cold beer in a local bar when Rags arrives with Father O'Mahoney, and we are dragged off to drink warm beer and listen to a dull lecture about agroforestry from an opinionated young Irishman. This is followed by Father O'Mahoney's potted history of Ethiopia. Both my lecturers assume I have never been to Africa before and know absolutely nothing about anything.

When we return to the hotel there is still no electricity. Using Patrick's torch we inspect each other's sheets. We strip back the blankets to find stains and pubic hairs. By the time we negotiate the filth-encrusted basins in the corridor we are all giggling insanely. Hysteria has set in.

At half past seven next morning, still dirty and tired, we arrive at Father O'Mahoney's to interview him. It does not go at all well and eventually – and fairly predictably – another interview ends up on the cutting room floor.

We set off next for northern Tigray. We arrive in a vast dusty plateau, a great brown stretch of stones like some hellish crater left by a prehistoric nuclear bomb. Tzvika sweeps the camera across the arid emptiness till it comes to rest on a group of small children. They are hunched over a pile of stones playing some kind of game. Their presence in this stony desert is extraordinary, because the place itself feels beyond death.

By the 1980's Tigray was a rebel stronghold. Then famine struck. Between 1984 and 1985 Mengistu stopped the delivery of food to Tigray in an attempt to starve the rebels. He restricted migration and then began a cynical resettlement programme. He had followed the advice of Mao: if you want to empty the sea of fish, you have to drain the sea.

Mengistu used the famine to his advantage. He rounded people up at feeding centres and forced them onto trucks. The Russians gave him planes so he could move people out of the area quicker. Thousands died in resettlement camps or by trying to escape them. 300,000 made the torturous five week walk to Eastern Sudan rather than trust government feeding centres.

We find a family which was forcibly resettled and has recently returned to their home. The man is ploughing his field. It looks to me as nothing will ever grow in that unyielding earth but he whips his oxen on, the old wooden plough forcing its way through stone and rubble.

His wife is rebuilding their house, literally stone by stone, lugging great chunks of rock around. In an effort to help I try to lift a stone and I stagger under its weight before it is six inches off the ground. For the first time I hear giggling coming from the grave children who have gathered to stare. I make a great show of trying to lift the stone and failing, and I soon have them all shrieking with mirth. Their laughter rings out under the vast sky and I begin to feel the slow dribble of life returning to this awful place.

The woman tells me she was forced onto a truck and taken south.

'Women's hair was all over the ground,' she says. 'We were crammed in like hay. Children were crushed to death. People were vomiting and fainting from the heat.'

The citizens who escaped the resettlement were bombed. In 1988 Hawzen, Tigray's main trading town, was viciously attacked. Civilian remains were found by the sackload. People had been burned to pulp.

We interview Major Petros, a pilot who flew government planes during that time. He wears aviator glasses and a leather jacket. Silver sideburns frame his smoothly handsome face. Under pressure from George he admits that many civilian villages were marked as military targets on their maps. It was 'unthinkable' to question those maps or to disobey orders. So they dropped their bombs, or faced prison.

The ancient town of Axum, home to some of Ethiopia's most treasured monuments, is our last stop. It was here that the notorious Aferworki, the Man in Red, terrorised the population. I am not sure how best to tell his story. Plenty of people are prepared to tell us about the atrocities he committed, but it is difficult to convey the atmosphere of a town at the mercy of a single man. I decide to do some reconstruction. We tie a red ribbon round the barrel of a gun and then, using a local man to play the Man in Red, we film him stalking the deserted town.

It is a nice idea but virtually impossible to implement. Hundreds of people swarm around, curious to watch us work. Every time Tzvika begins filming a child pops into shot and gapes at the lens. The more we try to control the children the bigger the crowd grows. Eventually it is so huge that Tzvika gives up. We have been trying to achieve these shots all morning in glare, dust and crippling heat. Tzvika turns off the camera and lights a cigarette.

'It's too hectic' he says, and shrugs.

I do something I never do on a shoot. I begin to cry. I am hot, tired, hungry, thirsty, dirty, fed up and furious with the children.

'I'll film if you want, but the shot won't be any good,' says Tzvika.

The minute he turns back to the camera, the children scream with glee and leap around in front of it again.

'You see,' says Tzvika and returns to smoking his cigarette.

Just then a pair of khaki-clad policemen arrive, armed with large sticks. Seeing our predicament they begin swinging their sticks at people's legs, beating children away from the camera. I am appalled, but I would be lying if I said there was not a part of me that was relieved. One of the police turns to me with a dazzling smile and implies we should carry on. By now the crowd has been forced back and are lined up against two sides of the square.

We begin filming again. Just as our Man in Red is making it to the end of the shot, the children nearest the camera edge into the frame. I yell with frustration, and the police begin thrashing around with their sticks again. We do that shot six or seven times before we give up. I light a cigarette, say every filthy word I can think of under my breath, and decide to call it a day. Surprisingly, the shots work.

On the plane back to Addis we can scarcely believe we have

finished filming. We decide to go to Castelli's for the wrap party. At this moment I would give up my entire fee to dine there again. George is so keen he telephones from the airport to book a table, and dine there we do. I buy some champagne, George the wine, and Rags treats us all to the rest. For a night dirt, squalor, suffering, pain, even our disagreements with one another, are all forgotten. I even find myself hugging Tzvika and telling him how brilliant he is.

It was immediately after this film that my father was diagnosed with cancer. He died two months later after a long and painful struggle. At the time I was able to be strong because whenever I wanted to break down and cry I remembered those Ethiopians who had watched their families being tortured and executed. Though in pain, my father was dying at home surrounded by his family, with excellent professional care. That thought kept me going.

The film was aired before he came home to die. He watched from his hospital bed with the expert eye of a top advertising man. The nurses told me he boasted to them how clever I was. To me all he said was: 'Not bad, old girl, not bad.'

7   A THANKLESS TASK
Uganda

Habitat, the arm of the UN which focuses on the environment and particularly housing, commissioned a series of short 'spots' from round the world. They had to be made by local women film-makers, and to look at issues which most affected their day to day lives. My assignment was to train and enable a group of women producers at Uganda Television to make five 30 second films as part of this series.

Fifteen female faces look at me. None smiles. None shows a sign of interest. I stand at the front of the classroom and want to give up, go home and cry. Instead I smile.

'Any questions?' I ask brightly.

One woman crosses her legs slowly. Two others close their notebooks. There is no other reaction. I have to resist the impulse to fling my piece of chalk at them and walk away.

I arrived in Kampala yesterday morning. I was eager to come to Uganda because it was supposedly having a renaissance after decades in the wilderness under Idi Amin, and then in the grip of HIV and AIDS. Under the recently elected president, Museveni, the country is said to be thriving – democracy works, the Asians are slowly returning and Ugandans are starting to rebuild their shattered economy.

Irene Zukosoka is the Director of Programmes at Uganda Television. Her dream is for UTV to make programmes that will be broadcast throughout the world, and she fantasises about starting a pan-African women's network. Irene has velvety eyes in a round, plump face and her hair is curled and fragrant with coconut oil. She is voluptuous, both in appearance and in her sensual appetite for food and drink. At lunch time she sinks her white teeth into half a fried chicken with lashings of hot sauce and chips. As she walks her plump body rustles in bright, tight, traditional African clothes.

At her request I arrive with a consignment of *White Musk* from the Body Shop. With an eager cry she sprays the scent into her hair and all over her ample bosom, which is becomingly draped in green and yellow fabric.

'It's so lovely and cool,' she says, patting her neck. 'It's so fresh.'

It does smell nice on her – on me it smells like caramel-flavoured urine.

UTV is housed in an old colonial hospital, set in generous grounds with an open verandah along one side of the building. This promising exterior houses an under-funded, depressed and struggling organisation. There are plenty of badly paid, gloomy staff but virtually no resources. As Irene shows me round we pass the news studio. I look in, eager to see how their set up differs from ours.

At one end of the cavernous, dark studio is a trestle table against a tacked up backcloth. On it stands a dusty bunch of plastic flowers in a tinfoil container. Behind it sits a solitary newsreader, reading from some hand-written notes torn out of a lined pad. He speaks to an unmanned Umatic camera on a wooden tripod. There is no-one to adjust the lights or operate the camera. The newscaster talks on alone in the middle of that big room.

Irene herself as Director of Programmes has no access to an electric typewriter, let alone a computer. Her secretary sits outside her office with a manual typewriter and a black telephone with one line. There is one women's loo to which Irene's secretary has the only key. The dank cubby hole stinks of rotting fish and bleach. The light bulb has blown and there is never any running water. Loo paper is acquired from a drawer in the secretary's desk.

Irene's office is dark, its brown walls decorated with UNICEF posters tacked up with yellowing sellotape. Irene is dwarfed by her untidy desk, behind which she keeps a supply of snacks, fizzy drinks and a bottle of *White Musk* body moisturiser.

What had seemed like an interesting challenge in London is fast transforming into one of the hardest tasks of my working life. There are seventeen women in my class, as opposed to four or five as I was promised. I complain to Irene.

'You can do it. You must teach them all to make films like you,' Irene wheedles,

'Please. We need your expertise here.' She offers me a crisp as she bustles off.

Later I learn that Irene rounded the women up and told them they had to attend my course. I am training not just producers but virtually the entire female staff of UTV. The women are on meagre civil servants' salaries without much hope of a pay rise, so they are not motivated to work hard or take an interest in their jobs.

My idea of a good course is one on which you get your money's worth. A course should push you and test your limits. Here this kind of European attitude is culturally alien and useless. Uganda has been overrun with aid and well-meaning non-governmental organisations for years, and a 'workshop' culture has developed in which people are paid to show up to the endless training sessions on offer.

Now I am faced with a group of hostile women to whom the idea of paying for training is unthinkable. They see no advantage in gaining new skills because they do not believe in a long-term future for their jobs. Money is the one and only objective. They sulk and I despair.

By my first lunch time I am ready to give up. Already we are slipping behind schedule. By five the same day I am exhausted. The women have warmed up, which has aggravated rather than allayed my fears about the course's success. I am trying to teach them the principles of telling a story within a tight time frame, and ask for their own short story suggestions. The first hand is tentatively raised. Rose, a quiet girl with complicated plaits, says she has a really good suggestion. She unravels a meandering and complex plot about an AIDS orphan to which a full-length feature film could barely do justice.

'Let me explain again,' I interrupt after about eight minutes and before the final act has started.

'You have a maximum of about ten shots with which to tell your story. It must be simple.'

I am met with blank, bored looks.

'Think of your shots,' I say. 'Draw a story board.'

Another hand goes up:

'What's a storyboard?'

At last I have something concrete to teach them, but my students are packing their bags to leave.

'I'll show you tomorrow,' I say. 'Thank you all very much.' They shuffle out of my class without looking at me.

I have heard that the Zimbabwe-based American John Riber is in town. I have met John several times in Harare, where he runs an outfit called Media for Development which makes films for the African cinema on a range of issues from AIDS to widows' rights. Such is his fame throughout Africa that Irene wants to meet him. He is in Kampala making a film, and tonight he is throwing a party at my hotel. I arrange for Irene and me to be invited.

The Equatoria is a big, concrete, unlovely hotel situated on one of Kampala's busiest roundabouts. Irene and I arrive, cross the astroturf by the pool and go into a beige-carpeted function room packed with a mainly white crowd. I have just spotted John Riber's clean-cut, blond features when I hear a Yorkshire accent:

'What the bloody hell are you doing here?'

I turn round to see Alan Graham, my one-time editor and colleague from Nairobi.

'Guess who's here?' he says into a mobile telephone, 'Charlotte bleeding Metcalf'.

He is talking to a cameraman I know in Nairobi.

'I don't believe this,' he is saying.

Irene giggles and tells the waiter to bring beers. When it comes to ordering drinks Irene is very assertive.

Always a bit of a wheeler-dealer, Alan suits the raw, emerging market of Uganda much better than the well-heeled film establishment in Nairobi. He has recently moved to Kampala and is already supplying John Riber's film with equipment and local crew.

'It's great here,' he says, smiling winningly at Irene as he produces a business card from his breast pocket.

'I can give you a great price,' he says, 'Call me. We'll do a deal. I'm here to help.' He winks at her. He hasn't changed. My spirits lift. One of the great things about Africa is bumping into people in unlikely situations. It is a vast continent, with a tiny circuit of white film people.

Irene drinks several beers extremely fast and starts to sway gently. Her eyes are bloodshot and her tongue seems too big for her mouth but she is determined to collar John, so we move into the crowd.

John hugs me ruggedly as if I was a man, patting my back and presenting me with a clean-shaven cheek. To Irene he boasts of his many cinema successes, a veritable Steven Spielberg. She absorbs everything he says as if it was oxygen.

But when she starts to ask him about how to raise money he at once starts to look bored and irritated. He is taking his team on to dinner and Irene and I are clearly not invited. It is time to leave. I lure Irene into the bar by the pool, where she orders Drambuie. Then she insists on driving home, chuckling at my concern.

'I'm fine,' she says and takes off with a screech of wheels.

I think about my class tomorrow and sit up late, making a blueprint for a blank storyboard form onto which my pupils can sketch their ideas, and start learning to think visually. Early next morning I go in to UTV to have it photocopied. I am directed to a department optimistically called 'Resources'.

From there I am sent to the Chief Administrator's office where there is a queue.

'I just want to use the photocopier,' I say.

'Wait please!' the woman behind the desk barks at me.

I wait over half an hour and start worrying about being late for my students. I go up to the desk again. The woman carries on tidying her pencils, ignoring me.

'Please,' I implore, 'I'm doing a course for Irene Zukosoka and I really need this copying.'

'Who is this Zukosoka ?' she asks, without raising her eyes.

'She's Director of Programmes,' I say sharply. Surely she knows this? Evidently not.

I show her my rudimentary storyboard. She handles it gingerly.

'What is this?' she asks, thrusting it back at me.

'It's a storyboard,' I retort. She shrugs and looks blank.

'Please wait,' she says.

She has forgotten me already. I persevere:

'My class starts in ten minutes and I'm going to be late.'

'How many do you need?'

'About fifty'. Her eyes bulge.

'Fifty? I thought you wanted just the one. You will have to see the Head of Resources. He's not in.'

I grab my precious storyboard and leave.

Out in the corridor someone points me along the verandah to a door marked Head of Resources. I go into a deserted office and see a photocopier. I manage to turn it on and I am starting to make copies when a woman comes in.

'Good morning,' she says, 'Can I help you?'

I try to sound airy as I tell her what I am doing. Her smile is chilly as she asks me to accompany her. I follow her red high heels down the corridor to another office where a man in a striped shirt sits behind a desk.

'Yes?' he says grumpily, looking up.

'I'm not sure what I'm doing here,' I say. 'I was just using the photocopier and...'

He interrupts.

'You were using the photocopier?'

'Yes.'

'What for?'

'I'm teaching a class for Irene Zukosoka and I needed some storyboards.'

'Where are you from?' he barks.

'London.'

'Why couldn't you bring these materials from there?'

I explain.

'Why do you take advantage of our resources? You are coming from the UK – why can't you bring a copier?'

I almost laugh but think better of it.

'Look, I'm only trying to run the best possible course for your television producers.'

He asks how many copies I have made..

'About twenty.'

He is absolutely furious. He demands payment for them. He does not know who Irene is either.

I arrive at my class late and cross. There are only five girls there. I fight the urge to cry as I distribute my storyboards, tell them each to plot a film and go in search of Irene.

She is sitting on a sofa in her office with her feet up, drinking a bottle of orange Fanta and nursing a hangover. She is feeling very sorry for herself and plans to go home as soon as she has drunk a nice cup of sweet coffee and read the paper.

'I can't go on,' I tell her. 'It's an uphill struggle'.

I describe my encounter with Resources.

'Can't you do the class without this story – thing?' she asks.

'Don't worry about it. Come and have a nice dinner at my house tonight and we'll talk about it then. Oh, dear, where's my coffee?'

Exasperated, I go back to my class and draw storyboards all day, while the class members struggle to invent storylines.

Irene sends her cousin, Cosmos, to pick me up for dinner. He is a skinny young man with owlish spectacles. Irene has wangled him a job as a cameraman at UTV. We drive east out of the city along the Kampala Road till it crosses the railway lines and tarmac turns to dirt.

We arrive at a cluster of Soviet-style apartment blocks. The buildings face each other across wastelands of churned up mud where little boys play football with a tin can amongst bonfires and chickens. The sound of dogs barking and babies crying drifts from the windows and women shout to each other up and down the stairwells. There is a pungent but homely smell of frying on-ions. Washing hangs from lines that festoon the buildings so that the blocks have a festive air, like ocean liners decked out with bunting.

Irene's flat is a monument to daintiness, with lace curtains, doilies and flock wallpaper. It is an African version of an Edwardian parlour. Irene is ensconced in a moss green velveteen armchair, wearing a hairnet and a pink vest that shows her dimpled, chubby arms. She watches three televisions at once. All of them crackle and fizz without producing a viewable picture.

Unusually, at thirty-eight Irene is unmarried. She lives with her cousin Rose, and Tony, a shy child of about ten, the orphan of relatives who died of AIDS. She also has a live-in maid.

Irene has prepared a feast: fried tilapia or Nile Perch, goat and potatoes, *matoke* – the national dish, a starchy mush made from green bananas – and then cheese and salad. We eat dinner on our laps from trays laid with embroidered cloths, in front of the televisions. Every so often the maid is called in to readjust one of the aerials but to no avail. We watch snow-like static and listen to its accompanying hiss.

We drink a quarter bottle of pink Moet and Chandon stolen from British Airways Club Class on one of Irene's recent foreign trips. She is often abroad attending workshops. It is how she found out about the Habitat films.

She shows me her collection of miniatures, smuggled off planes to and from Europe – Gordons gin, Smirnoff vodka, White Horse whisky, two quarter bottles of Soave and about six of Chianti, all stashed safely in a plastic bag. I admire them and Cosmos picks out a miniature bottle of Courvoisier to drink. Irene also has a supply of miniature salts and peppers and British Airways chocolates. She may have landed me in the job from hell but she is hospitable, and after lashings of goat stew I am starting to enjoy myself.

I take a taxi back into town. The driver is friendly and is playing some great Zairean music. The sky is still streaked with scarlet and the breeze wafts the soothing, smoky smell of African night into the open windows. I decide that whatever the assignment, it is great to be back in Africa.

Next day things start to improve. A man called George appears, announces that he has been assigned to the course as Head of Drama, and starts to recruit local actors. My students simplify and improve their storyboards. There are several usable ideas, especially one about a girl migrating from the village to the big city, and another dealing with domestic violence. Even a cameraman materialises. We are almost ready to start shooting. We spend a useful afternoon checking out locations, casting, and scheduling next week's filming.

It is Friday night and I am meeting Alan Graham in the Equatoria bar. He has with him his live-in girlfriend Catherine, a beautiful Kenyan half his age. She sits very still, long-lashed eyes cast down, nursing her bitter lemon and not speaking. I try several times to bring her into the conversation, but Alan talks over us.

The plan was to have dinner, but after a few drinks Alan announces they are off. Catherine shakes my hand politely and smiles. As Alan steers her out between the parasols he pats her bottom. He has left me with the drinks bill.

On Monday morning it starts to rain. When I arrive at UTV there is no camera, no cameraman and no minibus. George, the already invaluable Head of Drama, manages to rustle up a vehicle, but apparently I have no camera 'allocation' and our cameraman has simply disappeared. The minibus cannot leave the compound until the Chief Administrator signs a form. He is out.

After I've done a lot of shouting a grumpy man emerges from Resources with a very old camera. Irene's cousin, Cosmos, says he will step into the breach and film for us. We pile into the van and set off for our village location.

After the rain the village is muddy and ducks are wallowing in the puddles. I jump out of the minibus but my students are reluctant to follow. They are wearing freshly pleated silk skirts, blouses with lacy collars, tailored jackets and fluffy cardigans. They carry patent handbags or fake Chanel bags with quilting and gilt chains. I look in dismay at eight pairs of feet in white court shoes, patent pumps, high-heeled slingbacks, strappy sandals. I alone wear jeans and a T-shirt.

I try to explain the (to me) simple concept of practical working clothes. It is beyond them. Smart clothes denote a smart job and social position. They do not want to undermine this impression, especially in a rural village. They only descend from the van when I promise them we will use the monitor to look at shots, so they won't dirty their clothes. They step gingerly amongst the puddles and goat droppings, their heels squelching into the mud.

Cosmos is bossy and rude to the girls, and pays no attention at all to their first, uncertain attempts at direction. It seems to go against the grain for the girls to tell their male colleague what to do and, as the boss's cousin, Cosmos has even more reason to lord it over them. The girls are ready to give up and go home at five. They have lost interest in their storyboards and do not seem to care about the film at all.

The next day the van driver refuses to budge till eleven, when the Chief Administrator arrives to sign our form. A rather grand 'actress' arrives wearing a silk pleated skirt, white shoes and red jacket with gold buttons. She refuses to play the role of a poor, homeless girl because of her 'pride'. We have no option but to pay her a lot more money.

In the van my students are muttering in their own language. They refuse to meet my eye.

'I know something's wrong,' I keep saying. 'Tell me.'

One of them says that I am exploiting them.

'In what way?'

They say I have come to Uganda to use them as cheap labour on my own project. I am glorifying my own career on their backs.

'It's not my project, it's yours,' I explain wearily.

'Why aren't we being paid then?' says a girl who has been truculent from the start.

'You are treating us like slaves.'

I explain again the aim of the course but she turns away in disgust. One of the women makes an obscene gesture at me. Another shouts at me in her own language. I am fed up. I just want the damn films made so I can go home.

We are filming in a market when two men rush up.

'You are exploiting us,' says one. 'You want to show your

country images of poverty,' says another, thrusting his face at me: 'Go home to America!'

He has very stained teeth. I explain patiently that I am from the UK to help UTV make some educational films.

'You will have to speak to the boss,' says another man.

We are led through a maze of stalls to the centre of the market where a very fat man with bloodshot eyes presides over proceedings from a straw-roofed hut. He looks at me with dislike.

'You! You are from the BBC!' he accuses me.

I explain I am not but he does not believe me. Again he thinks I am undermining Uganda by deliberately filming poor people. Though I am exasperated and angry, I understand his point of view. The only Ugandan news which ever seems to reach the European networks is bad – usually stories of villages decimated by AIDS. For years news crews have descended on Uganda to sniff out the poorest, the sickest and the most wretched. Why should he believe I am any different?

At lunch time there is another row. My students have not been given a big enough daily allowance to eat in town, but going all the way back to UTV would waste well over an hour. Reasonably, they say they will be happy with a snack and sandwiches rather than waste the day, but Cosmos says he will not shoot another frame until he has had a square meal. He demands cooked meat with *matoke* and rice. He is sprawling in the back of the minibus complaining of exhaustion as if he has just come from a battlefield.

'Come on,' I say, 'Don't be unreasonable. We're on a really tight schedule here. We'll never finish if we flog all the way back out to UTV.'

He looks at me coldly and sneers.

'Is this the way you always treat African crews? Starve them?'

I give up. My students look deflated. They seem to be in awe of this skinny tyrant. We drive back to UTV so Cosmos can eat his lunch.

After Cosmos's lunch we lose our driver and it starts to rain. I try to find another driver. There are several sitting around doing nothing but, as usual, none can be allocated to my project without the appropriate official paperwork. Our own driver eventually wanders in, an hour and a half late, carrying a huge supply of groceries. Instead of being mollified by his hot meal Cosmos is in a poisonous mood, and my students are lethargic.

We drive back into town as the rain stops and the puddles start to steam in the heat. We are shooting a scene in the bus station. It is noisy, hot, muddy, filthy and crowded and we work shrouded in toxic clouds of carbon monoxide. The monitor has broken down so I cannot check Cosmos's shots. Each time I question him, he looks sullen.

'Do you want me to play it back in the camera?' he asks aggressively.

This is not an option. The camera heads are dirty and our first three tapes are already seriously damaged.

'No. Carry on. But please try and hold the shot a little longer.' I ask feebly.

The next day we begin to edit. The equipment is housed in a series of airless, windowless rooms with bars for doors. Editing equipment is fragile and needs air conditioning and a cool, dust-free environment. Our cramped, concrete cell is filthy and hot. Our editor's sweaty fingers slip and leave damp smudges on the dust-encrusted keys. The barred doors let in a little air, but also a lot of echoing noise from passers by.

We are due to start shooting our second story about domestic violence that afternoon. As usual there is a problem with transport.

'There is no allocation for your project,' says the man in Resources. By now, my loathing for Resources knows no bounds.

'Thank you for your help,' I say.

'No problem,' he says, my sarcasm lost on him.

I decide to steal the vehicle. It has a key in it, and we have a driver. The only problem seems to be who will take responsibility – or the blame. I am ready to. In fact I am spoiling for a fight with the Chief Administrator. We set off.

Our story is about a young girl who ends up on the street because her father drinks and beats her mother. I have invested a lot of hope in our director, Joanne. She is bright, relatively enthusiastic and today appears in shorts and a sweatshirt, ready for some action. I am delighted.

Sadly, as soon as we start putting together the shots Joanne loses interest. She sits on the ground and expects me to work it out for her. I have yet another row with Cosmos, whose camerawork has proved to be badly framed, unsteady and generally deplorable.

We are filming a strong scene. Father is late home, mother looks anxiously at the clock, smiles reassuringly at her children, then looks terrified as she hears her husband's violent banging at the door. It is a beautiful performance, but at the crucial moment our light batteries fail. My students stand around listlessly. It is nearing six, darkness is falling and they want to go home.

'Come on,' I say, 'This is a key test. Technical hitches are always happening. You have to finish filming today, so what are you going to do?'

Joanne looks at her watch.

'I really have to go,' she says.

'Don't you care about finishing your film?' I ask.

'I have to pick my child up from my sister's house. My husband will be angry if I am late.'

There is a general murmur of agreement from the other women. It is ironical that they have written a film about domestic tyranny when custom dictates that they put their husbands and families before their jobs under all circumstances.

'OK,' I say, softening, 'I understand. But let's just think of a way to do this one last shot shall we?'

They look exasperated.

'I've had an idea,' I say. 'Has anyone got a torch?'

Despite themselves they are intrigued, and we end up with a very effective, moody shot of the drunk father weaving home by the torch's unsteady beam, then his fist banging angrily on the door. At last it is a wrap, and the women flee gratefully.

When it comes to making our final masters, Irene does not have any new tapes.

'This is Uganda's main television station. There must be a tape in it somewhere,' I say, without conviction. After a prolonged search she presents me with two tapes. One has yesterday's news on it and the other last week's football match. It is the best she can do.

I think about these films going out at the Habitat Conference, alongside all the slick offerings from Europe and America, and I nearly despair. Yet I know that, however poor technically, our little films are powerful, especially the one about domestic violence. I am determined to persevere.

At last the films are edited, and Irene wants to go out and celebrate. Alan comes, bringing with him his flatmate Peter, some sort of computer expert. With them are their Kenyan girl friends Catherine and Natalie. What can these lovely young girls see in their middle-aged, raddled Englishmen? Peter has an unenviable moustache and bad teeth.

'Anything for a freebie,' he says, guffawing as he shakes hands with Irene. I wince inwardly. I am in for an expensive night out.

As a prelude to the party we drive to the Hotel Diplomate to watch the sunset. Kampala is spread across a range of hills which are soft and grey as doves' breasts against the coral sunset sky. As the dusk deepens and the lights start to come on far below us the city is like a cluster of glittering diamond necklaces displayed on dark velvet. I can physically feel all the frustrations, irritations and disappointments draining out of me. It is going to be a good evening after all.

The domestic violence film went down an unexpected storm at Habitat. Rather than detracting from it, the poor technical quality enhanced its value and said as much about the state of modern Uganda as the content did. The women of UTV were highly commended for their skills, later my course won a Commonwealth award and there were many demands for copies of the film. As a glimpse of one Ugandan woman's daily life it was both convincing and haunting. It had been worth persevering after all.

8 THE UNKINDEST CUT
Uganda

Female circumcision is common in many African countries, and varies in degree of severity. In Uganda it is practised only by the Sabiny tribe in a remote part of the country near the Kenyan border. When girls there reach puberty they have their clitoris and outer labia crudely removed.

Now there was to be a film funded by the United Nations Fund for Population, but only on condition there was an African producer on board. Irene, my friend and Director of Programmes at Uganda Television, agreed to take on the role but had no intention of cancelling a trip to New York to accompany me on the shoot. However, she did at least organise a local film crew. So it was back to Uganda for me.

I am tired and cross when I arrive at Entebbe. The flight is delayed and I have to wait at Nairobi airport, surrounded by the blue-rinsed women members of the Kenyan Bowling Team on their way to a tournament in Lusaka. In their maroon blazers and Liberty print shirts they fuss around me like a clutch of agitated hens. The driver I was promised has not materialised at the airport so I share a courtesy bus to my hotel with an American woman, swathed in beads, who asks ignorant questions about poverty all the way into Kampala.

To cap it all my room at Fairways Hotel is grim. It looks over a walled yard that contains a Pepsi machine, a brick bar and a thatched hut selling *nyama choma* – barbecued meat. My room is typically furnished: two single beds, a beige carpet which stinks of damp, a pair of brown velveteen armchairs, a rusting fridge containing a bottle of water, a broken television, a gigantic, elaborate sideboard made of fake teak and a mirror which would look more at home in a cocktail bar. In the bathroom the plastic shower curtain is mouldy, the grey towels thin and fraying, the loo paper rough and gritty.

I have dinner with Irene the night I arrive. She hugs me warmly, enveloping me in her customary smell of *White Musk*.

'So good to see you,' she says, 'Come on, let's eat. I'm hungry.'

She is always hungry. We eat in the parched yard overlooked by my bedroom. Tinny music is pumping out of a primitive tannoy system. Irene supervises the cooking of our *nyama choma*.

'You must try it,' she says, 'It's delicious.'

There is a lot of talk about the temperature of the griddle, and Irene repeatedly berates the teenage cook for using the wrong cuts of meat. He sweats anxiously into the flames where our meat is sizzling.

When it is ready I look with dismay at the fatty, gristly twists of burnt beef. The chicken is raw beneath soot-black skin. With her usual cheerfulness Irene thinks dinner is wonderful. She tells me that after living under Idi Amin's regime simple freedoms like being able to walk around freely at night are priceless privileges.

'This is great,' she says, waving a chicken wing at the yard.

'Let's eat some more!'

My cameraman, John Stephen Okurut, wants to be paid 50% up front so Irene's driver Alex drives me to the bank. Alex had written to me in England asking me if I would pay for his training as a car mechanic – $250 US – and I had to refuse, but now he is relaxed and friendly. That is always the way in Africa. One minute you are resenting people for asking you for money and the next, you are wracked with guilt about not having handed it over.

I emerge from the bank with a massive wedge of notes – there are thousands of Ugandan shillings to the pound. Okurut is waiting for me in Irene's office. He is a very tall, elegant man. The fine fuzz of white hair on an otherwise smooth bald head give him the air of an elder statesman. His manner is formal and he speaks softly and courteously.

I give him his advance. His face is like a stone carving, hard and closed, as he counts the notes. He folds them up and tucks them into one of his rather fine beige socks. I am surprised he is being so unfriendly.

'Everything OK?' I ask brightly.

'Fine,' he says.

'Are you sure?'

'Sure'. He avoids my eye.

'We agreed on the amount of money, didn't we?' I ask.

'If that's the way you feel, that's fine,' says he.

'What do you mean?' I ask.

He turns slowly to look at me, eyes dead. I try smiling.

'You've got the money you asked for, so, everything's OK then?'

He shrugs very slowly and looks rather disgusted.

I am becoming impatient.

'Okurut, if you don't tell me what's wrong I can't help you.'

He stands up. His posture is straight and proud.

'It's OK.'

I say:

'Well, I'll be going then.'

I think about shaking his hand, but he is stiff with resentment. I leave.

Two hours later, I am just settling into a book on my balcony when the telephone rings. It is Irene.

'Something bad has happened,' she says. 'Okurut is very angry.'

She sounds out of breath, stressed.

'I could see that,' I say. 'What the hell is wrong with him?'

'You only paid him 30,000 shillings and you agreed 300,000.'

With so many shillings to the pound, and such huge denominations of cash, I have counted in tens rather than hundreds. I kick myself, but it was an easy mistake to make and I gave him plenty of opportunity to point out my error. Instead Okurut chose to misinterpret the situation as though I was trying to cheat him. Doing business in Africa can sometimes be the most infuriating undertaking.

'Can you come back?' asks Irene.

It is the end of the day, the traffic will be solid but, if Okurut's precious dignity is to be saved, I have no option but to climb into a taxi and head back to the office.

Okurut is all smiles when I return with the balance.

'No problem,' he says, smiling and patting me rather patronisingly on the back.

I bristle. It is my turn to be stiff.

'See you tomorrow then, ' I growl.

It is not just Okurut who insists on advance payment. I am haemorrhaging money. Cash up front for the car hire, petrol nearly $100 to fill the tank, the sound recordist also wants to be paid in advance, plus a deposit for hiring an extra microphone. By the end of the first day I feel I have spent most of the budget.

To cheer me up Irene promises to take me out at the weekend. Our outing consists of driving miles out of town to a new but deserted 'guest house' which boasts both jacuzzi and sauna. A sleepy, slovenly girl appears, dragging her flip-flops.

Irene insists I have a massage. I am shown into a bare, whitewashed room by a mountainous, scowling woman. This is a far cry from the dimly lit, fragrant New Age massage parlours of London.

'Lie down,' she barks, indicating a high, plastic-covered bed. A spider scuttles into a corner.

I feel pale and vulnerable as I strip off and climb up. She kneads me vigorously with baby oil. My limbs are like twigs in her meaty fists. She pounds my stomach with a violence which verges on the criminal. She finishes by slapping the backs of my thighs till they burn.

'OK,' she drawls. 'You can go.'

I am so oiled that I slip like a seal from the treacherous bed and slither into an undignified heap on the concrete floor. For the first time my masseuse smiles.

Irene would stay in the sauna all evening, but I have to go back into town. I am dining with Elaine Eliah, an American journalist. She has written an excellent article about female circumcision and

I want to meet her.

Elaine is hunched and bespectacled. She wears turquoise shell suit trousers and a baggy T-shirt cinched at the waist by a money bag. She takes me to Kampala's most highly rated restaurant, Le Chateau. I want lashings of wine and huge helpings of steak. Elaine frowns and announces earnestly that she is teetotal and is only having one course. I wonder if I can last the evening.

I relinquish steak and order coq-au-vin as Elaine tells me her story. Having worked as a cook on a tug boat in Seattle, she left her husband and arrived in Uganda with nothing but a backpack. She went up north to see the gorillas, fell in love with the country and never left. She wrote restaurant reviews to earn her living, and fast built up a career as a journalist.

As if on cue the Belgian owner of the restaurant sashays up to our table, all floppy blond hair and clasped hands. He fawns over Elaine and thanks her for a recent newspaper article which has brought him new customers. He lavishes pistachio and banana ice-cream on us, then Belgian cake stuffed with frozen Bavarois. He even throws in an Irish coffee on the house.

'You must have written some article,' I say to Elaine, through a heavenly mouthful of brandy-laced cream.

'Sure, how else do you think I get to eat round here?' she says.

I am starting to like Miss Eliah.

Next day the rain is a grey wall, relentless and solid. A wet weekend in Kampala is no fun.

'I hate bloody Africa,' I mutter.

I am wondering what to do when Irene telephones.

'You have to come out tonight,' she says, 'It's a very big occasion.'

Irene and her friend come to pick me up. They are wearing glamorous black frocks, jewellery, and shiny crimson lipstick. Irene's *White Musk* battles with her friend's heavy gardenia scent. They take me to the Casino for the final of the Miss Kampala contest. We elbow our way through a pulsating, volatile male throng. Judges at round tables fill in piles of cards. We buy some drinks and find a spot where we can just about see the stage.

The compère is a light-skinned woman wearing a white, halter-necked evening gown and an expression of extreme boredom.

'Please, keep the noise down,' she repeats loudly and rudely to the crowd. This has no effect whatsoever.

There are about fifty contestants in bikinis and swimsuits. There are spotty, podgy teenagers. There are girls with huge, flabby bottoms, with tree-trunk thighs and invisible knees, solid, chunky girls, hefty girls with huge breasts. Only one or two are elegant by Western standards. I think: 'If only the obsessed-with-thin purveyors of British fashion could see this.'

The men are in a frenzy. They roar, wolf-whistle, cheer, laugh, clap and shout lewd remarks as each girl struts her stuff.

'Hey big legs!' or 'Fat bum, kiss me!' they shout.

The prize for the winner is a spanking new Mercedes wrapped in pink ribbon. Desirable as it is, it doesn't seem worth this humilation. Most of the girls look bewildered as they blink into the glaring lights and try to smile at the hectic crowd. One of them trips on her platform sandals. A roar goes up. Another one starts to leave the stage by the wrong exit. One is so mesmerised that she doesn't leave the stage at all, and is manhandled off the stage by the compère. The crowd hoots with merciless laughter.

Irene starts mumbling about the judges.

'It's all fixed up,' she says, watching them with narrowed eyes.

'Look at those men, they are cheats!'

The judges are downing glasses of white wine as they eye the contestants, the cards and the scores forgotten.

'I'm not staying around to watch this corruption,' says Irene haughtily.

Anyone would think she is talking about a human rights trial. I never find out who wins, but I think the lucky ones are those sufficiently discouraged to give up modelling for good.

The next day I set off for Kapchorwa. With me are Okurut, Godwin the sound recordist and Peter, our driver. For eight hours we twist up through the mountains along a raw, red clay road.

Peter is anxious about the rain, crouching over the wheel to peer out at the swathes of cloud above the lush valleys, green with banana trees and coffee.

We arrive at dusk. It is cold and damp. Kapchorwa is a grim cluster of mud and concrete constructions clinging to the side of the road. An albino in a battered hat stares vacantly as we draw up outside the Paradise Hotel. Children, wild with excitement to see my white face, come running along the road.

'*Muzungu, muzungu!*' they chant, 'White person!'

The Paradise Hotel is about as far from paradise as it gets. It is a shack with a corrugated iron roof, but it has the only bar and restaurant in town. Inside men sit patiently in the gloom waiting for the three hours' worth of evening electricity to come on. Till then there is nothing to do except stare at me. I am the best entertainment they have had in weeks. We are served sweet, milky tea from a filth-encrusted plastic jug.

Godwin tries to be chatty while Okurut gives me a ponderous Ugandan geography lesson. At seven the single bulb goes on. The men continue staring, but less avidly. They are concentrating on their food. We eat rice and beans, and drink more tea.

Okurut and Godwin are staying at the Paradise but the UN has arranged for me to stay at the town's official guest house, a big, white-washed bungalow that looks promising. A cross-eyed, backward boy with a limp shows me into a room with a red earth floor, furnished with a wooden bed. The one bathroom boasts a three-piece suite from Armitage Shanks in turquoise but there is no running water. The bath is ringed with grime and the basin sprinkled with pubic hair.

I ask the boy to bring me water and he shrinks away, giggling maniacally. Eventually I make him understand, and he reappears with a small jug. I wash as best I can in the dirty bath. We are so high up in the mountains that it is bitterly cold. I tuck myself up in my hard little bed and wait for the light to go out.

In the middle of the night someone arrives. He takes over the next door room, banging noisily into furniture and ordering the boy around. Then he gobs, coughs, spits, retches and farts.

Next morning, over tea and eggs, he looks startled to see me but quickly recovers his composure and is quite charming. He is the Ugandan Minister for Labour.

The backward boy's mother is now in evidence, bringing slices of white bread with small smears of margarine, and ferrying buckets of water to the bathroom with which to flush the lavatory. The Minister even arranges a jug of hot water with which to shave. He hums loudly as he scrapes away at his beard. I have gloomy thoughts about brushing my teeth over the even hairier basin.

Peter is supposed to pick me up at 6.45. He does not come. At eight o'clock I march down the hill, grumpily waving away the children who run after me. I find Okurut and Godwin tucking into eggs at the Paradise.

'Where were you?' I ask. 'I've been waiting for one and a half hours.'

Okurut opens his eyes very wide:

'Oh, we thought you should sleep, so we filmed the women getting water from the river,'

'Yes, well I should have been there,' I persist.

'Oh, there was no need,' says Okurut.

'There is a need, Okurut,' I say. 'I'm the director and I need to be present at all the filming so I know exactly what we have in the can.'

He shrugs, eyes narrow and hard. The shoot has not got off to a good start.

We then have to negotiate with the post office to charge our batteries. It is the only place in town with a reliable source of electricity. Once more a crowd gathers, intrigued by the strangers. A small boy keeps touching my bottom and then running behind his mother's skirts from where he peeks at me with an angelic, mischievous smile.

Dr. François Farah, the country representative of the UN's Fund for Population, arrives to chair a workshop. Born in Lebanon and reared in Canada, François speaks with a succulent French accent and oozes charm. He has a professional smile framed by a neatly clipped beard. His slightly greying hair gives him a dignified, authoritative air.

François is determined to wipe out female circumcision in Uganda. With a local ally, Jackson Chekweko, he has set up a community-based project named Reach and he is so certain of success that he has persuaded the UN to fund our film.

Jackson Chekweko is a skinny young man with a wide smile. His formal good manners and rather flowery eloquence mask a steely determination and an ambitious streak. Jackson became involved in the campaign because of his own story. His sister, Rose, was pregnant with her first child when her husband's family demanded that she should be circumcised. She nearly bled to death. Jackson decided there and then the practice must be abolished, but he understood how difficult it was to change attitudes.

'The problem with previous attempts to stop the practice was that they were coercive,' he says, 'They undermined the community's ability to reason for itself. Because of that, the reaction was negative. The community wants to protect its culture.'

Jackson also understands what so many campaigners fail to understand – in a male-dominated society, there is no point in targeting the women. Communities like Kapchorwa are built upon rules created by men. It is the men who will not marry uncircumcised girls, men who create the environment in which women have no choice but to conform. Jackson knows that the practice will continue until the men themselves decide to stop female circumcision.

Jackson takes us to a 'bar' where men squat on wooden stools round a small hut and drink cassava beer. The sludge-coloured foam is served in enormous Cowboy margarine tins. Even plastic cups are too expensive. Jackson sits down amongst them and the men listen as they drink. Soon they want more to drink, and their attention wanes as they shout to be served. Jackson, ever the politician, asks me for money to buy a round. It is absurdly cheap and worth every Ugandan shilling. Their tins replenished, the men are prepared to pay attention.

Jackson talks about the health risks of female circumcision, not just for the women but for the unborn babies. Cleverly he explains that these men's sons or grandsons might become stuck inside the woman's body, their passage obstructed by the tough genital scarring. Some babies could die before the midwife had time to cut the women open. The men listen gravely, absorbing the idea that their all-important male progeny could be at risk.

The workshop that François is chairing opens at the community hall that afternoon, and Jackson's mother-in-law is going to be there.

'You should see her,' says Jackson. 'Really, it's a terrible thing.'

He will say no more.

She arrives leaning on two clumsy wooden crutches. She drags her legs with a sickening lurch and twist of her body. Jackson helps her up the steps to the hall and she collapses gratefully into a chair. I am shocked by the extent of her injury. Surely this cannot all be put down to circumcision.

'I'm thirty-five years old,' she tells me in her own language, Jackson translating.

'What?' I ask, in disbelief.

Despite the lively eyes, her face is haggard and gaunt. Lines make deep troughs in her brow and round her mouth. Years of pain have withered and shrunk her features. She laughs, showing a mouth full of gums and very few teeth.

'I expect you think I look older.'

Her father arranged a husband for her when she was fifteen, and she was circumcised that season in 1976. In Kapchorwa the 'season' is in December on every even-numbered year. She was cut with a dirty razor blade and contracted a fever while her genitals suppurated and bled. She lost all feeling in her left leg as the poisoned blood coursed through it. Her leg became withered and paralysed. Three other women suffered similar mutilation that year. When she finishes her story Jackson's mother-in-law grasps me by the hand and smiles. I only have the strength to say to her:

'Thank you.'

Then we meet Rose, another active campaigner. She has been fighting the practice since she was circumcised in 1994. She agrees to talk but asks if we can go to a quiet spot.

We find a grassy mound about a quarter of a mile away. The view across the valley to the mountains is beautiful. In the distance a cock crows as Rose, in a barely audible whisper, begins to tell her story. Godwin edges closer with the microphone, trying not to break the spell. Okurut is still as stone, his eye pressed to the eye-piece. I am holding my breath.

Rose describes the evening before her circumcision. The girls to be circumcised are forced to dance to show they are not afraid or weak. They are beaten if they eat and drink because hunger and thirst are signs of feebleness. At dawn the girls are taken down to the river for a ritual bath. They are exhausted and cold and the icy water makes them shiver. A cow is slaughtered and the contents of its stomach smeared on their faces to form a stiff, white mask. The girls are taken to a central part of the village. They blow whistles maniacally and continue dancing to indicate their enthusiasm for what is to come. The circumcisors wait.

Rose's face becomes pinched. The sun is high in the sky now. Sensing we are reaching an emotional climax, Okurut stands up briefly from the camera and wipes his face. As she carries on Rose clenches her fist and frowns in an effort not to cry.

'I didn't want it but I was forced to do it to become a member of the community. After the circumcision there is a lot of bleeding and all that pain.' She pauses. When she speaks again her voice trembles.

'You have to swallow all that pain. You are not supposed to release it out. You are supposed to keep it within you. The circumcisor is supposed to cut you without you even blinking an eye.'

Her voice trails off and she looks away.

If a girl so much as blinks – let alone cries out – during the cutting, she is deemed a coward and ostracised. How brilliant of the men to have come up with such a tradition. What a clever way of ensuring the women take their punishment without a murmur, volunteering for it with grim determination.

After talking to Rose I go back to the guest house to compose myself, and find François entertaining the village Elders. About a dozen of them sit opposite each other on sofas. Most wear suits or traditional dress with flowing white scarves. There is a splendid array of hats, including exquisitely embroidered skull caps, a flat tweed cap and a floppy, khaki sun hat sported by the Chief Elder, Mr. Cheborion.

François is looking wan. Clearly the Elders believe the UN has limitless funds with which to revive their sagging village economy.

Mr.Cheborion stands and reads from a long, handwritten list. The Elders are demanding education for all, including a new school, schoolbooks, teachers and uniforms, electricity and radios for all the men. But they have agreed to shift their stance on female circumcision, and Mr.Cheborion is willing to be interviewed for the film. He wears heavy-rimmed black glasses and waves flies away from his face as they settle down in the comfortable shade of his sun-hat.

'I myself was one of those in favour of girls being circumcised,' he says. 'Now, I have learned how harmful it is and I am against it. So what I am advising is if a girl wants to be circumcised let her be circumcised, but if she does not want to be, let her alone.'

It is not quite the unequivoval condemnation that François hopes for but it is an encouraging start. If the Chairman of the Elders is outspoken against the practice there will be many men who will follow his example.

By the evening, weak tea with slightly sour milk at the Paradise Hotel tastes exquisite. Godwin is telling amusing stories about Ugandan white cowboys. If Okurut were not so elderly and dignified I could swear he is flirting with me. He takes every opportunity to touch my leg or arm, sit with his arm round the back of my chair and brush his thigh against mine under the cramped wooden table. He says men need women as 'blankets' in order to sleep comfortably, and goes on to bemoan the dearth of good blankets at the Paradise. I flee to the guest house.

Jackson has introduced a system of 'peer education'. Girls who have avoided circumcision warn their friends about the dangers of the practice. He takes us to the local school to meet Justine, his star 'peer group educator'. Justine is tall, and angular and her slender neck sticks out of her clumsy school shirt like a flower stalk.

The school stands on a hillside overlooking a valley, and during break pupils gather under the trees. This is when Justine seizes her opportunity to talk to them. Today there is a boy in the group.

'They say if you clitorise girls it will avoid prostitution,' he says.

I want to slap him but another girl backs him up:

'It's been going on since my great, great, great, great gran. How can I tell my parents I won't do it?' she asks, 'If I don't do it, they will get a rope and tie me down until I do.'

Justine soldiers on:

'They are just threatening this to harass you.'

Another girl pipes up:

'My brother says that if you marry a girl who is not circumcised you are putting yourself in problems because every time you are not there, she will be looking around for other boys and other men.'

'I think we will be followed by demonic spirits if we do not do it,' says a shy girl from under lowered eyes.

I feel sorry for Justine. She is not really equipped to fight centuries of superstition and tradition. All she can think of to say is:

'As for these spirits, I don't really think they will come.'

But there is hope. Judith and Grace are teenage sisters whose father objects to the practice on Christian grounds. Outside their thatched hat the sisters serve tea in flowered china cups while their father tells me how he is unable to tolerate harming one of God's creatures. His girls will never undergo the knife.

Grace has plans to go to university. She has a beautiful, rather placid face and her eyes shine as she speaks. Judith is more outspoken.

'So many girls here they don't go to school. Why?' she asks, thumping her fist into the grass.

She glares at me. I urge her to go on.

'Because of this circumcision!' she says. 'Once they go to circumcision, they finish school. It's terrible. It's a reason why there are no educated women here,'

Grace and Judith's father stands up. I realise he is about to make a speech. He says that God has brought us together and that he is honoured I have travelled from overseas to help them abolish this practice. His eyes water with gratitude.

I feel small and hypocritical, jetting in for a few days, shooting the film and then going back to my comfortable life. I am determined to persuade the BBC to let me come back to Kapchorwa and make a film so that people all over the world will know what is going on.

Thunder clouds like purple silk sacks have started to plump themselves up in the sky. By the time we arrive back at the workshop the rain is pulsating on the corrugated iron roof and inside the hall it is virtually dark. It is time for François's keynote speech.

He sweeps to the front of the hall, immaculately groomed in a lightweight grey suit. He begins by praising the custom of celebrating the passage from adolescence into adulthood. Though he approves of marking this transition, he deplores what he calls 'the cutting'. He does not use the term 'female circumcision' because of its association with male circumcision. He wants people to understand that slicing off a girl's genitals is much more dangerous than snipping a boy's foreskin. Yet he also eschews the widely accepted term 'genital mutilation'. He thinks 'mutilation' is a condemning, hostile word. Instead, he plumps for the neutral but accurate term 'cutting' and believes this non-judgemental approach is the key to combating the practice.

François speaks calmly but with passion. The women are

transfixed. The men look uncomfortable. He ends by saying that African mothers are probably the best in the world. No African mother will deliberately hurt her child, especially the vulnerable girl child. The reason mothers continue to inflict circumcision on their daughters is that they honestly believe it to be an essential part of their daughters' traditional rite of passage.

I have started to sympathise with these mothers' dilemma. In Kapchorwa an uncircumcised girl is an outcast. She cannot milk a cow because people believe she will sour the milk. She cannot gather grain from the granary for fear she will wither the crop. She certainly cannot marry. A mother who does not circumcise her daughter is jeopardising her child's future. No wonder mothers put their daughters through such suffering when the alternative is so bleak.

That night I actually find myself enjoying the Paradise Hotel. Okurut is now definitely flirting. The blanket references border on the lecherous, but he is chuckling away benignly as we share a plate of fried cassava. The postmaster arrives on a yellow motorbike and we treat him to several beers to thank him for his electrical supply. He writes out his address and asks me to send him gifts from London.

'What kind of gifts?' I ask. He shrugs:

'Just gifts.'

'Well, like what?' I persist. He thinks hard.

'Perhaps even you can send me some soap and a magazine about motorbikes.'

The next morning the community gathers to honour François. He, in turn, is handing over a new jeep to the Reach Project. We sit in rows while one Elder after another stands up and makes fawning, dreary speeches. The jeep is a shabby old thing and already muddy and dirty but it is revered as though it is the latest Ferrari.

I am on the point of dozing when I feel Jackson by my side.

'I think as the white visitor here it is now your turn to make a speech,' he whispers.

Sheer vanity makes me baulk at the thought of standing in

harsh sunlight to be scrutinised by hundreds of curious eyes. I have not been able to wash my hair since I came to Kapchorwa, and it is scraped back into an unbecoming knot. My face is bare of make-up and my nose is blistered and pink where the sun has caught me unawares. My crumpled denim shirt is tight across my stomach, swollen after a diet of beans and *matoke*.

But I stand up. There is no choice. Some of the women in the front row giggle and whisper to each other. There is a stir of expectation. I have no idea what I am going to say, but the laborious translations help me to stay a jump ahead of the game.

I thank them profusely for their generosity and cooperation. Then I explain how the film might be used round Africa. If the Reach project succeeds in Kapchorwa it can be used as a blueprint elsewhere. I praise them as a community for having the courage to embrace change. Mr. Cheborion nods vigorously. Grace and Judith are grinning. Rose beams. By the time I sit down and the applause starts I am almost enjoying myself.

I was still entirely confident that somehow or other I could raise the money to film the circumcision season in December. I had no idea just how difficult it was going to be.

9 WELCOME TO WOMANHOOD
Uganda

*It was a dreary December day in London and I was planning a
Christmas shopping spree. I had decided to forget about going back
to Kapchorwa. I had pestered everyone I could think of to raise
funds, but with no luck. The circumcision season was starting in
a few days and it was highly unlikely someone would commission
the film at this late stage. I had given up.*

I am walking into Harrods when my mobile rings.

'How quickly can you get a flight to Uganda?' asks the Editor
of the BBC's *Correspondent*.

Now *Correspondent* is a presenter-led programme, and a
culturally sensitive topic like female genital mutilation needs a
black female presenter. The Nigerian journalist Donu Kogbara
is available. She wrote an article that resulted in a Harley Street
doctor being struck off for circumcising the daughters of wealthy
Africans. I ring her immediately.

Her drawl is fruity and upper class but she has a good throaty
chuckle. She sounds fun, but does not sound quite as keen on the
project as I might have hoped. She will have a problem leaving
her baby for more than a few days. She also hates flying, and is
reluctant to go to Uganda unless she can fly direct. Perhaps most
important of all, her views on genital mutilation do not exactly
gel with mine.

'Quite honestly Charlotte,' she says, 'I haven't too much
sympathy with these women. They're so passive. My grandmother
smoked a pipe, which was considered pretty rebellious in her
day, and she didn't give a shit. I don't see why these girls allow
themselves to go through with it.'

'They have no choice,' I counter.

'Oh I don't think so,' says Donu, 'They're just pathetic.'

At this late stage it is Donu or no-one. I am confident she will change her mind when she sees the situation for herself.

Donu's preference for flying direct means she has to wait for a flight, but I must leave immediately if I am to reach Kaphcorwa in time for the start of the season. Donu will just have to catch me up.

The BBC does not want to risk a Ugandan camera and crew, so I arrange for Tzvika and Peter to come in from Harare with their equipment. I fly into Kampala ahead of them, hire a car, go into town to collect some necessary supplies, then set off back to the airport with my driver Okulu, to meet Tzvika and Peter.

I have not slept much on the plane from London. Lulled by the noise of the car engine I fall asleep. When I wake with a start we are driving along an empty rural road. My watch reads 5.45. We should have reached the airport at least half an hour ago. This does not look like the approach road to Entebbe.

'Where's the airport?' I ask Okulu.

'Yes,' he says smiling.

I repeat myself very slowly:

'Where is the airport?'

He looks anxious beneath the smile. He still cannot understand the question. I feel the stirrings of an incipient panic.

'Airport. Airport,' I repeat.

'Airport, yes,' he says, pleased he has understood.

'Where is it?' I spell out. Okulu waves his hand,

'Oh it is very far!' My voice rises.

'What do you mean, 'very far'? Where's the bloody airport?'

He looks at me and laughs.

'Stop the car,' I say.

He carries on driving.

'Stop!' I repeat.

He looks at me uncertainly but keeps going.

'Stop the bloody car!' I yell.

He brakes so suddenly that we both lurch forward. There is a noise of metal rattling as we catch our breath. Okulu looks frightened.

'Okulu,' I say, trying to sound calm, 'Where are we going?'

'To Kapchorwa!' he says.

I put my head in my hands.

'But I told you to go to the airport first. We have to pick up the crew.'

He looks very grave.

'Oh,' he says.

'Turn the car round. Hurry.'

I have not thought to make an alternative arrangement with Peter and Tzvika because I could not imagine anything going wrong. Now I am two hours the wrong side of Kampala. It will take at least three and a half hours to go back to Entebbe. Their plane landed at 5.30. They will be through customs and waiting for me at 7.00 latest. It is now 6.00.

Okulu switches on the engine. It coughs and dies. With shaking fingers, he turns the key again. There is sputtering and then silence. He risks a smile. My face is hard as granite.

'Shit!' I say.

'Madam?' he ventures.

Fifteen minutes later Okulu emerges from under the car bonnet, his face smeared with grease. He holds two chunky bits of oily metal, obviously some crucial part of the car engine. Night is falling, fast and thick as a blanket. I ask Okulu how far is the nearest town. He does not understand. We will have to hitch a lift – somewhere. Anywhere is better than out here in the middle of nowhere.

We push the brute of a vehicle to the side of the road. Then I remember my luggage. It would be stupid to leave it in an unaccompanied car. I heave my bags out of the back seat.

In this part of the world a white woman lugging her bags along a deserted rural road at nightfall is a pretty rare sight. The first pick-up truck that passes stops. Okulu and I climb into the back amongst sacks of maize and six farm workers on their way home from the fields. They stare at me curiously. I look back at them glumly.

We reach a scruffy little town. Okulu seems to know his way around and leads me to a busy street, full of kiosks selling everything from soap, biscuits and Fanta to sewing machines and car parts. Oil lamps flicker. One of the vendors knows a mechanic. Someone goes to find a pick-up truck, and three men armed with spanners and oily rags hop into the back with us and drive back out of town to find our car.

There is a new moon and the inky sky is peppered with stars. A light wind flutters my hair round my face as we drive along in companionable silence. I feel a surge of gratitude towards these men. People in England would never be so helpful. We arrive at the car and the men start work on the engine. Soon there is a pile of twisted, greasy metal on the road. Okulu rubs his hands and grins at me apologetically. Time passes.

The men give up. By now most of the engine is lying on the road. I am demented and desperate for a telephone. We drive back into town and are directed to a public telephone. There is a queue. When I finally pick up the telephone I need a card.

One of the men in the queue has a card. I offer him a wedge of dollars. He takes the notes, counts them agonisingly slowly and hands me the card with a big grin. I have given him about $US 50. This is going to be one of the most expensive telephone calls I ever made.

'Philip has just this minute left,' says a woman's voice when I get through to the car hire company.

'It's fantastically urgent,' I blither, 'Please run after him.'

I sense her irritation and reluctance.

'Please,' I wheedle, 'It's a desperate emergency.'

There is a sigh and then I wait. I am terrified the card will run out. Finally I hear footsteps and Philip Asheyo is on the line. He rented me the car and assured me the driver knew exactly what to do.

'Thank God,' is all I can think of to say. Half a minute later and I would have missed him.

Philip is soothing and apologetic. He says he will go straight to the airport and pick up the crew.

'There's no time,' I say, 'They may try and leave to find me. Besides I have no idea where we are.'

Philip is calm.

'Let me talk to Okulu. He can describe the place.'

To my immense irritation Okulu puts the telephone down before I can speak to Philip again. When I ring back the lines to Kampala are busy.

All I can do is establish myself at the meeting point arranged between Philip and Okulu. We go to a garage at the edge of town. It has closed for the night.

'Are you sure this is the place?' I ask.

'Oh yes Madam,' says Okulu.

Nothing I have learned about Okulu so far inspires confidence.

There is nowhere to sit so I resign myself to standing in a garage forecourt in the dark for the next few hours. Okulu goes to find a tow truck. An hour and a half later he has not returned. I am alone in the middle of Uganda with my luggage. Yet I feel safe and, surprisingly, almost content. There is nothing to do but admire the stars. It is really quite relaxing.

A few cars drive by and slow down, surprised to see a lone white woman in the dark. Word filters round town. People drive into the forecourt just to look at me. One car stops. It is full of men. The driver winds down his window and examines me quizzically.

'Are you alright?' he asks in English.

'Oh I'm having a wonderful time,' I say, grinning. He laughs.

'Can I help?'

'No, really, I'm OK,' I say. 'I'm waiting for some people.'

'Here? At this time of night?'

I grin like a lunatic.

'Well, good luck,' says the man and drives off laughing.

A minute later he drives back.

'Are you sure you're all right?' he asks. 'I can give you a lift somewhere.'

His face is kind and concerned.

'Really, I'm fine. Thank you very much.'

I am glad that we broke down here rather than anywhere else. I would have been far more anxious in the same situation in other parts of Africa or even in England.

Eventually Okulu returns with the tow truck and car. In the car are my supplies, fruit, bread, ham and cheese. Okulu looks startled by such European delicacies. Cheese is specially rare in Uganda. We tuck in, laying out our supper on the car bonnet.

The food makes us drowsy. Okulu stretches out in the back seat with his feet out of the door and falls asleep. I try sitting in the front, but Okulu's snores distract me. I count the minutes as another hour ticks by. I walk to where I can see the road and squat down.

Watching the odd car go by keeps me occupied for about half an hour. It is quite cold so I pace up and down to keep warm. This goes on for another hour or so. I am beginning to think we must be in the wrong place. It is then that I see Tzvika's unmistakable spikey hair as a car sweeps up.

So, finally, after a maddening and seemingly unending series of disasters crew, baggage and functioning transport are all in one place, albeit in the small hours of the morning. After a great deal of hugging (me almost whimpering with relief), mild hysterics and lengthy explanations, then an even lengthier search for somewhere to lay our weary heads, we eventually get some much-needed sleep before hitting the road again next morning

Jackson is waiting for us when we finally arrive at Kapchorwa.

'Ah, Metcalf!' he says, 'I knew you'd be back.' He shakes my hand vigorously.

'Come, the Elders are waiting.'

He takes us straight up to the Reach offices where about ten Elders have gathered. There is no sign of Mr. Cheborion.

'You may remember Metcalf,' begins Jackson. He pronounces my name with relish and emphasis. Calling me Charlotte is too informal. The Elders nod.

'She requests permission to film the ceremonies,' says

Jackson.

'You are very welcome,' says one of the Elders.

The ceremonies are opening officially the next day, a couple of hours drive away. We should leave immediately. I know that Donu will be unhappy to find us gone but we have to make a start.

About two hours into our drive we hear chanting, a sign that the season is starting. A crowd of people is approaching over a distant hill. They wave leafy branches and dance towards us, chanting and drumming. The three men in front lift their legs up very high and twist their bodies in time to the rhythm.

For a moment they disappear into a dip in the road. As they reappear over the brow of the hill they whirl a cloud of dust into the sun with their branches. We can make out the colours now. The men in front wear pink skirts and beads criss-crossing their bare chests. They have painted white dots on their faces. They blow whistles maniacally. It is an eerie sight, vibrant with undercurrents of blood, violence and insanity.

Late in the afternoon we reach a dilapidated farm house with a sagging tin roof. A tall woman stands at the door. She wears gold earrings, and elegant sandals on long, shapely legs. She smokes a cigarette and looks both cross and uneasy. I know at once it is Donu. She must have been there for hours on her own. I step towards her and hug her.

The house has been turned into a bar with some bedrooms. There are a lot of drunk men round a huge television from which a football match blares through hissing static. We eat beans and *matoke* while Jackson tells Donu why the Sabiny people continue to circumcise their girls.

'Men here feel that once you are the wife of someone you should have less sexual desires,' he says, 'They strongly feel that when a female is circumcised her desire for sex decreases. They don't understand that the desire for sex comes from the brain. No! They feel and strongly feel that the desire for sex comes from the clitoris, so it is removed.'

Donu and I share a room which rustles with cockroaches.

Our two metal beds stand head to head and are supplied with stained mattresses and dirty blankets. There is a filthy cracked basin which has been put to a use never intended by the makers. Donu has drunk a tot of rum or two and a lot of Guinness. She takes charge very firmly. Soon the boys who work in the bar are running around with buckets of water, cloths and soap. Jackson hovers, embarassed.

'Really Jackson, I'm ashamed to be African,' says Donu. 'No Nigerian would ever offer accommodation in this disgusting state. It's quite appalling.'

The boys scrub, averting their eyes.

'Harder!' she barks. Her gold bracelet tinkles as she waves her hand at them imperiously.

'I don't know how you put up with it, Charlotte,' she says scornfully. 'There's no need to slum it just because we're in Africa for God's sake.'

She nicknames me the White Nigger. I nickname her the Black African Princess or BAP. We are going to get on just fine.

Next day we gather at a large clearing high in the foothills for the opening ceremony. A crowd has assembled and there is a lot of shrieking and wild dancing. The women are mainly topless, their breasts bouncing as they gyrate to the beat of the drums. They wear grass skirts and great clumps of grass on their heads.

People wave makeshift flags and leafy branches and above the crowd someone is jiggling a wooden pole topped with a formless lump of wood, like a severed head after an execution. The girls and boys due to be circumcised come marching up the hill, waving feathered wands and blowing on whistles that hang from beaded chains.

Suddenly everyone settles down and organises themselves into tidy rows in front of a trestle table. Behind it stands a senior district representative, a neat little man in a suit. The crowd sit meekly as he declares the circumcision season officially open. It is more like being at a church fête than at the start of a gruesome and bloody ritual. But the circumcisions themselves will not take place until shortly after dawn tomorrow morning, at even greater altitude

Which is why sun-up finds us high in the mountains, where the cutting will take place amongst a group of huts. The sun washes the sky pink as it rises above the thorn trees. The breeze rustles the tall grass, golden in the early morning light. I feel I have never been anywhere so remote. It is like being on a lost plateau on top of the world. Smoke drifts from the first village fires and an old woman sits smoking a pipe.

Soon we hear the sound of whistles and chanting in the distance. We can make out two tiny figures in the landscape below. Then we see several more. They are running. There are dozens, then hundreds of people rushing towards us through the grass. Within minutes we are surrounded by a jostling, excited crowd.

In its midst are the girls and boys to be cut. Their faces have been painted with the contents of a freshly slaughtered cow's stomach. The boys and girls look dazed, the whites of their eyes yellow against their spookily pale faces. Beads hang from their floppy hats and festoon their breasts. Boys and girls alike wear pink and wave feathered wands.

First the boys stand in a row, continuing to blow their whistles. Above the crowds I can see their arms reaching up on either side of their heads, their hands pointing skywards, as a sign of courage and willingness. The crowd surges round, laughing, shrieking, chanting. There is a collective shriek as the circumcisor goes to work. I see an arm start to tremble. Then the arm collapses and disappears below the crowd altogether. There is a collective groan. The boy has shown a sign of weakness and is already an outcast. He will never marry.

I find the disgraced boy sitting on a stool with two other circumcised boys. They are huddled in blankets, motionless with shock, and they gaze unblinking into the camera. At their feet is a blood-spattered sack. Beneath the boy whose arms have betrayed him, a thick pool of blood is congealing in the hot sun. In it I see a terrible shred of flesh. It is not just his foreskin, it is the end of his penis. He may die from loss of blood or an infection. He can hardly walk. At dawn the teenage boy was a proud warrior. Now he is a cripple and a pariah.

The girls are circumcised in makeshift corrals made of blankets and wooden stakes. They lie down in the dirt, legs and skirts drawn up. The crowd throngs round the opening of the corral and stands on tip-toe to peek over the blanket. Then the circumcisor, a gnarled old woman, kneels down and goes to work with her razor blade. She saws off the clitoris first, then the outer labia. The girl's eyes roll. The crowd shrieks as blood is drawn. The precious flesh lies in the dirt as the circumcisor throws dust into the gaping wound to staunch the flow of blood. Donu, Peter, Tzvika and I are speechless. We cannot film. This is torture far too terrible to be recorded on camera.

'You've taken us to some hectic places and we've filmed some terrible things,' Tzvika says to me later, 'but this is radical. In all my years in Africa I've never seen anything like this. Ever.'

Donu wants to say something to camera. Behind her the girls limp towards the huts. Donu points towards them and says:

'Young women walk away, their clothing stained with blood. They can hardly walk. This is what we call a welcome to womanhood.'

Her emotion is genuine. On camera it is brilliant. It becomes the film's centrepiece, and her phrase its title.

The circumcisor sits, still clutching the bloody razor blade in filthy, cracked fingers with black nails. Her face is a withered, gaunt mask, her eyes yellow, bloodshot and cold. I suspect she is drunk.

'What do women gain from circumcision?' Donu asks the old woman.

'Personally I gain nothing,' she replies, shrugging, 'But girls earn esteem from going through this cultural practice. No-one forces them to do it. They come freely from miles around.'

'Were you circumcised?'

'Of course I was, but I didn't die. You can modernise many things but not this. Our grandfathers and grandmothers, even donkeys and baboons are circumcised. Among the Sabiny people this practice will never die.'

Some teenage boys who are listening snigger.

Women are now raking over the blood and burying the discarded flesh in sacks. Jackson watches, distraught. Despite all his efforts this is still happening.

'Don't you sometimes feel you're fighting a losing battle?' asks Donu.

'I have hope,' says Jackson hesitantly, 'that with continuing education we can teach people to realise this thing is bad.'

One of the women burying the sacks cackles. Jackson gets angry.

'I sometimes wish I was director of resources in this country,' he says.

'If I was, I would insist that at least 50% of all resources should be given to us, so that everybody can be educated and know what's bad about this practice. It's a matter of life and death now.'

We visit a 13-year-old girl who has been circumcised. She lives with her family in a red mud hut. We just about squeeze into a tiny room. A beam of light from a miniscule high window falls on the girl who lies on the floor under a blanket. The rough blanket is fibrous and dirty and I try not to think about its proximity to the bleeding mess of pulp that was her genitals. Donu kneels down and begins stroking the girl's forehead. The girl looks up at her as if she was an angel. I am unable to speak. I direct Tzvika by sign language to start filming.

'It's hard to understand why she's not crying,' Donu says to the camera, 'There must be so much pain.' The girl continues to gaze at Donu.

'You're a very, very brave girl,' Donu says to her.

I cry. I turn away because I know Peter and Tzvika are also on the verge of tears.

The girl's mother agrees to talk to us for money. She wears a spotty frock and a perky, red checked scarf round her head. She has dressed up for this big day. Donu is also a mother.

'How can you bear to see your daughter in so much pain?' she asks.

'Oh I understand the pain. I was circumcised myself,' replies the mother in a matter-of-fact monotone, 'There's nothing wrong with pain. She'll be all right. She had to do it for her ancestors. It was God's plan for her to do it.'

'Don't you want a better life for your daughter?' asks Donu. The woman looks blank.

'Don't you want your daughter to grow up and be someone who can work and travel like me. Or do you want her just to be a typical Sabiny woman and go on suffering?'

'How dare you talk to me of something which can only be a myth!' says the woman.

'For us people living here, we can't even begin to think about a better life or a soft life, even if we wish it otherwise. It's God's will for us to suffer.'

Yet there is some hope. Jackson takes us to another coming of age ceremony. The girls wear the traditional pink skirts and white beads and blow whistles and dance towards the circumcision corral. But instead of lying down and being brutally mutilated, they emerge intact, wearing new dresses. They are given a goat each and their heads are wrapped in a turban to symbolise their progression into adulthood. Their father, Motil, presides over the ceremony wearing a monkey skin outfit and a complicated feather headdress.

Sadly, Motil's motives are not so pure. He has three wives and fifteen daughters. He has decided not to circumcise his girls because 'of the money'. When Donu asks him what he means, he says it is very expensive. Relatives expect to be served with food and plenty of alcohol. Donu then asks him if his wives have been circumcised.

'Oh yes,' he says.

'And do you think they suffered?'

'They did, but you know, I myself I also suffered.'

'How did you suffer?' asks Donu, stern behind her designer sunglasses.

'I was circumcised myself! I suffered very much.'

Donu leaves it there. There is no point in explaining to him the difference between cutting a foreskin and gouging out essential lumps of tissue, muscle and flesh. At least he is not using his own suffering as an excuse to inflict it on his daughters and for that we have to be grateful.

On our last night Donu storms into the kitchen at the Paradise Hotel and shouts at the cowering cooks. Boys are dispatched to market to buy eggs and vegetables.

'Just look at the state of this – it's a disgrace!' says Donu, waving a greasy, black frying pan at us from the kitchen doorway.

'Get me some soap and a scrubbing brush,' she orders a sulky boy, 'And I don't mean tomorrow, I mean now!'

The staff's surliness turns to admiration as Donu produces clean plates piled high with pepper and onion omelettes. Even the displaced cook starts to smile and soon everyone is drinking rum and having a good time. Even Peter has a sip of alcohol.

Jackson is sad to see us go. He hugs me warmly.

'You keep your promises, Metcalf. I hope you will come back,' he says.

'Perhaps,' I say, and hug him back.

We are hysterically happy to be back in Kampala. Filthy and stiff from our long journey, we arrive at the Kabira Country Club. On a verandah overlooking a sweeping lawn people are eating dinner by candlelight. There are clean cloths and flowers on the tables. There is lobster and steak on the menu. We are in paradise at last.

Donu and I agree that much of Sabiny tradition is extreme sexism – men's absolute certainty of the inferiority of women – masquerading as culture. Where we disagree is where to lay the blame. Donu is disgusted by the passivity of the Sabine women and the way they embrace suffering as something necessary and God-given.

Personally I believe that, given a glimpse of another possible life, most women would rebel. Yet Kapchorwa is so remote and inaccessible that for most escape is not a reality. Many Sabinys have never come down from the mountain. It is a matter of taking the world up to them. Otherwise, how can girls possibly imagine a world beyond, let alone aspire to it?

I don't even really blame the men for circumcising their wives and daughters. Their sexism is based on deep-rooted habit and ancient tradition. Once they understand the harm they are doing, many men are happy to abandon the practice. The problem is that Jackson cannot persuade the entire population single-handedly. But this season 400 out of a total of 1,200 eligible girls resist the blade. He is at least making some headway.

The film was a success and Donu and I received a commendation from the Head of Current Affairs at the BBC, for our sensitive handling of a difficult issue. The film went on to win a Silver Apple Award in New York, and a Golden Spire prize in San Francisco. Better still, after seeing the film, a group of women in Surrey clubbed together, gave a garden party and raised £200. They sent the money to Jackson. The film would have been worthwhile for that alone.

10 WHITER THAN WHITE
Zimbabwe

In Africa most people are so ashamed to give birth to albino babies that they hide them away or abandon them. I had heard stories of mothers killing albino babies at birth, either by drowning or by swinging the baby by its legs and cracking its skull open against a palm tree. In some parts of Africa albinos are believed to possess magical powers but in Zimbabwe they are feared and despised. They are outcasts. They are probably the most invisible and persecuted minority in Africa.

I arrive in Harare armed with £200 worth of Uvistat Factor 15. A customs man asks me why I have so much of it. When I tell him it is a gift for an albino he sniggers, as if I have told him a dirty joke, and waves me through.

In a neat but drab office at the university Professor Makumbe, a brilliant and internationally renowned political scientist, sits in a corner hunched over a computer screen. His paleness is startling. His skin is so white that it glows against the dingy walls. His head is round and smooth as an egg, which makes him look like Humpty Dumpty, and he wears a fluffy pink cardigan.

'Did you bring the sunscreens?' he asks. Our film is going to be built around him, so he and I have spoken at length over the phone – amongst other things, about sunscreens.

I hand over the bag and he puts it carefully into a cardboard box, already full of sun tan lotion.

'Stupid Americans,' he says, following my glance, 'USAID sent a crate of Factor 30 and we can't wear it. The chemicals are too strong for our skin.'

His voice rises to an indignant, high-pitched squeak.

'It's useless. Absolutely useless.'

He chuckles, folds his chubby hands over his ample tummy and looks at me curiously with his head on one side.

'So, you are going to tell the world about our plight?' he asks.

He is making me rather nervous. Jolly and genial as he is, there's a razor-sharp intellect at work and he is not a man to be trifled with. I realise that his readiness to cooperate with me and the BBC is driven only by his determination to draw international attention to the suffering of his kind.

Makumbe has formed the world's first ever Albino Association. Its initial goal is to compile information. Makumbe reckons there is a very high concentration of albinos living in Zimbabwe and Uganda. He thinks there are about 5,000 in Zimbabwe alone, but since albinism is so hidden, gathering statistics is a slow and difficult process. He has no funding and the Association survives on good will and sheer determination.

He has located a relatively large proportion of Zimbabwe's albinos and now plans to bring them together. The Albino Association Assembly is to take place in three days. Makumbe hopes it will attract publicity and put albinism firmly on the map so he can begin lobbying the government for action. He still needs money to hire a room.

'Perhaps the BBC can contribute?' he says, with a shrewd smile.

'Perhaps it can,' I say, grinning back.

I am delighted to be able to help. He giggles like a mischievous child.

'Oh I love the BBC!' he says.

John Makumbe has reached the ripe old age of forty-nine. Albinos' life-expectancy is low so Makumbe's fitness, both physical and mental, is testament yet again to his determination to survive and stamp his presence on a hostile world.

He is lucky to be alive at all. He nearly suffered the fate of so many albino babies.

'When the midwife saw me so white and pale she wanted to kill me on the spot,' he says,

'Traditionally albinos and cripples are killed at birth and I was white as a dish.'

His mother stopped the midwife from strangling him. He giggles and shrugs as if to say, 'And here I am.'

Donu has not yet arrived, but with my camera crew – Tzvika and a Zimbabwean sound recordist I have not worked with before – we drive out to the suburbs in search of two albino sisters. When we get there we spot them immediately. They are walking along the dirt road towards the water pump. In the morning glare their skin shines with a greenish intensity. A little boy jeers and makes a face at them as they walk past.

Abigail and Pauline were born to a dark mother unexpectedly. Albinism is a recessive gene that can skip generations, but in their family no-one could trace the gene's source. Both girls are in their twenties. Pauline has yellow buck teeth. Abigail has a moon-shaped, mournful face, blighted with skin lesions. She has a frizz of hair, whereas Pauline's is cropped close to her skull. Albinos' hair is not white but varies between apricot mousse and pale butter. Their eyes are red, liver coloured. All albinos need glasses.

Pauline and Abigail's mother Laina welcomes us into her home. Her daughters are an eerily luminous presence in the gloom of the pokey sitting room. Laina sits between her daughters and holds their hands tightly, protectively.

Pauline has never worked. She cannot even find a job selling vegetables. People believe that buying anything from an albino brings bad luck and that albinos contaminate food. While Pauline talks a baby starts wailing in the next door room. Abigail disappears behind a flowered curtain and reappears with her son. He is plump, dark and glossy as an aubergine.

Abigail had been engaged to a dark man. When she became pregnant, her fiancé's parents forced their son to cancel the wedding. They were terrified of having an albino grandchild. Abigail was abandoned and returned to her mother's house to give birth.

Abigail bounces her son on her lap, holding his feet in her scaly hands. He giggles delightedly. Seeing me, he reaches out his arms. The colour of my skin is reassuring, familiar. Just then Laina begins to cry. She wipes her eyes frantically with her apron.

'What am I going to do?' she wails, 'I get so depressed thinking about my girls' future that I think of suicide. But if I die they'll have no home at all and who will look after them then?'

Pauline stares at her mother, her big jutting teeth giving her a slightly gormless, vacant expression. Abigail's baby starts to whimper.

'What about John Makumbe?' I ask, looking for something to say that might comfort these people.

'He will change everything,' says Laina with conviction, 'He is a great man.'

She blows her nose noisily into her apron. I worry about the camera intruding on her grief, but Tzvika quietly goes on filming, and in the final edit Laina's lament looks so dignified that there is no sense of an invasion of her privacy.

Pauline's employment story is common, and Makumbe wants the laws changed to prevent discimination against albinos in the workplace. I meet one of his closest aides, Felicity. She has six 'O' levels and a secretarial diploma but, like Pauline, has never worked.

Felicity wears her yellow hair scraped back and is dressed in jeans and sneakers. Apart from a slight squint and the fact that her neck is red and lined, she looks healthy and cheerful. Yet for the last sixteen years she has watched women far less qualified walk into the jobs for which she has applied.

'When you tell them your qualifications on the telephone, they want to interview you,' she says.

'But as soon as you open the door and they see you are an albino, you know from the look on their face that there's nothing there for you.'

She suggests putting this to the test, so we buy a newspaper and she circles five or six jobs that require her qualifications. We go to a telephone box and film her as she starts making calls. She omits to mention she is albino until the last moment. Her potential employers are enthusiastic about her application until they find out she is different. Then the lame excuses start.

At Harare's specialist cancer hospital there is a queue of albinos waiting for treatment. Once again I feel squeamish about filming them, but Tzvika is subtle and unobtrusive. Places for radiotherapy are limited here. One woman sits under a floppy floral hat. Her neck is red, raw and scrawny like a recently plucked chicken and her eyes are set deep in heavily puckered skin. She smiles at me, revealing rotten gums and a handful of yellow teeth. I put her age about seventy.

In fact, she is thirty-three. The sun has ravaged her fragile, unpigmented skin. Black lesions have eaten deep into the flesh of her legs. The young woman doctor who examines her shakes her head and sighs. She looks tired.

'It's really too late,' she says once the woman has left.

'The cancer is very well advanced. If only she had just covered her arms and legs. But they never do.'

Makumbe can do a lot to educate albinos about health. Telling them to wear trousers and long sleeves is relatively easy. It is much harder to fight prejudice and superstition.

Tracey is the only dark woman who sits on the Albino Association's committee. Two of her children are albino. Her nine year old daughter Kuda is being persecuted by her teacher, who is pregnant and thinks physical contact with Kuda may result in her giving birth to an albino baby. She places Kuda at the back of the class, as far away from her as possible. Like all albinos Kuda's eyes are bad so she cannot see the blackboard. She falls heavily behind in her lessons.

During break time we find Kuda's little brother Tony in the playground. He stands alone, clutching his lunch box. Children surge around him. He peers out through his thick-lensed glasses from under a floppy hat pulled down low over his face. To protect him from the sun he wears grey trousers and a long-sleeved jumper. All the other boys wear shorts and short-sleeved shirts. I watch an older boy throw a stone at him and run away. Tony just stands there. There is nowhere else to go.

After break there are games. The teacher, aware of the camera, tries to encourage the other children to pick Tony for their team but they go on choosing their friends till he is the only one left.

Back at home Tony complains to his mother about school. Tracey is cooking okra stew with a dark baby on her arm. Kuda is sitting on a stool eating a biscuit. She nibbles away at it like a rabbit, throwing us furtive glasses from under her hat. Some of the boys in Tony's class have stolen his pencils, laughed at him and called him bad names. Tracey takes him by the arm and shakes him.

'Don't you go listening to them,' she says, 'Stand up for yourself. You must fight back!'

He looks at her doubtfully. When she turns back to the stove, he clutches at her skirt.

'They beat me too,' he says in a tiny voice.

Infuriated but tender, Tracey lifts him up onto a stool.

'Now look, these bad names are stupid. They can't hurt you.'

He looks down at the floor and sniffs.

'Tell us all about it,' I suggest.

His urge to be listened to is stronger than his shyness, so he sits down on the stoep outside the kitchen door. The homely smell of frying onions drifts out. Clean washing flaps in the breeze which rustles the avocado tree. There are bright marigolds planted in painted tins.

'The only time any children ever talk to me is when I'm at home,' Tony says.

'Why at home?' I ask.

'Because then no-one can see them doing it. They only come when no-one else is around.'

He winds his jumper round and round his fingers till it is stretched and misshapen. I have nothing to say which can comfort him.

Tracey hopes that by the time they are grown up things will be different.

'Thanks to Makumbe?' I ask.

'Oh yes. He's a wonderful, wonderful man,' she says.

Her luminous jade eyes shine with hope. I wonder if Makumbe realises how much people are counting on him.

Makumbe is married to a dark woman and has three dark children. When we arrive at his house he is sitting at the dining room table helping them with their homework. After the children finish their prep he sits down with his wife on a sofa and puts his arm round her.

His wife was awe-struck by Makumbe's charisma and courage, though it was by no means love at first sight. Her love grew from her admiration.

'But I loved her from the very beginning,' says Makumbe giggling.

Their home is a comfortable, happy one but his main concern is that his children have a strange-looking father. His daughter came home from school one day after being teased. She asked her father why he was different. He explained that the colour of his skin did not make him a lesser man.

'My motto is, you know, I can do it. And I'm doing it,' he says.

The next day Donu arrives. Together we are renting a mock Tudor house which would not look out of place in Surrey. Donu is days late because her small son has had an accident. He is now doing fine, so she is in a good mood She has braided her hair, which accentuates the elegance of her profile with its high, sloping forehead. After she has inspected our kitchen we go straight to the supermarket.

'I must have meat,' she says, loading large chunks of meat and a bottle of Scotch into her trolley.

When we get back to the house she promptly tells the maid to wash the dishtowels.

'Look at these, they're a disgrace,' she says. Then she gives orders about preparing the vegetables and promises to cook me chicken Nigerian-style with peanut sauce. After approving the kitchen arrangements, she drinks a stiff Scotch with Coca-Cola and chain-smokes several cigarettes.

'That's better,' she says as we set off to meet the members of the Albino Association.

Donu's journalism is not informed by compassion. She believes people owe it to themselves to fight and she cannot bear people who present themselves as victims. She reacts to the albinos exactly as I predicted – she is deeply unimpressed by their apparent helplessness.

In the evening I introduce Donu to Paul Hughes who runs Mighty Movies. It is from Paul that I hire my crews, including Tzvika and Peter, and my camera equipment. The Hughes family live behind an electric gate in high walls. Dobermann Pinschers lunge at the car as we arrive. Donu is frightened, and shrinks into the back seat until they are dragged slavering into their kennels.

Typical of old Rhodesia the house is an ugly, modern bungalow with mullioned windows. It is squat and functional with a bar at its heart. Here men gather, the master of the house dispensing beer and whisky while the women chat at the other end of the room, usually dominated by the television.

Paul is a Falstaffian figure with a penchant for Scotch. His wife Maureen is large and lugubrious but Liam, their son, is a chip off the old block. At sixteen he already smokes and drinks and constantly cracks atrocious filthy jokes.

For dinner there are two whole garlic chickens, one of which Liam devours single-handed, allowing the juices to run down his chin. There is a small salad, a mountain of chips and violently hot sauces that Maureen makes herself.

Maureen married Paul when she was very young. She does not believe in mixed marriages and approves of social separation. However tonight she takes care to be charming to Donu. The talk turns inevitably to race. Maureen complains about the racism that still exists in modern Zimbabwe. For a moment I think she is taking a liberal stance till I realise she is talking of her own experience.

'This black man in the post office was so horrible to me. He told me I would have to wait my turn. He was so rude. So hostile. I was really upset.' I do not dare meet Donu's eye. I fear the whisky might loosen her tongue, but she smiles politely.

Later Donu laughs it off.

'Well what do you expect?' she says. 'She's not exactly having a very exciting life is she? Let's face it, Harare's a dump!'

Donu has been in Harare less than twenty-four hours but her

mind is made up. Part of me agrees with her. I too find the hard-drinking, joyless culture depressing. Many of the white people seem to have little to do except sit around the Scotch bottle.

Next morning at the British Council aid workers and expatriate wives are surprised to see a crowd in the entrance hall – and shocked by its appearance. British people going to the library try not to stare at the excited, chattering albinos. Felicity is dashing around greeting everyone. Laina arrives with Abigail and Pauline. I introduce them to Donu.

'They're not lookers, are they?' chuckles Donu. I respond by looking po-faced.

'Oh come off it,' she says, 'Admit it.'

Donu's complete lack of political correctness almost always has the ability to undermine my prudish seriousness and make me smile.

I am struck by a man who looks European from a distance. He has dyed his hair black and wears it in dreadlocks. He hides his red eyes behind Ray Ban dark glasses. In his sharp black suit he exudes confidence. Just then Makumbe arrives sporting a Hawaiian-style pink and brown shirt. With him is the Deputy Minister for Health.

Never have so many albinos assembled in one room. Makumbe is making history. News crews have gathered and jostle for position on the edges of the crowd. Only my camera crew is allowed to wander freely.

When Makumbe stands to deliver his keynote address he begins pacing up and down in front of the crowd. Surprisingly, he proves to be a natural stand-up comedian. He imitates the average African crossing the street to avoid an albino. He apes reluctant employers trying not to catch the eye of an albino interviewee.

The crowd roars with laughter. He talks about the way albinos' basic human rights have been systematically eroded by centuries of prejudice. Now it is time to stand up and demand them back.

'We can help the government to make changes, but we cannot expect them to do that without you…or you…or you,' he says, pointing into the crowd.

'There is no excuse any longer. We must all work together.' His voice rises to its characteristic high-pitched squeak.

When he finishes he gets a standing ovation. Then the man with the dreadlocks stands up. He tells us how he has survived, by using his dreadlocks both as a makeshift form of sun helmet and as a disguise and protection against prejudice. He is witty and self-deprecating but his litany of woe is depressing after Makumbe's rousing words. He is a highly qualified academic who has lost job after job to men far less able.

'It has to stop,' he says. The crowd rumbles its assent.

This is a crowd full of hope but it does not look physically fit. Many are bent over their notes, unable to see to write even with their glasses. The evidence of skin cancer is everywhere. Makumbe marches into the crowd and takes hold of a small boy. Under a yellow baseball cap his face is shiny and looks as if it is covered in an enormous black bruise. Makumbe takes the boy to the front of the room.

'Look at this little guy here,' he says, lifting him up and yanking back the baseball cap so people can have a better look.

'This is skin cancer. How can we tolerate this?'

£1,500 would pay for the treatment but it is way beyond the family's means.

Then the Deputy Minister stands up, beautifully groomed in a white suit and pearls. She adjusts her spectacles and pats her careful coiffure. Ever the politician, she takes hold of an albino baby and coos at it. She turns to the cameras for her photo opportunity and then she addresses the crowd.

She promises to recommend a series of reforms to the government so that albinos can be classified as disabled people and thus receive spectacles and sunscreens as well as cancer treatment. She says she will address the issue of discrimination in the work place. The crowd roars its approval and then it is over.

Afterwards the mood is ecstatic. The presence of a government representative has persuaded people that Makumbe has real power and is leading them into an enlightened age. Only our man with the dreadlocks is cynical.

'We can go on trying,' he says, shrugging, 'But I believe we'll be waiting a long time for change.'

We join Makumbe and some other members of the Association in a celebratory meal. They choose a grisly ice-cream place in one of Harare's numerous soulless shopping malls. They sit under a parasol near the car park and order milk shakes and French fries. Donu sits down amongst them and begins talking while we circle with the camera.

Donu steers the conversation deftly towards sex and marriage. Makumbe says dark women are attracted to albinos because they are so charming, and everyone at the table roars with laughter.

A white man in shorts comes past with his two little girls. They stop and stare open-mouthed.

'Daddy, Daddy,' one shrieks, 'Look at those funny people.'

Her father yanks her by the elbow and drags her away. Meanwhile the albinos are recovering themselves, wiping their eyes and clearing their throats. Even Donu is momentarily unsettled by this bout of hilarity.

'Of course there are a lot of black guys wanting to sleep with white women but they are essentially adventurers,' continues Makumbe more soberly.

'They have no intention at all of marrying the poor things.'

'Well you're all married to dark women. What's wrong with albino girls?' asks Donu, sharply.

The answer comes from an elderly albino man sitting across the table.

'We must not encourage people to marry albinos.' he says,

'Albinism is an inherited disability and we must not allow that because we don't want our children to inherit it.'

Donu is back footed.

'Don't you think there's something sad about that?' she ventures.

'I mean you're effectively hoping that you'll breed yourselves out so there won't be anyone who looks like you.'

Makumbe is vehement and squeaky:

'Yes, and that's a beautiful thought. Why should we embrace

our disability? Why should we pass it on to our children?'

I looked at Felicity. She is sitting quietly the other end of the table. Even her own kind spurn her and dark men are likely to run as soon as she becomes pregnant.

'I don't think I will ever marry,' says Felicity.

She looks sad but her devotion to her leader is unquestioning. She looks at him as she continues:

'I don't think we should marry if we risk passing on the disability.'

She looks away, unable to confront our scepticism, knowing this level of self-sacrifice is pitiful.

Later Donu interviews Makumbe in depth and he talks again about his daughter.

'I tell her that skin colour is not important and that in another life her father will not even be an albino.'

'What will you be?' Donu asks.

Makumbe thinks for a moment and then smiles serenely.

'I think I shall be a spirit.'

For all his achievements, Makumbe dreams of an afterlife in which he is nothing more substantial than a colourless vapour.

Donu asks him what he would like his epitaph to be. Makumbe puts his head on one side and smiles.

'I would like them to say, "He did it, he did it."'

'It being?' asks Donu.

He breaks into a mischievous grin.

'I have absolutely no idea.' He laughs. 'But I would like them to say, "He did it".'

The BBC was delighted with the film but it did not air immediately. They were 'rescheduling'. In the end they never showed it and I was not told why. I was used to current affairs editors dropping programmes, but Professor Makumbe was relying on the film to generate the international publicity he needed for his cause. If he reads this, all I can say is: 'Sorry.'

11 FOUR WEDDINGS AND A SHEIKH
Nigeria

Television Trust for the Environment was commissioned by the United Nations to make another series of films about global population issues. Pleased with the films I had made in Uganda, they asked me to go to Nigeria and make a film about polygamy and its consequences. Things were looking up.

The Emir arrives on the same plane. Those of us in economy class are prevented from disembarking while he alights. Out of the window I can see his acolytes prostrating themselves, bottoms raised skywards, their foreheads pressed to the tarmac in obeisance. We can hear their reverential murmurs through the open door. By the time the rest of us are allowed off the plane the Emir and his entourage are being swept away by a convoy of black Mercedes.

I'm a seasoned veteran of African airports but nothing has prepared me for Kano. I stand helpless as person after person shoves me aside, elbowing forward and using hand luggage as battering rams. Soldiers bristling with guns saunter amongst us but do nothing to maintain order. People are shouting and arguing with a ferocity that successfully inhibits any attempt on my part to fight for my place in the queue.

Two hours later I am finally alone, the last in the queue. I am thirsty and have a thumping headache. An official in one of the glass boxes stretches and yawns. Another beckons me without looking up. A soldier orders me forward with a nonchalant thrust of his rifle. As my passport is stamped the official starts joking with one of the soldiers over my head. He hardly gives me a glance.

The other side of immigration baggage handlers in blue boiler suits are struggling with crates, bundles and tottering piles of assorted luggage. A suitcase has burst open and spills its colourful guts onto the conveyor belt – a twisted heap of socks, underpants and leaking toiletries winds its way round and round. There is no sign of my luggage. Half an hour later I find it lined up in a row with a set of purple Samsonite suitcases.

Luckily Ihria is waiting for me. Ihria has come up north from Lagos with a crew and the camera equipment, and is to act as my local producer and fixer. Behind wire-framed spectacles his anxious expression reassures me immediately that he knows the hurdles we are taking on – he is as worried as I am about the shoot ahead. It is not going to be easy for a white woman and three men from Lagos to tackle the taboo subject of polygamy. But that is the assignment I accepted, and here we stay until it is completed.

The cameraman Abraham Adetutu is a tall, grave, elderly man with a languid walk. Ihria assures me he has an excellent international reputation, and has been working on and off for the BBC for years. Femi, the sound recordist, speaks very fast and excitably in high-pitched pidgin English. He is a Lagos homeboy and scorns dowdy northern Kano, especially its food. He is also extremely funny, with an utterly infectious laugh.

Our only local help is Marliyah, who is to double as our translator and our finder of polygamous households to interview and film. She turns out to be rather upmarket, affluent and proud, reluctant to discuss money, and worryingly vague about what she has managed to arrange. She alarms Ihria but I soon learn that if I trust her she will usually deliver at the last minute, just as we start to panic.

Away from the clumsy, bungled attempts at modernisation, the old city of Kano is a beautiful medieval backdrop for a ceaseless parade of humanity. Here mud houses rise rounded and elegant behind crenellated walls, and people thrust their way through murky, smoky alleys in multi-coloured robes – fuchsia, vermilion, amber, lilac, indigo, scarlet – like a vast swarm of butterflies. Nigeria is Africa's most populated country and I feel overwhelmed by the massive, moving, noisy, colourful throng.

There are even more people than usual taking to the streets because there's a petrol shortage and queues stretch for up to two miles. We have to limit our own driving to daytime, so at night I am stuck in my hotel while the crew drive downtown. My hotel, though grotty, is expensive and they prefer to save as much as possible of their per diem accommodation allowance for themselves.

Our regular restaurant is a dusty, fly-infested, concrete shack, which serves big bowls of okra cooked to a slime with gristly, occasionally hairy, morsels of goat which I find quite disgusting but which Femi adores. We eat it with our hands accompanied by *fou fou,* a grey, gluey goo. It sticks to my fingers, clogs my nails and my hands stink for hours after each meal.

We begin shooting almost immediately. Alhaji Aminu is a fifty-five year old used car dealer and lives with his three current wives in a traditional compound. High windowless walls conceal a courtyard, on one side of which is Alhaji's air-conditioned room that he keeps locked. Opposite are three smaller rooms, none with air-conditioning. In each lives a wife with her children and possessions. One morning I count twenty-two children in the compound, the next twenty-seven. They swarm around, mainly naked, queuing to be washed or fed.

Alhaji is out at work when we arrive and his oldest wife Hawa welcomes us. She is a hefty woman with beautiful almond eyes. At forty-seven she has been married to Alhaji for thirty years and borne him eleven children, nine of whom have survived. She continues to bear him children – her youngest is just four. Yet Alhaji has wanted new, younger wives.

His second wife Zadia is the daughter of Hawa's best friend. Alhaji married her when she was thirteen and she is now pregnant with her second child. Though Zadia is still only a teenager, very pretty and clearly fertile, Alhaji has tired of her and taken yet another wife who has also recently given birth.

Hawa's bedroom is dominated by a high, lumpy bed covered in a pink, sateen quilt. Two of her older sons loom in the doorway, protective of their father's territory and property. We crowd into the room as best we can. Hawa motions to us to sit down on the floor beside her.

There are several children in the room, not necessarily Hawa's own. As the oldest wife she is the household matriarch. A small boy sits in her lap and stares at us, picking his nose and eating the snot with intense concentration. A baby, naked except for a rag nappy, screams on the floor beside her. The baby has flu but Hawa has no money for medicine. The vitamins she has bought in the market are two years past their sell-by date. Another small boy solemnly plays with Hawa's bare feet, counting her toes under his breath.

Hawa examines me shyly as Marliyah explains what we are doing. The young men get bored with women's talk and amble off. Immediately Hawa's diffidence dissolves and she starts giving me warm, conspiratorial smiles. She talks openly, knowing her husband is highly unlikely to come home from work in the middle of the day.

I ask her how she felt when Alhaji married Zadia.

'When she was first brought here to be honest it wasn't very pleasant,' she confides, 'She was my friend's daughter, a mere child. But later I realised living together was the Will of God. So we forgot our differences.'

Most of the childcare duties, like the daily wash, are left to Hawa. The children queue up naked by a red bowl where she sponges them down briskly, pouring water over their heads from a jug to rinse the suds. The other wives and some of the older daughters prepare food and chop vegetables. Chickens and goats roam amongst the newly washed children.

When Adetutu begins filming he sits down in the dust with the camera balanced on his knee. I ask him why he is not using the tripod. He shrugs and says he prefers to work without it. I watch as he zooms in and out.

'I hate zooms,' I venture.

'As you wish,' he says.

A minute later he uses the zoom again.

'Please can we just take some static shots?' I ask.

He insists his shots are excellent. There is no way of checking because the monitor has arrived from Lagos without the right leads. Adetutu is not the kind of man you argue with. He has a quiet, authoritative manner and an air of wise maturity.

'Perhaps we can use the tripod on this next interview?' I ask, hoping for a compromise.

'Sure,' he says.

By now I am desperate for a loo. There is no obvious place. I ask Hawa, who shows me into the kitchen hut. Two young girls squat by a low fire where a pot simmers. Hawa shoos them out. A hen scratches around in the dirt. I realise I am expected to squat down by the fire and pee. There is nothing else for it and I am bursting. The hen chooses the worst possible moment to run at me flapping and screeching. I fall over. When I rejoin my crew I am scuffing my pee-spattered shoes in the dust to conceal the telltale stains.

I am glad to escape into the gloom of the middle wife's room. Zadia sits on the only chair, its foam rubber innards bulging from a filthy yellow cover. Behind her are some makeshift shelves on which are displayed three rows of white pans with an orange floral pattern. They look as if they are never used. Once they were proudly exhibited to demonstrate Zadia's value. Now they are gathering dust like forgotten trophies.

Zadia speaks in whispers, unable to meet my eye. She picks continuously at her fingernails. She was brought to the house at thirteen and found it impossible to relate to her co-wives because they were so much older. At the time Alhaji had yet another wife who has since died. Zadia was his third and now Alhaji is on his fourth.

'They are the same age or older than my mother,' says Zadia, 'Even their children are older than me.'

She never leaves the compound and all hopes of finishing her schooling have evaporated. She has wept every day for as long as she can remember.

'As far as Alhaji is concerned, we are all living here in peace and harmony. But you would not believe what he does to me,' she says, and her voice trembles.

Later Alhaji returns. Cold, hooded eyes look out from a self-satisfied, fleshy face. Zadia scurries forward to minister to him. She puts an armchair outside his room where he sits fanning himself with a whisk, lashing out irritably at flies. The fourth wife brings him a glass of water. He takes it without looking at her. He will not be interviewed, waving us angrily away as he surveys his realm from his throne. It does not matter. We have captured the moment on camera, and his whole manner is a very clear expression of his views.

Alhaji's implicit stance is endorsed by local religious leaders. At an Islamic education centre we meet Sheikh Mohammed El-Hassin, who chairs seminars in Islamic studies. He arrives on a Vespa, sky blue robes flowing behind him, his embroidered hat neat on his fine head. He might be handsome but for a certain shiftiness about the eyes.

We interview El-Hassin in a dreary office, bare except for a desk and chair. On the wall behind him is a tattered map of Nigeria. He begins by explaining why he supports polygamy.

'It has come to solve many of society's problems. That is why Islam enshrines polygamy as one of its principles.'

I nod encouragingly and, to my astonishment, he begins talking about women's periods:

'A woman has a menstrual period. During that period a man sometimes has a natural urge for another woman. What does he do? How does he satisfy himself?'

This is not a rhetorical question. He looks at me intensely as if waiting for me to answer. Ihria is sitting behind me and I can hear him tutting under his breath. I shrug. El-Hassin goes on.

'Islam says: "Alright, take another wife! This way you do not have to leave your home for extra satisfaction. Both wives will now fall under your canopy."'

El-Hassin smiles smugly before adopting his lecturing stance again:

'So far as Islam is concerned, a woman's number one duty is to give comfort to her husband.'

He tells me how stressed he is. I think he expects me to sympathise.

'Right now, I am so tired. I have to see so many people during my day. When I go home, I need my wife to provide me with some comfort. It is her duty.'

He looks at me challengingly. Behind me Ihria's breathing becomes more agitated. He does not like El-Hassin one bit.

Other than carnal and domestic duties, El-Hassin is pushing a more serious agenda.

'Islam is very concerned with population,' he says.

If a man marries a barren woman he does not discard her 'like old clothes'. Instead, Islam gives him permission to 'retain' her while marrying another woman who can reproduce.

It is of course this preoccupation with fertility and reproduction that leads to half the population in many developing countries being under fifteen. Estimates show that if women like Alhaji's wife Zadia were allowed to delay giving birth till say twenty-three, population momentum would be reduced by nearly half.

The chances of women delaying pregnancy till twenty-three are remote in a region in which religious leaders condone, even encourage, sex with children as young as six.

'Are you saying that little girls of as young as six are ready for sexual relationships with their husbands?'

I enunciate clearly. I do not want there to be any room for misunderstanding.

El-Hassin's eyes glitter. He looked at me with hostility and mild disgust.

'Exactly!' he answers. 'It's very straightforward. There is nothing wrong. These small girls are ready for sex. It's explicit.'

His words are chilling but it is hard not to smile.

'Got you!' I think.

'I wanted to hit him!' says Ihria later. 'How did you keep your temper?'

'There was no point losing it,' I reply. 'We gave him enough rope to hang himself.'

'Let's go and eat *fou fou!*' says Femi, stretching. 'That horrible, horrible man has made me hungry.'

First we have to attend a seminar chaired by El-Hassin and attended by about twenty scholars. The classroom is hot and dusty; it seems an insalubrious setting for such academic luminaries. The scholars, all men, take the class very seriously. For our benefit they speak English.

'Islam insists on early marriage,' begins an elderly man in a dark green robe.

He explains that girls should marry young to grow up under the guidance of their husbands. Girls need to be 'taught' how to be responsible members of society.

'Polygamy is something from Almighty God,' asserts a splendidly-dressed man with a fine head of silver hair and a thick, square beard.

Another eyes me shrewdly as he makes mischievous references to a 'so-called great world leader' and his immoral behaviour 'consorting openly with some young lady'.

After the seminar a man approaches me:

'Excuse me Madam, may I enquire as to the nature of this filming?'

I explain that we are trying to understand polygamy.

'But these fellows here I think are from the South and they do not believe in it,' he says, indicating Ihria, Adetutu and Femi. He turns to our translator, Marliyah.

'We know this woman here to be against it, though she says she is a good Moslem lady.'

Marliyah looks furious. He turns back to me:

'Now this lady from Europe has come to portray us in a bad light to her people.'

Some of the other scholars have gathered round us in a tight circle. I begin to feel uncomfortable, on top of which I do not trust Femi or Irhia to keep their tempers.

'I am truly interested in your point of view,' I say. 'We want to examine the issue from all sides.'

'So then lady, are you saying you would embrace a polygamous marriage?'

I hesitate.

'No!' You would not!' he crows. 'I think you are against us and have come to say bad things about us.'

I decide my best policy is to stay silent.

'Are you a Christian?' he asks, and as I hesitate he goes on:

'Do you honestly think your Jesus was not polygamous?'

He looks at my blank face and smiles. He has got me.

'Ah, my dear lady, you have not read your Bible.'

I see my opening:

'That is why I want to learn.'

For three days he bombards me with courteous, flowery notes and a selection of turgid, pompous and didactic pamphlets, with titles like *Combat Kit – Against Bible-thumpers* and *The Islamic Way of Life – Conquering Christianity*. I am touched by his obviously sincere belief that I will come round to his view.

Next, as a counterbalance to the determined rhetoric of El-Hassin and his scholars, we interview a deeply impressive and highly effective woman named Mairo Bello who runs a centre for runaway or divorced adolescents. At first I find her daunting. Her round face looks out sternly from the frame of an orange headscarf, and a deep furrow between her eyes gives her an angry look.

Mairo takes us to her centre where in a sunny room painted a cheerful pink we find her girls learning how to make clothes. The noisy clatter of sewing machines combined with giggles and chatter are reassuring. I think of Zadia, barely able to raise her voice above a timorous whisper. Mairo also teaches self-assertion and leadership skills.

'These girls must learn to speak out. They must find a voice, and you can help,' says Mairo, eyeing me sternly.

'They have been brainwashed from day one. From the minute they were put in their cradle they have been told that all they are useful for is marriage and that they have no other function in life than to start bearing children. These girls in early marriages are treated no better than dogs, forced to live on the leftovers after the day's meal.'

Treating girls like breeding machines means that Nigeria's population continues to grow at a terrifying rate. Mairo implores the West to take notice. Polygamy and early marriage are not just quirky, cultural practices. They are ruining the lives of this and the next generation of women, and seriously undermining Nigeria's chances of development.

'What keeps you going?' I ask.

Mairo answers without hesitation:

'When I see a girl carrying her books to school or to university, her head held high because she is learning, that is the most beautiful sight in the world for me. I will never give up so long as there is a chance for girls to go to school.'

A Lebanese doctor I know from London has given me an introduction to his brother François who is married to the French Consul in Kano, and the night we finish filming I go to dine with him. François collects me in his sleek, comfortable car and as we purr along the road I start to relax. The film is made, I am going home tomorrow – I can afford to let my hair down and celebrate.

The Consulate stands in an exotic garden. I can smell jasmine and gardenias on the warm evening air. We walk up a path flanked by burning torches and into a vast, luxurious space on several levels. There are comfortable sofas, a blazing fire, ethnic sculpture, a state-of-the-art music system, a well-stocked bar, modern art, candlelight and vases of lilies and roses. Two huge, glossy dogs slouch around, banging their tails in friendly greeting. After night after night in the fusty, deserted dining room of the Prince Hotel, it is all too much.

François's wife, the Consul, is beautiful in an Audrey Hepburn sort of way. An ethnic necklace made of antique silver and rare stones accentuates her slender neck and fine collar bones and provides the perfect counterpoint to her understated Parisian chic. Servants bustle as François opens a bottle of chilled white wine. It tastes sublimely of smoke and damp earth and honey.

By the time we sit down to eat I am so excited by the thought of good food I could eat the tablecoth. Servants bring in thin slices of beef cooked to perfection, succulent on the inside and slightly charred on the outside. There are lashings of fresh vegetables and salad, potatoes cooked with onions and thick, golden cream and cheese, with pudding to follow. I have seconds and then thirds of everything.

Now that I have eaten enough for six, I am ready for conversation. I begin to tell François about our film. When he hears we have been shooting without official permission, he becomes stern. My inner glow chills and I sober up fast as he begins to question me:

'This is a police state. Where are your tapes?'

'In my hotel.'

'How are you proposing to leave the country with them tomorrow?'

'I hadn't really thought,' I stammer.

I hear myself sounding irritatingly naïve. From being an entertaining guest I am becoming a headache.

'You don't really expect to walk out of Kano airport with those tapes in your luggage, do you?' asks François.

'This is a police state,' he reiterates. 'Do you honestly imagine they're not all aware of you here? This place may be teeming with people but it's a small town. Word will have got around. They'll be waiting for you.'

I sense the first sour stirrings of panic in my stomach.

'I'm afraid I won't be able to help,' he says.

'We can only help French nationals. We cannot possibly be seen to interfere with a case which isn't ours. If there's any trouble you'll have to depend on the British Consul.'

'What do you suggest I do?' I ask, my voice small with anxiety.

François shrugs.

'Whatever you do, do not think of trying to take those tapes on the plane with you.'

I have twelve Beta tapes, too large to hide even if I had a place to stash them. Next morning I confide my fears to Ihria. He says he has no idea what to do.

'If this was Lagos, it would be easy,' he says. 'I'd know exactly who to bribe. Here, I simply don't know anyone. We'll have to talk to Marliyah.'

Marliyah has a cousin, Hassan, who works for KLM, the airline with which I am flying. We try calling him but the telephones at the airport are down, so we drive straight there and find him in the KLM office. Marliyah does not tell him that we have made the film illegally because she thinks it will compromise him. She takes another route.

'If those fragile tapes go through the airport scanner, they will be ruined,' she says.

'Don't worry,' says Hassan, 'I'll make sure you don't have to put them through. I'll speak to the security guys myself.'

This is not working.

'Maybe instead you can take the tapes onto the plane for her?' ventures Marliyah.

Hassan narrows his eyes and looks at me suspiciously.

'There is no need,' he says. 'I'll ask the guys not to X-ray your luggage. They will hand search it as usual.'

'Actually,' I say, clearing my throat nervously, 'It's very difficult. Even if they say they won't put the tapes through the scanner, they always make me. And I'll lose my job if anything happens to them.'

'What's on the tapes?' he demands.

'A film about Kano,' I say. He looks at me closely.

Marliyah begins talking to him fast in their own language. It does not appear to satisfy him. He turns to me again.

'Why do you want me to carry these tapes?' he asks.

'Because even if they go near the machine they will be damaged,' I repeat.

'That is not so. Many tapes and films go through our machines.'

We are no nearer persuading Hassan to carry the tapes for me. I begin to tell him a lie about wiping a whole film at an African airport.

'Which airport?' he interrupts.

'Nairobi,' I answer. This seems to please him. He chuckles.

'I think we can assure you it will be very worth your while,' Marliyah says quietly.

Hassan eyes me as if estimating my worth while he switches back into his own language to talk to Marliyah. They seem to be arguing quite fiercely. I feel helpless just standing there but Hassan is my only hope. Suddenly both of them break out in smiles.

'OK,' he says, turning to me. 'Come back at six o'clock with the tapes in a bag.'

God knows what Marliyah has promised him but I know I will have to leave her with a hefty wedge of petty cash. Next step is to find a big but unobtrusive bag for the tapes. The only bags we can buy are red and white check laundry bags, which would be too conspicuous to carry onto the aircraft. Then I remember the Prada tote bag that my sister-in-law gave me for Christmas. It is big enough to hold the tapes and would not look out of place slung over a man's shoulder.

Later that evening the crew takes me to the airport. Ihria and I go to find Hassan. I feel a pang as I watch him shove my prized Prada bag into a cupboard. I regret the bag almost as much as the tapes. I wonder what my bosses in London would say if they knew I was handing their precious material over to a virtual stranger. Still, I have no choice.

The crew and I go to the bar for a final drink. We are the only customers in a filthy concrete room overlooking the runway. A television blares. Ihria, Adetutu and Femi drink beer, and I have something horrible, like rum, as a much-needed bracer. A cockroach scuttles over my foot as we sit at a sticky tin table. Though I am sad to say goodbye to the crew, I am not sorry to be leaving.

Beyond the passenger barrier armed soldiers are rifling through everyone's luggage. My bag is searched twice. The first soldier uses his gun barrel to sift through my clothes. I cannot take my eyes off it. Then he ushers me towards another soldier, who asks:

'Where are the tapes?'

'What tapes?' I ask brightly, smiling and swallowing hard.

'Have you not made a film here?'

My stomach churns, but I dare not hesitate.

'No,' I say. My jaw aches from smiling.

'Show me your passport,' he demands.

He examines it, looking hard at the picture and then at me and back again. He orders a third soldier over, who searches my bag again.

'You have no tapes?' asks soldier number three. This one smiles disarmingly.

I think my legs may give way. I feel light-headed.

'OK,' he says suddenly. 'Go.'

He shoves my clothes back into my bag and zips it up. But it isn't over.

Hassan has told me he will meet me in the departure lounge but I cannot see him. I pace up and down and try to distract myself in Duty Free but there is nothing I want to buy. I try reading but I cannot concentrate. I wonder if I can even remember what Hassan looks like.

My flight is called. I have a last desperate look round, but there is nothing for it but to go to the departure gate. A jolly, plump KLM official is tearing our boarding passes.

'Hassan will meet you by the plane,' he says under his breath. He does not once look up. I think I may have imagined it. I look round to see if anyone else has heard, but the other passengers are making their way out and onto a coach. There are a couple of white families but otherwise the passengers are Nigerian.

The coach starts across the tarmac towards the plane, and I see several soldiers with guns standing round the foot of the plane steps. I feel sick. Flight attendants greet us as we leave the coach. Through the crowd of passengers I spot Hassan. As we inch closer I see he does not have my bag. He stands next to a soldier. I draw level with him. He ignores me. In my panic I have forgotten his name. Just as we are about to move forward,

I remember it.

Perhaps he didn't recognise me in the crowd, because as soon as he sees me he grins. He walks nonchalently over to a KLM car, opens the boot and takes out my Prada bag. He brings it over to me, right under the eyes of all the soldiers.

'Have a good flight,' he says.

I make it up the steps in a trance. I could kiss the smiling air stewardess who points the way to my seat. I stow the precious bag with its illicit contents in the overhead locker. I am sweating. I sit down, close my eyes and wait. For once I find the tinned muzak soothing. The doors are closed and for the first time I start to feel safe. I begin to relax.

At this point I hear the Captain announcing a short delay. Before I can take it in the doors open again and four armed soldiers come down the aisle. They peer closely at everyone as they make their way steadily towards me. I am sure I am going to be sick. I shut my eyes and all I can hear is my heart beating.

Minutes later they have left the plane. I see them on the tarmac, lighting cigarettes and laughing, their guns slung casually over their shoulders. The doors close, the engines roar and the plane takes off. I have been genuinely frightened. I promise myself that never again will I film without permission in a police state. It is a promise I have kept.

A few days later I watch the footage. The camerawork is appalling. I berate myself endlessly as I look at the wobbly zooms: why, oh why did I not insist on using the tripod? Worst of all, the heads of the camera were so dirty that the tape is scratched and the picture feathered and torn. On three of the tapes the camera was in such bad shape that the footage has come out in black and white. A lot of it is entirely unusable. The insurance company agrees to pay for some reshooting but the last thing I want is to return to Kano. I send a list of shots to Ihria, and tell him to hire a cameraman, and then DHL us back the tapes.

The film is a turning point for me. The drama with the tapes has destroyed my carefree rather slapdash approach to permits and officialdom. I realise too that from now on I will have to be much sterner and more authoritarian with my cameramen. As a film-maker I am finally coming of age.

In the end despite the bad picture quality the film was powerful, and Channel Four aired an edited version including my question to El-Hassin about sex with six year olds. But I still feel depressed when I think about Kano. Today northern Nigeria is under Islamic Sharia Law, and El-Hassin and his colleagues are dictating how women live.

I wonder if Mairo's centre has survived. Hers was a mighty voice but a lonely one, and her outspokenness against the prevailing culture will not have endeared her to the sheikhs. Yet she was so right. Polygamy is only viable if women are totally dependent on men for their survival, and until girls are allowed to go to school women will remain so.

12 AMINA
Ethiopian Somaliland

The Hatasheikh Refugee Camp lay outside the town of Jijiga on a great plain near Ethiopia's eastern border with Somalia. It was set up for Somalis fleeing the bloody conflict between rival warlords in their own country. Five years earlier Hatasheikh had the biggest population of any refugee camp in the world, and was still home to 50,000 Somalis.

Amina was a Somali and a qualified midwife working in the camp. With the support of the UN's High Commission for Refugees, she had single-handedly set up a programme to stop female genital mutilation. Her success rate was so extraordinary that UNHCR commissioned me (with my friend, cameraman Bill Locke) to make a film about Amina's work.

Through the dark I can just make out the whites of Amina's eyes and the glint of her teeth. The hot, concrete room smells of sweat and the heavy, greasy food we ate earlier. Amina has wriggled down her mattress and lies on her stomach with her head close to mine. She is whispering so as not to wake Monique on the other side of the room.

'A woman showed me this magazine,' says Amina. 'She had been a servant to a French family in Mogadishu and must have found it when she was cleaning. I tell you, you have never seen such terrible things.'

'Like what?' I ask.

Amina expels air through her teeth in disgust,

'I saw women with…. No, no, I can't tell you this.'

She pauses and the only sounds are our breathing and Monique's faint snores.

'The women had penises in their mouths.'

'Oh,' I say.

'Can you believe that?' she hisses.

I am so curious to hear what she is going to say next that I hold my breath.

'But there was worse,' she whispers, 'Much, much worse.'

Her clothing rustles as she edges nearer. Her voice has dropped so low I can barely make out the words:

'Men were doing these terrible things.'

'Like what?'

'I can't tell you,' she says, 'I can't describe it.'

I hear Amina sit up and rummage around. Suddenly she turns on a pocket torch and shines it at her own face. She looks ghoulish in the feeble yellow beam.

'They were touching the women's parts with their tongues – like this,' and she makes a darting movement with her tongue, in and out of her mouth like a snake. She stares at me with big, dark eyes full of wonder and horror. Then she snaps off the torch and falls back onto her mattress. I simply don't know what to say.

Amina and I are in a makeshift dormitory in the administration block of the Refugee Camp. We have two disused offices between us, so while Bill has his own room, I am sharing with Amina and Monique, a young Dutch field officer for UNHCR.

Amina has worked in Yemen as well as in her native Somalia. She has seen the impact of genital mutilation on childbirth time and time again. The Somali version of infibulation involves removing the clitoris, the labia majora and minora and then sewing up the wound, often with thorns. This is carried out without anaesthetic when girls are five or six years old. On the day we arrive in Addis Ababa, before we have met Amina, Monique shows Bill and me a video of this practice.

A child smiles joyfully at the camera as she is tempted onto her mother's lap.She has been told this is her special day and she is enjoying being the centre of attention. She wriggles on her mother's knee and giggles as an old woman comes into the frame.

The woman has a gnarled face and wears a dirty headscarf.

With a rope she ties the child's legs tightly to her mother's thighs. The child thinks this is a nice game and looks up lovingly and trustingly into her mother's face. Then her mother spreads her legs and lifts her daughter's dress up.

The old woman crouches down as the camera zooms in on the tiny unformed cleft between the child's thighs. The old woman prods it with her finger. With filthy fingernails she tries to pinch out the clitoris. The child lets out a yell of surprise. The sound rises, slithers up an octave and explodes into a heart-wrenching shriek of agony as the old woman begins to carve away at the flesh with a rusty razorblade.

The child's eyes bulge in horror and disbelief as she tries to turn to her mother. Her mother claps her hand over her daughter's eyes and holds her head. The child struggles but her legs are tied firmly. Her plump little arms wave helplessly. Her mouth becomes a strangely distorted hole from which the screams of pain soar, tearing the air. The blood spurts, obscenely bright, as the old woman works.

The camera zooms into the ground to a row of thorns, long, cruelly curved and black, with which the old woman will sew up the bleeding pulp between the child's legs...

I cannot watch any more. I think I am going to be sick. Bill is pale and has wrapped his arms round his chest. I ask Monique to turn it off. She looks surprised. Surely if I have made films about this before I must be used to such footage? Never, never, never, never, never. At this time 98% of Somali girl children are forced to undergo infibulation. It is an intolerable statistic and I will do anything to help change it. It is why I've agreed to make yet another film on this grisly subject. I feel it is the least I can do.

We are staying with Monique in Addis to save money on hotels. Monique hides her youth and her prettiness behind wire-rimmed specs and under shapeless skirts with elasticated waists, T-shirts in muddy colours and clumpy, sensible sandals. She stands with a stoop, skinny arms crossed over her narrow chest. I wonder about her life far from her home, family and friends in Holland, but can find no trace of personality in the drab, bare flat near the airport.

Later, over dinner in an Italian restaurant, she reveals herself to be surprisingly ambitious, prepared to stick out her stint in the field so that she can rise to a well-paid and prestigious desk job in Geneva. Bill and I order wine but she refuses it. She answers our questions in a rather high-pitched, expressionless monotone, but seems not to know how to continue a conversation.

Now after a few days at Hatasheikh I am beginning to like Monique. Her colourless, flat persona is a clever carapace. It gives her a competent, unruffled air and suggests an unsentimental toughness.

Though I respect Monique's coolness I feel more at home with the passionate and sensual Amina. Amina is beautiful. High cheekbones stand out under almond-shaped eyes and over a dazzling smile. Only the deep furrow between her eyebrows hints at her suffering. Below her lovely face Amina's body is running to fat, the result of an enormous appetite – especially for goat stew. She will gnaw on a bone, tearing at the flesh with greasy fingers as the fat dribbles down her chin, eyes slitted with pleasure.

We first meet Amina the day we arrive in Jijiga. We fly up in a tiny chartered plane. I sit in the front, excited by the prospect of flying over Ethiopia. Before we take off the Moslem pilot, glamorously smooth in his Ray Bans, bends his head over the instrument panel and prays as the propellers roar into life. He calls Allah's name out loud then flashes me a grin, white teeth filled with gold in his immaculately shaved face. Moments later we are airborne. The plane drones in a straight line over brown, barren country and a few hours later we land in a field outside Jijiga.

Amina is waiting for us. Monique is staying with a field officer from UNHCR who does not have room for Bill and me, so Amina takes us off into town to look for somewhere to stay. We stop at several grim-looking hovels masquerading as hotels or guest houses, but none have any rooms. Amina is not one to give up.

'OK, we will go and see Elizabeth,' she says decisively. In this setting I am surprised to hear such a European name.

We arrive at an unpromising compound where a sheet of corrugated iron serves as a gate. Several Somali women are cooking over fires in the courtyard. Despite her pale German skin and red hair, Elizabeth is dressed like a native Somali, swathed from head to toe in floaty cotton the colour of sherbert orange. She is the only white woman who lives there.

Elizabeth embraces Amina warmly and leads us into a comfortable sitting room. Along two walls are bench seats covered in ethnic drapes and cushions. She offers this room to Bill and me. We accept gratefully and (after a torch-lit journey the length of the compound to the hole in the ground that serves as a loo) Bill and I take a bench each, wrap ourselves in our sleeping bags and fall asleep.

Next day, driving towards Hatasheikh, I can make out some strange movement in the distance. At first it looks like hundreds of birds hovering just above ground level. As we draw closer I see thousands upon thousands of shreds of plastic flapping in the air. Everywhere we look strips of plastic have attached themselves to thorn bushes and trees. These ragged, seedy, self-made flags now flutter for as far as the eye can see. The entire plain appears to be decked in some kind of bizarre post-apocalyptic plastic bunting. If anyone is in any doubt that plastic is one of the environment's greatest enemies, this is the place to come. The plastic is going to be here long after any of us.

The camp is strictly policed and it has taken all Amina's charm and the might of UNHCR to secure us our two rooms in the administration block. My heart sinks as I see the three mattresses on the concrete floor and the shed with its hole in the ground that serves as loo and shower to the entire camp staff and us. I cheer up a bit when I realise that most of the staff push off at night, leaving only a few guards, and also that there is a tap from which to fill buckets. It will be possible to be clean, important for morale as well as health when working in the heat.

That same afternoon we enter the camp itself. It is beautiful in a strange way. Traditional Somali huts or *tukuls* are nowadays made from plastic sheeting stretched over wooden branches forced into an igloo-shape. These round *tukuls* stretch as far as the eye can see, as if hundreds of bubbles have drifted in to settle amongst the

167

palm trees.

Somalis have the most intact culture of any nationality I know. Their dress, their housing, their food, their language, their use of song and poetry – their entire way of life is so much their own that you can tell a Somali anywhere in the world. The women are tall and beautiful, long-limbed and straight-backed, their fine-boned, narrow faces exquisitely framed by their veils. The elegance of their slender bodies is accentuated by the caressing sweep of their robes.

Just as the jewel-like colours of sari silk flatter the golden flesh of Indian women, so the vivid, hot hues of their robes enhance the aubergine sheen of Somali women's complexions. The men too are handsome, though somewhat prone to a red-eyed, glazed expression caused by chewing *ghat*, a mildly narcotic leaf.

The *tukuls* are cool, spotlessly clean and comfortable inside. They are also surprisingly spacious. Somalis line the walls and ceilings with cotton sheets and the floors are strewn with mats and cushions. You are tempted to lie down and stretch out luxuriously amongst the pillows, their cotton covers cool against the skin.

On our first day of filming Amina takes us to a wedding. She wants to show us the dire impact of infibulation on a young bride. Outside the wedding *tukul* women are waving palm leaves and ululating as they sing and dance, stamping their feet and whirling around. Some hold up umbrellas against the sun, and these flap above the vibrant, swirling colours like crows. Plastic oil drums serve to bang out an insistent, irresistible rhythm.

Inside the *tukul* the floor is strewn with flowers and petals. Paper chains and tinsel, identical to the cheap, glitzy decorations we might hang in a classroom or office at Christmas, festoon the walls and ceiling. It is cool and dim and there is a strong scent of myrrh mingling with the smell of sweat and fried meat.

Ayaan, the sixteen-year-old bride, crouches in a corner. She wears a veil the colour of poppy petals with embroidered, scalloped edging. Her feet are hennaed in an intricate pattern. Her eyes remain steadfastly on the floor. She frowns and chews at her lip. Under her dark skin she looks ashen. Near by sits Abdi, the groom. He is a skinny man of about thirty with a moustache, pitted skin and anxious eyes. He sweats profusely. He wears an ugly, though clearly prized, Western puffa jacket in synthetic, luminous yellow.

The women in the family clap as we come in. We are asked to sit on cushions opposite the bride and groom. A girl sprays us with scent from an imitation bottle of Yves Saint Laurent's *Paris*. The smell is sharp and chemical and immediately I feel my skin prickle. I am violently allergic to some scent and know my neck and arms will be inflamed and itchy in minutes. Yet there is no question of refusal, just as there is now no refusing the tin tray of food which is put before us. We are honoured guests and have to behave graciously. We pick at the sugary sweets and popcorn. I look at Ayaan and see her move, and then wince with pain.

When a Somali girl marries the women in the groom's family gather the night before the wedding to inspect the wound between her legs. If the wound presents itself as a solid ridge of scar tissue, she is pronounced intact and the women leave ululating joyfully. If the flesh has torn and been infected, making the scar messy or ragged, the women reject the girl. They leave silently and then dig a hole outside her *tukul* to suggest the girl's 'open' and non-intact status. The girl is unmarriageable from then on.

Ayaan's scar was all too intact. She had been so tightly sewn up that on her wedding night she was impenetrable. Her husband's family called the circumcisor to cut her open. Thanks to Amina's patience, and her ability to translate without interrupting the flow, we begin to extract Ayaan's story,

'She cut me messily and badly,' she says. Then she looks up at us and her voice shakes with outrage:

'She was half blind.'

The couple have been married six days and the wedding festivities are still in full swing. Since her wedding night Ayaan has been fainting constantly and feeling dizzy. She has bled so much she has become anaemic. Despite the bustling merriment and celebratory mood of the women around them, the couple look miserable.

Abdi sits silent, motionless except when he flicks a fly away from his face or wipes the sweat from his forehead with a cloth. He had not been prepared for this joyful occasion to be so overshadowed by pain, blood and trauma:

'When I see her face and her pale complexion and all the pain and the blood and the parts which are hurting, my decision is to advise others not to be circumcised in the future. I really advise them not to do it,' he says.

Amina knows that until men begin to speak out against infibulation no amount of women's pain and suffering can stop it. For her Abdi's statement is a minor victory, yet it is still dreadful to contemplate their future as husband and wife. Amina doubts if Ayaan can survive childbirth. She will die from loss of blood.

Later Amina introduces us to Dr. Noor, a Somali gynaecologist who supports her work. Two of Hatasheikh's biggest problems are the lack of medical facilities and doctors. Women rely on traditional birth attendants or TBA's when delivering babies. On our way to meet Dr. Noor, Amina launches into a story about TBA's.

'When I meet TBA's and ask them about their equipment, they show me a very bad, old, blunt knife wrapped in a dirty cloth,' says Amina, shaking her head and sucking in her breath.

'It is very bad. They tell me that is what they use to cut women, to get the baby out. When I was a midwife I used to see babies with scars on their heads where the women had cut them by mistake. These TBAs are half blind. They are old women and they use filthy equipment. They cut open women before the baby is even ready to come out, so the mother bleeds to death. If she doesn't die then, she dies of infection later. It's terrible.'

Dr. Noor is a city man with a patrician manner. He wears a green baseball cap and Western clothes under his white coat. Half-moon spectacles give him an intellectual air. We try to attach a tie microphone to his lapel but he demands the 'big' mike. Bill cleverly suggests we use both so I run around after Dr. Noor swinging the boom pole for all I am worth. Bill dresses up the microphone in its furry wind-shield, so it looks as big and important as it can.

In one hut we find a woman lying on her side, in great pain.

She is heavily pregnant. Dr. Noor examines her with a hint of impatience. He barks orders to her family. He says to the woman:

'Your problems are all caused by infibulation.' He says to her relatives:

'You must take her to a clinic in Jijiga immediately.'

The woman's contractions have started but the vaginal opening is so tightly sewn that she needs to be cut open as fast as possible, using sterilised instruments.

Outside the *tukul* Dr. Noor is angry. I ask him what is the biggest health problem facing women in the camp. He turns round and glares at me.

'Of course the biggest problem is death,' he says irritably. He looks over his glasses at me as if I am a stupid child.

'At least 20% of women die from infibulation. 20%. That's a lot. It's clearly a major problem. We have enough problems in Africa. We really don't need this one on top of them all.'

With that he picks up his Gladstone bag and stomps off. I like his anger. Anything is better than complacency.

Complacency is Amina's biggest enemy. When she first arrived at Hatasheikh people laughed at her and treated her as an eccentric busybody. Amina imitates them:

'Ha ha ha,' she goes, contorting her face into a cruel sneer, 'That's what they say to me, "Ha ha ha. You must be crazy, you are a mad woman. You should not go round talking about the clitoris and our private parts. Don't you have any other work to do? You poor thing! If you can't find other work, we will share our wheat rations with you, you poor woman – you are obviously insane!"'

I wonder about Amina's own experiences of infibulation. Which is indirectly why we end up whispering about sex late into the night. Each evening we return to the administration block about five thirty and take it in turns to fill buckets and wash. Dinner is cooked in a nearby restaurant and brought to our room.

Then Bill, Amina, Monique and I perch on the edge of our mattresses round a big tin tray of pasta. Somalis have inherited many of their culinary skills from the former Italian colonials, and their pasta is delicious, usually made with tuna, tomatoes and onions. After we have eaten we lie back on our mattresses and chat till dark. Then we sleep, often as early as half past eight at night.

In the mornings we are up by five thirty. We eat breakfast in a restaurant just outside the camp where they fry up eggs with hot green peppers on a sizzling griddle, and bring us tiny, chipped cups of scalding, sweet, black coffee. Breakfast never tasted so good as in that dingy, filthy hovel, surrounded by flies, with the sun beating down onto the tin roof and cockroaches crunching underfoot.

Though it is exhausting working in the heat, after a few days I have had far more than my usual amount of sleep and it is making me restless. One night I can hear Amina is awake. It is then we start talking. She explains how infibulation has come to be so central to Somali culture.

Somalis believe it is a practice dating back to the Pharoahs, hence their name for it, *faronica*. They also believe it is encouraged by the teachings in the *Hadiz*. On a cultural level, they believe that women who remain uncut are hideous in the eyes of God – like goats or cows with their genitals flapping obscenely, open to dirt and corruption. To be sewn up neatly is to be clean, pure and beautiful.

So how has Amina managed to rebel? She was infibulated herself but says she will never be ready to speak about it.

'It was too terrible. I cannot.'

Instead, she begins to tell me about her time as a midwife. She has witnessed hundreds of deaths. Yet what shocks her most is the attitude of the men:

'They come to me after their wives have given birth. "Oh please Amina," they say, "Can you sew her up again and make her nice and tight like new?" There are their wives, barely alive, and all they care about is their own future pleasure.'

While Amina rejects the phsyical act of infibulation, she embraces the social restrictions that the practice implies. She deplores the liberal attitudes of the West. Women who have sex outside marriage are whores. It is then she tells me about the pornographic magazine.

'I know you are not married, Charlotte,' she says, 'But I know you are a good person. I know you have not been with men. I know you are not a whore like many of these European women who come here.'

I am glad it is dark so she cannot see my face. I am torn between the desire to maintain her high opinion of me and the more urgent need to tell the truth.

'What those men were doing to those women in that magazine was so disgusting,' she rasps.

'Actually Amina,' I venture, 'Most people do that in Europe.'

There is a sharp intake of breath.

'I don't mean in groups like in the magazine,' I continue, 'But in Europe people don't see anything wrong with enjoying sex,' and I take the plunge: 'Even outside marriage.'

'That's terrible,' she says, after a pause.

'Why is it terrible?' I ask. 'Men have sex outside marriage all the time.'

'That's different,' she says.

I know I am in for a long, hard night of arguing. An hour later and we are still going strong.

'If a man treats a woman well, loves her and gives her pleasure, she will stay with him, right?' I persist.

'Of course,' agrees Amina.

'So why does he need to cut her and sew her up?'

'So another man cannot enter by the back door,' she says. I know Amina is thinking about her second husband. Her first husband died in the fighting and she has married again. She is wondering whether this has been a wise move. I know she does not sleep that night.

The circumcisors themselves are Amina's most formidable enemies. Infibulation is a lucrative and respectable business, and circumcisors are believed to have superhuman powers. Amina tells me about one who promised to give up her work but found she could not. Her mother and her grandmother had been circumcisors. Circumcision was in her blood, a noble heritage handed down through generations. Apart from that she made good money.

173

Yet the real problem was more basic – she was having withdrawal symptoms. She missed the sensation of slicing flesh. At first she had begun carving up chicken carcasses to stem her hankering. This soon failed to satisfy her. What she really missed was the flow of blood and the shrieks of pain that accompanied it. She had resorted to buying live chickens and cutting their throats. Now she could no longer control her cravings and had gone back to work.

'Believe me,' says Amina, 'That is not the worst story I have heard these people tell.'

When I meet the circumcisors it is easy to believe her. The old women huddle round the entrance of a *tukul*. They greet Amina coldly and eye Bill and me with hostility. They agree to be filmed and so Amina squats down on a stool and starts talking to them.

'You mutilate little girls, you shed their blood, you make them cry! Where's the benefit?' Amina demands.

'It gives me an income for me and my children,' says one of the women.

'Are you thinking only of your own children? You're not thinking of others?' shouts Amina tearfully.

The circumcisor stands her ground:

'Yes. I'm putting my children first. Doesn't everyone?'

'That's immoral!' shrieks Amina.

She has lost the argument.

But elsewhere there are signs of progress. Amina introduces us to Hawa, who has decided against circumcising her youngest daughter Efra. One of Efra's sisters died in a fire. Her legs had been bound together after circumcision and she had been unable to flee the flames. Now Hawa has had enough. Efra is an angelic child of eight with huge, velvet-black eyes and a trusting smile – a rare commodity amongst girls who usually learn from the age of six never to trust an adult again. Hawa invites us to Efra's coming of age ceremony. First Efra is groomed. Her hair is massaged with coconut oil and tightly plaited. Her nails, on both hands and feet, are pared to the quick with a razor blade. I watch one of her aunts go to work on this rudimentary manicure with her stubby fingers. It is hard to look at any blade without thinking of what might have been. Efra is then bathed and dressed in a purple cloak.

Plates of sweets and the great staple of the Somali diet, popcorn, are laid out for the children outside. The women gather inside a *tukul*. Hawa throws myrrh onto tiny braziers filled with red hot coals and soon the atmosphere is thick with the sweet, fragrant smoke. It mingles with the sour reek of sweat and the rich smell of meat and fat. Then the women begin to sing and clap. Amina loses her pink scarf which has been tied tightly round her head, and her long hair flows as she sways trance-like to the whirling rhythms of the singing.

Amina is happy because Kadra, a one-time circumcisor, is there to bless the ceremony and ward off the evil eye, but not to cut. Hawa has paid Kadra half what she would have paid her to perform the gruesome operation, as a token of respect and to ensure Efra receives her blessing. Then she invites Kadra to join in the feasting and dancing.

As I watch Amina clapping and singing, I wonder who on earth can match her resilience, enthusiasm and passion. Earlier I have heard that Amina is leaving the camp to work on a project providing virtually fuel-free stoves. In a country in which many cannot afford the wood or charcoal with which to boil water, this is an important and worthy issue. To me it seems a somewhat petty project compared with Amina's work at Hatasheikh.

I ask Monique who is taking over. She gives me a vague answer. Amina's groundwork is like a newly planted garden. Without constant nurturing and watering it will die. I plague Monique with questions. Surely Amina is wasted on fuel-free stoves? Couldn't UNHCR persuade her to stay? Monique smiles patiently.

'That's life,' she says.

On camera Amina sometimes comes across as larger than life, a caricature of an over-emotional zealot. Watching her through a lens, shielded by a layer of glass from the power of her dynamic personality, I think about her underlying attitude. While she deplores the physical side of infibulation, part of her still fails to accept that women have equal rights. Saudi Arabia is her model country because women are spared the knife, but still remain devout Moslems and obedient to men.

It does not occur to her that the Saudis use many other extremely effective methods of supressing women. She has been so traumatised by the extent of the physical suffering she has witnessed that she cannot see the social dynamics which make it possible for it to continue.

Amina's swansong is a big workshop in the camp. For weeks drama groups and musicians have been rehearsing a play that Amina has encouraged them to write. She hopes it will help draw the crowds, and it does. The community hall is so crowded that many cluster round the windows to watch.

In the play the men are portrayed as idiotic bullies and the circumcisors as wickedly funny witches. The actresses play women who suffer, faint and even die, but somehow the players make it hilarious. The women in the audience clutch each other and shriek with helpless laughter, thrilled that the all too familiar subject matter can be replayed to them as comedy. For a few the scenes bring back painful memories.

I watch Amina comfort two women who are weeping into their veils. Amina puts her arms round them and cries too, but on the whole it is a joyous occasion. We are expected to join in with the dancing which follows the show. As I jig around under the paper chains with a toothless but exuberant old man, I once again feel that there may be some grounds for hope.

We made a Somali version of our film for aid workers in Somalia. I thought we had made a wonderful and useful film. At the time I was caught up in the excitement of Amina's success rate, and enamoured of the kindness and warmth of the Somali women with whom we spent so much time. Yet looking back I still feel frustrated.

I worry that I was looking at the work of women like Amina through a Western lens which distorted my perception. Despite all our late night exchanges of views, deep down Amina still believed women belong to and are ruled by men. And it is a view I know I can never share.

13 SIX AFRICAN DREAMS
Ghana

Ghana declared that its dream for the new millenium was to emerge from the ranks of the world's poorest nations and become a middle-income country by 2020. Channel Four decided to put Ghana's dream to the test. We would assess Ghana's progress as a nation by following six characters over twenty years – an ambitious and very longterm project. Alison Aylen, a researcher and assistant producer, was dispatched to Accra to find some likely candidates and at the end of September I set out to join her.

Alison has golden skin and a silky mane of blonde hair. She is tiny and voluptuous like a ripe plum. She is also quick-witted, funny and an excellent listener, with a gift for making friends. Documentaries depend on people with a talent for chatting people up, and of the six characters we seek for our film we have already clearly identified four. I am delighted to have her on board.

We are staying at the Shangri La Hotel within minutes of the airport. The rooms are cool and clean, if dark. Around the swimming pool there is a landscaped garden with fountains, streams, wooden bridges, bamboo, palms and tropical flowers. I am used to a very different kind of African hotel so for me this is utter luxury.

In the morning we go to Korle-Bu, Accra's main teaching hospital, to meet a likely fifth character, a doctor. Paths twist through stubbly lawns fringed with scrawny oleander bushes, and then disappear amongst the sprawl of squat buildings that make up the hospital. We pick our way amongst upturned paving stones, cement mixers and rusting drills, lying around as though a bold plan for modernisation has suddenly been abandoned.

Doctors, nurses, workers, patients and visitors swarm round kiosks selling kebabs and Coca-Cola. We are sent from building to building in search of our doctor but eventually track her down in a dark cubby hole which smells of cat food.

'We can talk here,' says Dr. Elsie Mensah, heaving herself up onto a high, unmade iron bed where she perches jauntily, swinging her plump legs.

'Sit, please,' she says.

I sit in the one chair and Alison sits on the bed next to her. Elsie's giggly manner is delightful but does not conceal her underlying ambition and intelligence. In her twenties, she is determined to become Ghana's best pediatrician.

She shows us round the Premature Babies Ward. There is a brace of twins swaddled together, and a normal sized baby with breathing problems who looks gigantic amongst the rows of tiny, wrinkled, under-formed babies in incubators. Elsie tells us the infant mortality has risen to 40% in the last month alone.

She agrees to take part and for once we have no serious problem working through the layers of bureaucracy to gain formal permission to film. Five down, one to go.

So we set off to meet our next candidate. I want someone in industry or commerce and I have heard that the man who heads Armitage Shanks in Ghana might be willing to take part. I remember what Dr. Piri said about the importance of plumbing during the cholera crisis in Zambia, and I have the idea that a working lavatory can be a metaphor for a developed country.

Mr. Armitage Shanks's offices are on an industrial site, above a showroom full of bathroom suites in liverish pink and beige. After keeping us waiting for half an hour Mr. Armitage Shanks takes us into the showroom, where he pontificates about plumbing. We stand around amongst the urinals and ceramic tiles while he boasts of his prowess in the bathroom market. There is no way we can have this man in our film. Our audience would be asleep within minutes.

In search of a replacement we go to meet Teresa, who is big in real estate and owns a company called Manet Properties. Her office is on one of her own housing estates which are made up of executive homes – row after row of identical, neat, pink boxes with tiled rooves.

In the marble lobby we are greeted by a vampish looking receptionist dressed in mint green, who at once ushers us into an office where Teresa sits behind an untidy desk, signing cheques with a chunky gold pen. Her long nails are painted the colour of dried blood. She wears a chic black and brown linen dress and her straightened hair is styled in a sleek bob. White teeth gleam behind glossed, blueberry-lined lips.

Teresa is not only a single mother, rare in Ghana, but has built up her empire entirely on her own. She has a successful hotel on the coast and dreams of expansion, envisaging a vast, global, property company in the next decade. She is perfect for our film but there is a problem. She has an appalling stammer. Each time she reaches a problem word her eyes roll backwards in her head, her face wobbles, her tongue protrudes and her mouth contorts in a frantic effort to force the sound out.

I think her stammer makes her achievements all the more remarkable, but I feel nervous about how she will look in close-up. Nevertheless, I decide to take the plunge and go with her. We now have all our characters in place.

The next day our crew arrives from London – Yang Shu, the Chinese cameraman and Tony, our sound recordist from New Zealand – and we set off for Obuasi to film with our first character, a nineteen-year-old footballer named Mike.

Obuasi lies in the heart of Ashanti country, where the gold mines are, and the road is tortuously long and rough. On the verge people are selling food: smoked flattened rats, giant snails and 'bush meat' or grass-cutters, which are huge rodents. Children hold them out by their bushy tails and thrust them through the car window. We shoo the children away, much to the disappointment of Charles, the driver, who adores bush meat.

Obuasi Goldfields are among the top five football teams in Ghana, and Mike is one of their star players. He is tall and athletic with intense eyes in a long, rather lugubrious face, and he looks much older than nineteen. It is only when he smiles that he looks like a naughty child.

'My dream is to be a world-famous footballer and very rich!' he says, chuckling.

Top footballers in Ghana earn about £25 a week – roughly five times the average wage – but the real goal, for which there is fierce competition, is to be one of the fifteen or so Ghanaian footballers bought each year by European clubs.

Tomorrow Goldfields are to play the Cape Coast Dwarves in the last match of the season. If they win they will qualify for the Confederation of African Football Cup. It will be a crucial match for Mike.

Next morning we get to the Stadium at 5.45 but the footballers are dawdling, yawning and wandering vaguely in the direction of breakfast. Their Dutch coach is shouting at them and muttering about discipline, but it is not until 6.45 that the bus rumbles off.

Mike bounces around on the back seat like a schoolboy on an outing. He is full of upbeat cheer and convinced Goldfields are going to win. The other players sleep, their long legs dangling into the aisle. Half-way through the long journey one of them feels ill and lies moaning in the aisle. The coach gives him an injection and coconut water to drink.

'They just won't learn,' he says, shaking his head, 'You can't tell them what to eat or drink or how to behave. There's no will-power or discipline at all.'

At last we reach Cape Coast. Miles of pure white, palm-fringed sand flick past the windows. Beyond growls the grey, thunderous Atlantic.

At the stadium it is scorchingly hot and there is no shade. Already supporters of the home team, the Cape Coast Dwarves, have gathered in force and are wildly waving flags and scarves in the team colours of green and gold. They beat drums, blow whistles, sing and dance. They are in carnival mood.

I set off into the crowd with my mini DV camera while Alison operates another camera on a crudely-made platform near the press boxes. Boys underneath it are sniggering and trying to look up her skirt through the gaps between the planks. She puts her handbag between her feet to block their view, so they do their best to saw it open and extract our precious expenses budget, fortunately without success.

From the start the referee seems biased towards the home team, to the delight of the home crowd which roars its disapproval and hatred every time a Goldfields player makes a tackle. The Dwarves score an early goal and the crowd goes crazy, leaping into the air, screaming, scarf waving, drums, whistles, the lot.

Things get worse in the second half. The referee is now blatantly on the side of the home team. The Goldfields coach is constantly on his feet pointing out foul play or players that are off-side. The Goldfields' despondency turns to anger and soon a fight breaks out on the pitch which enrages the jeering crowd.

As soon as the match ends the Cape Coast crowd tries to storm the wooden barricades which form the Goldfields' enclosure. When they cannot force their way through they throw bottles and plastic bags full of water.

Mike sits woebegone on a bench, staring glumly at his boots. He does not have the energy to take them off. Without stopping to shower or change the Goldfields make a dash for their bus, and we film as it honks its horn and slowly navigates its way through the jubilant but still hostile mob.

We follow the bus until it stops for petrol. Despondent and exhausted, the boys are slumped in their seats. The coach is not pleased that I want further interviews.

'The boys need to get home,' he says 'They're knackered. But Mike has spotted Alison and is thrusting his way out of the bus. The coach resigns himself to the boys having a quick drink with us.

Attached to the petrol station is a tiny bar. There are tables, chairs, a bead curtain sporting an advertisement for Guinness, and some Club Beer posters. We buy some drinks, and within minutes the air of depression has lifted and the team bursts into song.

Mike sings as if his life depends on it, waving his bottle of beer around.

'We are sad but we should make merry,' he slurs to the camera, 'It's a game. We shouldn't take it in heart. There should be a winner and a loser. So, if we are a loser we should learn from our mistakes and take good chance next time!'

Then he grins, delighted with himself, and shouts for Alison and more beers, banging his bottle on the table.

In no time Mike is hopelessly drunk and fawning over Alison like an over-excited, over-sized puppy. Alison flirts with him kindly but not provocatively, occasionally wriggling away a little nervously when he clasps her too tightly.

As the beer flows, spirits soar. Only Sammy the Captain remains mournful. A small, anxious man in his thirties, he knows what losing this match means to his career. It has been a crucial match for him.

By the time we leave the coach is indulgent:

'What can you do with them? I give up,' he says, shaking his head fondly and clucking gently at them as though they were a clutch of naughty hens.

Next day the weather changes. The skies are bruised and sagging, and it drizzles steadily. It starts to rain very heavily which makes filming impossible, despite all our mackintoshes, umbrellas and plastic sheeting.

So we set off to film with our next character, Leticia, a law student at the University of Ghana. We pass through Ashanti country again, stopping to eat at a place called Desperados. Inside it is desperate indeed, a murky Tex-Mex barn. On the walls are garish cartoons of Mexicans in huge sombreros, cowboys and Indians. In the lavatory someone has scrawled 'FUCK NIGGERS'. At the bar white gold-miners in khaki shirts and baggy shorts drink beer with gloomy determination.

We are happy to reach Leticia's home village, Sefwi Wiawso, in the heart of Western Ghana. Her mother's house has a rather festive look, surrounded by a bright pink picket fence. Her mother is robustly plump with a wise and wizened face, and she welcomes us warmly.

We do some shots of mother and daughter cooking over an open fire and talking about Leticia's life at the University. Leticia is wearing a black vest and as she pounds and cooks, she begins to sweat. Her face glistens in the fire light and she wipes it with her skirt.

Her mother listens intently, her head to one side, while her daughter relays her news from the city. Occasionally she clucks softly to indicate amazement.

'My mother is someone I look up to in terms of inspiration in all that I do, ' Leticia tells us.

'From the start she taught us how to trade, to farm, to cook and she sent us to school. Looking at her, if she'd been able to go to school like I am lucky to be doing now, maybe she would have been a great woman.'

In rural Ghana over half the women are illiterate and only 41% of all Ghanaians go to secondary school. Letitia was the first girl from her school to make it to the University of Ghana.

'I want to come back here and bring the women together to educate them and empower them,' says Leticia earnestly, 'If you educate a man you educate an individual, but if you educate a woman you educate a nation. A woman will see to it that all her kids are educated.'

After we have finished filming Leticia and her mother feed us up on *banku*, a gluey dough with fish sauce. It is hot, delicious and filling.

We say goodnight to Leticia's family and return to our guesthouse. It has dirty beds, no top sheets or towels, one stinking lavatory and a cold shower with a basin in the corridor. Situation normal.

Early in the morning we go back to Leticia's house. Cocks crow, and turkeys and kid goats scratch around in the yard as Leticia pounds yams with her brother, preparing *fou fou* for our breakfast. They serve it with fish and – a special treat for us all – bush meat. Charles the driver rubs his hands gleefully and tucks in, gnawing at small bones. Normally adventurous when it comes to food, even I cannot face stewed rodents so early in the morning, but I do my best.

After breakfast we make our way down the red muddy paths through the palm groves and banana trees towards the market, where the people are friendly and relaxed, either ignoring the camera, or eyeing it with benevolent curiousity as they pass. Women carry trays or baskets on their heads piled high with tomatoes, bananas, dried fish, giant snails, onions or bolts of brightly coloured material.

Leticia's mother has a stall where she sells waxed cloth. The fabric is beautiful, so we buy four lengths. She charges us 60,000 cedis, about £18 each – roughly the average monthly salary, clearly a special price for rich Europeans.

Later we visit Leticia's old school, housed in a series of long low buildings surrounded by wooden verandahs. Her old Latin teacher comes rushing out to meet us.

'What have we here? Are my eyes deceiving me?' he cries. He is acutely conscious of the camera and I enjoy the way he hams up his part, greeting Leticia like a movie star.

Leticia offers to address a class, and I am interested to see what the kids will make of her. She has poise and presence and she stands confidently at the front of the classroom, commanding total attention.

'I'm more concerned about the ladies,' she says, making eye contact with the girls,

'I'm pleading with you, don't mess up. You all want to be somebody in the future, am I right?' There is a general rumble as the girls concur.

'I believe that many of you girls in this class have boyfriends and that is very bad. If you are able to keep your virginity till the right time that a man shall marry you, he'll find you the perfect woman. If you pick a boyfriend now, he won't marry you. So one thing I want to advise you, please, please, please be careful about your life.'

Leticia has seen many of her classmates thwarted by early pregnancy, who are now illiterate, hard-working, child-bearing women. In a small village like this, once a girl is pregnant she is not in a position to complete her education, let alone leave home for the capital and university.

We decide to film Leticia returning home to Accra, and we want some shots of the minibus driving through the bush. We set up the camera beside the road and the driver enjoys himself whizzing past and splashing through the puddles.

Then we ask him to turn the minibus round and go back, so that we can repeat the shot from a different angle. Eagerly he begins a three-point turn on the narrow track which hugs the side of the escarpment. The minibus lurches suddenly as the back wheels slip over the edge of the precipice. We hold our breath as the minibus teeters. The driver laughs out of sheer terror. Another six inches and the van with all its passengers will plunge hundreds of feet below.

Slowly, carefully, the passengers ease their way out, and somehow the driver manages to manoeuvre the minibus back onto the road. I find myself hugging Leticia out of sheer relief. We decide to stop filming for the day.

Next day we go back to Korle-Bu Hospital to do some filming with Elsie. We follow her around as she inspects tiny babies with meningitis, talks to mothers who cannot pay bills, and bemoans the lack of CPAP, a machine which delivers oxygen continuously to a baby's lungs. It is a standard piece of equipment in American or British hospitals, and without it Elsie is losing babies at ten times the British rate.

Compared with Britain's 95,000 doctors, Ghana has 750. There is one doctor for every 26,000 people and only 50% of births are attended by trained personnel. In this context it is astonishing that Elsie is able to remain cheerful. She describes her job as 'fun' and bounces around the ward with her infectious giggle.

The next morning we continue our punishing schedule, setting off at 5.30 for Tamale in the northern region to film with our next character, Chief Nanton-Naa the Second.

Nanton-Naa means literally Chief of Nanton. Nanton-Naa is sixty-five years old, has been a chief for well over a decade and has twelve wives and seventy-five children. He is one of the top twenty chiefs in his region, reigning over about 6,700 people. Today he is hosting a gathering of neighbouring chiefs.

We drive through flat but lush and beautiful countryside, dotted with villages of brown mud thatched huts with wooden shutters, and we arrive at Nanton after midday. The celebrations have already begun. The talking drums are throbbing and a big crowd has gathered. It is baking hot.

'Chinky! Chinky!' the children cry gleefully, spotting Yang Shu.

Nanton-Naa's hut is large and thatched. The portal is bright blue and decorated either side with paintings of lions. We walk through a large, cool, dark room strewn with grass, into the inner sanctum.

This is the long, low throne room. Light filters through shuttered windows, striping the beige walls and floor. At one end of the room stands the throne, a hefty pile of cow hides behind which the wall has been painted hot pink and decorated with a yellow leopard to indicate the Chief's strength.

On the throne lies Nanton-Naa, propped up on an elbow. He is rotund with a white beard which encircles his jolly, round face. He has a gravelly voice, and grunts when he moves his big bulk around. He follows Alison's movements with beady eyes and laughs uproariously and gratifyingly at everything she says. He is clearly very taken with her.

Later we follow Nanton-Naa outside to where another throne has been set up. As he walks towards it through the crowds a scarlet, fringed parasol jiggles over his head and musicians throng round him. A drummer kneels in front of him, leans backwards and sings. Nanton-Naa walks very, very slowly and bobs in a dignified way in time to the music, nodding this way and that in response to the admiring throng. Finally he takes his throne. Either side stands one of his beautiful wives. They are tightly bound in bright dresses with matching headwear. Their sole purpose is to fan their husband. They wield the fans with all the vigour and concentration of aggressive carpet-beaters.

The dancing begins. The chiefs wear head-dresses that look

like old-fashioned nightcaps from a Dickens novel, and waisted blue and white striped tunics over a series of petticoats. Their hide boots are beautifully embroidered with flowers. They look more like Cossacks or Whirling Dervishes than African chiefs. As they dance, spinning like tops, their tunics flare out and swirl around them.

After Nanton-Naa has danced we are all ushered to the inner throne room. Nanton-Naa decrees that Alison is to be made a Sub Chief. She is told to sit in a plastic chair opposite Nanton-Naa and then she is dressed in one of the heavy, layered tunics with a headdress perched on her golden hair.

Nanton-Naa names Alison 'Chief of Repairs' and explains to his subjects that she has brought us all from far away over the seas to help them obtain the electricity they so desperately need. Alison thanks the Chief and then does the obligatory twirl in her new tunic, which thrills all the old men. An appreciative cackle ripples through the crowd, while Nanton-Naa looks on dotingly.

Next day the weather has turned savage and I wake to the noise of torrential rain beating on the roof. We drive to Nanton through the downpour, windscreen wipers screeching.

We find Nanton-Naa in the throne room, dressed in splendid robes and wreathed in necklaces made from leather, horn and stone. He talks about his dream for electricity. All he really wants is a little factory and some grinding machines to produce oil.

After the interview food is produced and the Chief produces gifts, a big sack of yams and four live guinea fowl trussed up by the claws. We are all now formally friends and the atmosphere in the throne room is relaxed. The courtiers start to make amused remarks about Yang Shu who is eccentrically dressed in a sleeveless vest, Chinese combat trousers and a very flamboyant cerise and yellow cowboy hat, a gift from our translator, Nantogma. Emboldened by the laughter Yang Shu begins to make jokes of his own.

'The girls like Ghanaian men,' he says, referring to Alison and me. I make a face, suggesting he zip up his mouth. When it comes to Alison the Chief does not need encouragement. Nanton-

Naa takes this in good spirits. Nantogma's translation is obviously euphemistic and tactful.

'What do you like about Ghana?' the Chief asks Yang Shu.

'Your women,' he replies promptly.

I catch Alison's eye and groan inwardly.

The Chief is barking orders at someone and Nantogma is signalling to Yang Shu not to continue.

There's a commotion at the doorway as Nanton-Naa's most beautiful daughter is thrust into the room. Yang Shu's eyes bulge with astonishment. Nantogma swallows hard before translating.

'You can take her as your wife if you wish,' he says.

The courtiers chuckle and Nanton-Naa puts his head on one side like a naughty old owl to watch the reaction.The girl bows and gives Yang Shu a dazzling smile. She is exquisite.

'Thank you,' says Yang Shu, 'But I have a wife at home.'

'You are married?' Nantogma asks with a puzzled frown.

'Yes my wife is in London,' says Yang Shu.

Nanton-Naa's smile disappears as Nantogma translates. He irritably waves away his daughter.

'He thinks you do not like her,' says Nantogma.

'Oh no! She's very, very beautiful,' says Yang Shu. 'If I was not married I would like her very much.'

Whatever Nantogma says when translating, this seems to do the trick. The Chief begins to chuckle and soon all the courtiers are snickering and pointing at Yang Shu.

'Right, time to go to the farm,' announces the Chief and belches very loudly as if to announce proceedings are at an end.

We follow the Chief's bouncing pickup truck to his farm. As he passes people drop to their haunches as a sign of reverence. His workers are toiling in the maize fields or gathering ground nuts when we arrive. As soon as the Chief begins to patrol they, too, all stop what they are doing and sink to the ground to greet him.

'Naa! Naa!' they say as he strolls amongst them. He waves his arm around his land, proudly showing it off.

Thirteen round ochre-coloured thatched huts make up the

compound of Nanton-Naa's wives. They are built in a circle round a central area where they cook and socialise. Each of the twelve wives has a hut and the thirteenth is kept empty and ready for a potential new wife. I hope fervently that the Chief has not got Alison in mind for hut number thirteen.

The hut doorways are decorated with pieces of broken pottery baked into the mud so that they look like delicate mosaics. Doves roost and coo at the tips of the conical thatched roofs. Groundnuts are laid out to dry in the sun. A fire crackles in the middle of the compound, where a vast black pot is already simmering.

The first wife is better dressed than the others, in thick, green, gold-embroidered cloth from Nigeria and an impressive matching turban. She wears chunky, expensive gold earrings and a necklace from Accra. She sits regally outside her hut, slightly apart from the other wives and clearly in charge.

Custom dictates that it is the newest wife who ministers to the Chief, so wife number twelve is not in the compound. Her role involves doing everything that he needs from bathing and dressing him to cooking for him and accompanying him everywhere.

The eleventh wife, recently superseded in this role, is beautiful. She is about thirty and has given birth a month ago to the Chief's youngest son. The tiny baby already has two ritual scars burnt into his cheeks and peers at us between bouts of greedy breastfeeding. Wife number eleven admits that she is relieved to be living here in the compound with time to look after her children, rather than having to look after the Chief all day every day, which she describes as virtual slave labour. Nevertheless she is clearly proud of being a Chief's wife.

The other wives are cooking and pounding yams and maize together, clustering round the fire and laughing and chatting as they work. They eat together and feed the children, shoving big handfuls of *fou fou* into their mouths. One wife emerges from her hut proudly carrying a shiny black Singer sewing machine on her head. She sits outside for a while and then takes the machine off her head and begins to sew some scarlet cloth. Others lay down mats and pray to Mecca, touching their foreheads to the ground.

Others bring firewood for the fire.

I gather all the wives together in a group and interview them. Number One takes her place at the centre. Babies crawl and tiny children toddle in and out of the shot as we film. The wives become very giggly, especially when I ask them if the Chief has a favourite, or if they ever have arguments or become jealous. Wife Number One orchestrates the entire interview and they await her instructions before they speak.

'Speak! Speak!' she says, raising her arm imperiously.

Then they talk, some shy, some giggling so much that they have to cover their faces. They become fiercely animated when I ask them about electricity and what they would most like.

'A fridge!' they cry.

'A grinding mill!' says one.

'A fan,' says another, which prompts a serious outbreak of giggling.

'A water pump,' says someone else.

'A toilet,' says another, a sentiment which is greeted with shrieks of delight.

'TV,' shouts one and then, in chorus, they all begin: 'TV! TV! TV! We want TV!'

Just then the Chief marches into the compound with Wife Number Twelve tripping after him in red. He leads us out to the main compound. Everywhere are signs of impending electricity – great coils of cable, huge wooden drums of green wire, boxes full of transformers. They lie around amongst the tethered horses, bicycles and goats.

The Chief moves amongst these abandoned boxes of equipment reverentially. At one end of the compound two goats have climbed onto a crate of invaluable parts and are nosing around curiously, defecating happily. Electricity seems so very far away. The light is fading so we hurry round the village to take some shots.

This is the magic hour. When the sun is dropping, Africa always seems idyllic. The sweet smell of woodsmoke drifts up from the huts. Doves karoo, goats bleat and there is the soothing, rhythmic beat of the women pounding yams. Men cycle home to their families at a gentle pace. Children shriek happily as they run amongst the huts.

The sinking sun bathes everything in golden light, and the soft glow of oil lamps and the first fires of the night look inviting through the dusk. Everyone here has a blind faith in modernisation, an unequivocal belief in the benefits of electricity with no concept of what they might lose. Perhaps this untouched village looks like paradise to me because sometimes we Westerners yearn, romantically but unrealistically, to return to a simpler life.

Next day we fly back to Accra to finish our filming with Leticia. She is waiting for us at Ghana University, an elegant campus inspired by Chinese architecture. It is made up of long, low white buildings with red tiled roofs and shuttered windows. There are archways and lattice-work and walkways with vistas, fountains and cool sunken courtyards.

Leticia wears a neat, fitted pink suit with court shoes and carries a sensible handbag. She has done her hair and looks quite the prim young lady. She is a long way from the girl who sweated in her vest over a hot fire as she cooked *foufou* with her mother.

She takes us to the fusty law library and then to the common room, a big airy room adorned with portraits of men in academic robes. We begin the interview and she seems very certain of herself and for a twenty-two year old extremely determined. Only when I ask her about boyfriends does she lose her aplomb and giggle like a child.

Next day we drive out to Greater Accra to film our final sequence with Mike, the footballer. His home town, Tema, is a deserted little place by the sea made up of clapboard houses.

Mike takes us to the house in which he lives with his father. As the result of a car crash his father has been paralysed since Mike was a child. In the back room he lies under a threadbare sheet on a thin mattress. Despite being unable to move he has quick, intelligent eyes in a kind face framed by a thick grey beard. He is friendly and welcoming.

He allows us to shoot Mike shaving him. Mike bends over his father and scrapes away with a knife, then trims his beard with scissors. All the time father and son chat away, mainly about football. I am very moved that Mike's father displays no trace of bitterness. He is proud of his son and his one fear is being a burden.

Later Mike enjoys showing us round the new house he is building right behind his father's. In Ghanaian terms it is a palace, and a measure of his success. Yet what Mike really wants is enough money to take his father abroad in search of a cure. I am touched by his naive faith in Western medicine.

We still have a couple of scenes to shoot with Elsie, who lives in a doctors' block behind the hospital. Her ground-floor flat is dark and dusty and looks over raw concrete to an identical block opposite. The only cheerful sight is the brightly coloured washing hanging out to dry.

The sombre flat is transformed by Elsie's little girl, a toddler who exhibits such capacity for joy that it is impossible not to be affected by her. She waddles up to us, confident and curious, or peeps out shyly but coquettishly from behind her mother's skirts. She is one of the most beautiful children I have ever seen.

She personifies Elsie's biggest dilemma. Elsie has decided she has to go abroad to finish her training. In Ghana it will take her far longer to qualify as a pediatrician than the three years it would take in the States. She has already started researching American medical schools. Her ambition tells her she has to go, but she is going to have to relinquish her beloved daughter to her mother. She should not have to make such a painful choice.

Next day we set off down the coast to Ada to film Teresa's tourist hotel, the Manet Paradise. The terrace overlooks the lagoon and the opposite shore, which shimmers in the heat as elegant, painted boats slide by.

Teresa's dream is to turn this piece of coast into the Miami of Africa. Tourism has increased over the last three years but Ghana is still not a major holiday destination.

'Whatever we are doing is nowhere near getting people into

the country, as they would go to Florida or Las Palmas or Hawaii or any of those places,' says Teresa. I am not sure whether to admire her ambition or wonder at her naivety. She certainly has a very long way to go if her hotel is going to attract an international crowd. Yet Teresa is not the kind of woman to give up. She has just negotiated a loan equivalent to £1.8 million, despite the punitive interest rates.

On Teresa's new estates, the most expensive house for sale is £75,000, three hundred times the average income.

'The success of everybody is judged by his ability to own a home,' explains Teresa, 'I have a big dream – to build beautiful affordable homes and to make a difference in this society.'

She takes us round one of these dream 'executive' homes. It is furnished with pink curtains, lots of doilies and a big shiny oval table with stiff, striped chairs. Her target market is young executives working for banks or international institutions.

In the bathroom Teresa tries the flush. It jams.

'Our b-b-biggest nightmare is always the p-p-plumbing,' she stammers, aware she is on camera, 'I'm always scared when a c-c-client c-c-calls but, as you can see, things are excellent here.' With a lot of effort she manages to flush the lavatory.

I want a shot of Teresa walking away through one of her eerily empty sterile estates. To do this we hire a crane which was built for a feature film in 1928. It's a vast old monster but it's the best Ghana has to offer. It is manned by a gangster-like grip in Ray Bans called Francis. When we first meet he asks three times where the director is, before I can make him understand he is talking to her.

I want to see the shot from the crane myself, so I ease myself gingerly into the bucket seat while Francis and his men remove the weights. The crane rears up into the air at alarming speed. My stomach stays on the ground.

I am high up above the red tiled rooftops, from whence the estate looks like a toy town. There is no harness, nothing to prevent me from falling the huge distance to the ground below. We are breaking every rule in the Health and Safety Guidelines, but there is no other equipment in Ghana to achieve the same cinematic shot.

Teresa has a big red jeep. As we drive to one of her construction sites she begins to tell me how much she misses her father. She has recently returned from his funeral. Her colleagues are shocked that she has gone back to work so soon after his death.

'People expect you to mourn for a month,' she says. 'But you know, I couldn't leave my business alone for that long.'

We are friends by the time we arrive at her vast construction site. We sweep up in a cloud of red dust. It is not yet midday, but there seem few people around. In the distance is the desultory sound of a single hammer. Teresa clicks her tongue disapprovingly, frowns and begins marching towards the noise of the hammer.

On the way we come across a group of workmen sitting in the shade.

'What are you d-d-doing here?' demands Teresa, looking at her elegant gold watch.

'We are relaxing,' says one.

'Re-re-relaxing?' barksTeresa.

'We are tired,' says another.

'You are t-t-tired,' says Teresa contemptuously.

'There is no work,' says another. 'The cement is not here.'

There has just been a delivery of cement. It is standing in the sun, untouched. Teresa points it out.

'Start w-w-working now please,' she snaps, and storms off.

'We need carpenters, plumbers, masons and we need them educated,' she says to camera.

'We have to deal with people who haven't been trained, and it makes our work very difficult. If these people are trained it will help the economy. The success of the economy will depend on this huge middle group.'

Teresa is probably right. There is a massive demand for the kind of homes Teresa is building but she can only meet a third of that demand.

Later I sit her down to interview her. I simply have to ask her about her speech impediment. It will seem strange in the film if I do not address it. I am afraid of offending her so I leave it till last.

'Didn't having a stammer make it even harder for you to succeed as a woman?' I ask tentatively. To my relief, she smiles.

'Stammering's definitely been an obstacle,' she says. 'It made me very reserved by nature. I had to internalise. Sometimes I think much of my strength has come from there, so it is also an asset.'

I admire Teresa and want to keep in touch with her. She assures me that next time I come to Ghana she will have built an estate with a thousand homes on it. Her ambition and determination are beyond question. What will let her down is the quality of her workers and the culture of doing as little as possible for the money.

We are nearing the end of our shoot. Our last task is filming with 'KSM', Ghana's best known 'shock jock' and a stand-up comedian. I never learn his full name, he is KSM to everyone. He is late back from performing in South Africa, so we only have a day and a half to do all the necessary filming. I have to make some swift decisions about scenes to drop.

KSM is tall, with hooded eyes in a long, fine-boned face. He is handsome, like a classical African carving, which gives him a confident air bordering on arrogance. I think it is essential to film him conducting his live radio show, *Talk Shop*. Headphones on, KSM stands rather than sits at the control panels, looking out of the window across Accra.

He calls himself 'The Voice of Reason' and today's show is about corruption. He rants about African presidents who steal money from their countries, and singles out General Babangida of Nigeria who has pocketed billions of dollars, now safely stashed in Swiss bank accounts. He talks about the culture of bribery and nepotism which prevents talented people from reaching the top.

Callers jam the lines, wanting to tell their own stories. KSM is brilliant and debates live for two hours. It is a veritable tour de force. With half a million listeners it is by far the highest rating talk show in Accra.

KSM lived in the States for fourteen years, but decided to return to Ghana to help his country develop. Seeing that people were sick of politics, he turned to radio and television.

'My dream is simple,' he says, 'to change Ghana through the media.'

He also has a television production company called Sapphire, and is directing Ghana's first sitcom. His aim is to build up the television industry to compete on an international level.

'I'm looking forward to having Sapphire programmes on Channel Four,' he says, twinkling.

'World class, made in Ghana by Ghanaians.'

He has not returned to Ghana half-heartedly. He wants Ghana to pull itself up by its bootstraps so his own children will not want to desert their country for America, as he did. Yet he knows too that Ghana has problems to overcome.

'One of the biggest problems is complacency,' he says. 'People are comfortable with just enough to get by, they don't have the drive. We're in a global world and it's not just a matter of meeting deadlines, but exceeding them and getting competitive. Culturally, most of our priorities are wrong.'

We go to watch him do a much anticipated comedy turn in Accra's equivalent to Ronnie Scott's Jazz Club. There is a bar and lots of little tables and chairs, facing a small stage with a painted backdrop. The place is packed.

KSM's show is a vicious but hilarious attack on the complacency he so hates. First he pokes fun at returnees:

'In the first year they are full of big ideas like, "Hey, we have to build a subway in Ghana." '

The audience fall about laughing as he imitates a pompous returnee, explaining his plans for a line between one end of Accra and the other.

'In the second year they are getting more realistic,' KSM says, and pauses while the audience shrieks.

'"Oh, I think we need some more buses on the street," Yeah, they're getting more realistic.

'In the third year...,' and KSM slumps, drooping his shoulders as he ambles across the stage with a hangdog expression. He gives a huge shrug:

'Oh well, who can change Ghana?'

The audience roars its approval, recognising their own inertia and weeping with laughter at their hopelessness.

'I know we can do better,' KSM says later. 'I know we have the brains and are capable of doing it. So part of my frustration is that I know we have the potential. Wherever we are now, Ghana is the gateway to Africa.'

Back in London our commissioning editors at Channel Four kept changing their minds about the kind of film it should be. The Head of Programmes insisted on calling it 'The Ghana Generation' which I thought made it sound like a geography lesson. With a title like that the film passed unnoticed except by one or two critics, who said it was an excellent and interesting film 'despite the unpromising title'. Meanwhile the original idea, to return and track the progress of our six characters over time, has completely lost momentum, and I think Channel Four is hoping I will stop pestering them about it.

I doubt if Nanton-Naa has electricity yet or if Elsie went to New York. Leticia has been in London twice and is doing well at Law School. Mike has been in London, looking for a team. I have lost track of him but I hope he found one. Teresa has not yet finished her dream estate. The government took away KSM's radio frequency because his shows were too subversive. The latest news is that he has it back and is as outspoken as ever.

Whatever happens to the film series I hope, passionately, that our magnificent six will all achieve their goals.

14 YOUNG WIVES' TALES
Ethiopia

The Civil Code in Ethiopia sets the minimum age of marriage at fifteen but in the countryside the rules are frequently waived. Cameraman Bill Locke and I were making a film about child marriage for the UN Fund for Population. We were filming in Bahir Dar, a relatively lush part of the Ethiopian uplands, near the shores of the great mosquito-infested Lake Tana. It is here that early marriage is most common.

Drums throb and the crowd coils round a group of dancing women, shaking their shoulders and hips in a sensuous frenzy. Those closest to the dancers clap with rhythmic intensity, echoing the insistent beat of the drums. The women pant and sweat, though it is cool and a grey sky hangs low over the plain like a damp dishcloth.

Bill, the cameraman, and I work our way through the throng, pushing into a breathing, pulsating wall of flesh. We reach the dancers in the centre. Someone has gone to fetch the bride. The dancing becomes more frantic.

The four year old girl is being married to a boy of nine. Though the bride is bawling, her father continues to smile. He picks her up and holds her out towards the camera. She squirms and buries her face in his shoulder, snot and kohl-stained tears leaving black slime on his jacket. He murmurs to her gently, twisting her face round so we can have a good shot of her. With the instinct of a superstar hounded by the paparazzi, the tiny bride thrusts out a chubby hand, jangling with silver bangles, and pushes our lens away. Bill and I pack up the camera.

We have arrived at this wedding full of self-righteous indignation about the rights of the child and imagining the parents to be cruel and heartless. Yet the bride's father, despite his apparent happiness even in the face of her tears, seems tender and loving as he smoothes her crumpled dress, gently dabbing at her make up, whispering consolingly into her ear.

Later that day the bride leaves for her husband's new home. The official practice is for the bride to live with the boy's parents till she reaches puberty. During that time she is brought up as part of the boy's family and learns to regard her future husband as a brother-like figure. She does not move to her husband's quarters until she menstruates. That may sound almost reasonable, but there is ample evidence that this cultural practice is being widely violated.

The next day we set off to another wedding, armed with pots and pans and bolts of cloth as gifts. We arrive at a small settlement, a huddle of round, thatched *tukuls*. The preparations for the wedding are well under way so we start to film. A group of women cooks *njira*, the rubbery pancake which serves as bread, on round hot plates over a fire. They pour the fermented *tef* from jugs onto hot metal plates; the liquid squirls, hissing and bubbling as it hits the hot metal. When the *njira* is ready they flip it onto flat baskets.

Boys lug skinned carcasses to a meat hut, carrying whole haunches of cow over their shoulders. Blood dribbles into the dust behind them as they lope along in their bare feet. Myrrh-scented smoke wafts its sweet, blue swirls into the air from the hot coals on which girls are roasting coffee and pouring the bitter black elixir into tiny glazed cups.

Nibret the bride is just eleven and small for her age, with huge mournful eyes. They are swollen as if she's been crying. Her hair is tightly cropped and she wears a cream woven dress, thick with embroidery. She stands blinking in the sunshine. Soon she is dutifully playing the happy wife-to-be and starts to dance with one of her sisters. She may wriggle her shoulders, expertly suggesting a precocious knowledge of her sexuality, but her gestures – the way she giggles, hides her face behind her hands and peeps through her fingers – are those of a child.

I try to talk to her. My translator and local producer Alemayehu is reassuringly solid and avuncular. If anyone can draw Nibret out, it is he. Nibret sits on a three-legged stool. She sniffs, twists the skirts of her dress round her finger and studies the ground in front of her.

'What do you feel about getting married?'

She shrugs, sniffs and stares into the distance. We try again:

'Do you know your husband?'

She indicates that she doesn't, and looks at the ground.

'Are you nervous?'

She wipes her eyes, puts her chin in her hand and gazes at some fixed, far away point.

'Are you going to miss your home here?'

She picks at a piece of embroidery on her skirt and says nothing. We ask her again. Her jaw juts in an attempt at dignity and then we ask the next question.

'Aren't you sad to be leaving?'

Her chin wobbles and a juicy tear runs down her face. I cannot carry on. Her unhappy face tells us all we need to know.

Nibret's parents are dead. Her grandparents have raised her and they agree to talk to us. The grandfather is an elegant man with a white beard framing a chiselled face. Granny is voluble and vivacious. She talks emphatically, using her long, slender hands to make a point.

'We're not sure we're going to live for long and besides we don't trust our cattle to survive,' she says. It is hard to tell how old they are, haggard with years of toil, but they are probably not much over fifty.

'We want to make sure Nibret is secure and looked after in case something happens to us. Besides, we all gain new relatives.'

She smiles and her husband nods in agreement. I realise how much they love their granddaughter. They are doing what is best for her, protecting her future, ensuring she is in safe hands with a degree of financial security. But before I am completely won over I remember that they stand to gain a good price for her.

'So, how did you choose her husband?' I ask.

A 'mediator' finds a suitable groom and then acts as go-between for the families. The bride and groom do not meet until the wedding night, and the groom cannot see the bride until she is safely delivered into his parents' home.

The groom's party is arriving that very night. As darkness falls we sit round an oil lamp outside a hut, moths fluttering around the flame and mosquitoes feasting on our ankles. The stars peppering the sky are brilliant but there is no moon. The African night stretches out around us. Alemayehu curls up and sleeps, blissfully happy. The place reminds him of his childhood in his grandmother's village. Bill and I chat companionably, as various people come to greet and sit with us. Women bring trays of *tibs* with *wot*, meat with hot pepper sauce, to have with *njira*.

Every so often there is a creak of a twig or a rustle in the bushes, and a murmur of expectation runs through the settlement as ears strain for the sound of the groom's arrival. Another hour passes and I start to feel drowsy after so much food, but coffee is made and we are alert again. Then we hear the distant sound of shouts and singing.

Minutes later the groom's party bursts out of the bush. While the fire is built up and stoked by the women, the men are given an enormous feast. After the food the men gather round the fire and dance. Unlike the sinuous writhing of the women, their dancing is jerky and brittle. To hand claps and shouts they stamp out a staccato rhythm in the jagged firelight. I wonder which is the groom: the fierce old man in ragged trousers who shouts as he dances? The young, grinning one who claps his hands hypnotically? Or the man with glazed, bloodshot eyes who jumps too close to the flames, as if in a trance?

Meanwhile since bride and groom are not allowed to see one another, Nibret sits hidden in a dark hut chaperoned by her older married sister of thirteen. The two girls crouch like frightened animals, holding each others' hands. Their eyes are huge and watchful in the darkness and they wince at the shouts and hoots and the harsh pounding of clapping hands and feet which symbolise the male world that Nibret is about to enter.

Early next morning the men gather behind the settlement to finalise the contract. There are no women present. Boys bring coffee and *njira*. The mediator sits on the ground in the middle. He is a sleek, sloe-eyed man with a sly face. He is wrapped in a pale blanket, his knees drawn up, surveying the proceedings. On his left sit Nibret's grandfather and various uncles, brothers and cousins. Nibret's grandfather looks anxious and tired, and huddles against the dawn chill in a dirty blanket.

On the other side of the mediator sits the groom's party. A bearded man in a blue nylon anorak, a potent symbol of urban sophistication, perches on a hussock of grass with a Bic biro and a piece of ruled paper torn from an exercise book. This piece of paper is to be the marriage contract that decides Nibret's future. The mediator's manner is imperious. Nibret's grandfather is eager to please. He is scared of not receiving the right price for his beloved granddaughter.

Turned off by these mercenary negotiations, Bill and I go in search of the groom. He waits in a hut with his best man amongst his retinue. He is a handsome boy of fifteen or so, rather the worse for wear after the revelry of the preceding night. The best man is very aware of his own dazzling good looks, shown off by a purple hat which he wears at an angle calculated to accentuate his high forehead and fine, dark eyes. Beside him the groom looks wan.

The other boys and men make way for us and sit down to listen, like a theatre audience. I ask the groom what he is looking for in his bride. He says he doesn't really care what she's like as long as she isn't lazy, in which case he'll just chuck her out. This draws a great snigger from the crowd which encourages him to keep up his macho stance. His best man nudges him conspiratorially and whispers something obscene. I feel I am in a locker room at a boy's boarding school, the atmosphere seething with adolescent tumescence.

'Are you nervous?' I ask the groom.

'A bit, I suppose,' he admits, while his best man suppresses a snort of derision.

'But are you looking forward to getting married?'

'What's there to look forward to?' he says, regaining his swagger.

The boys around him titter and smirk knowingly. I want to give the groom a good slap, but his posturing bravado is encouraged and condoned by his peers and elders as the correct male attitude towards his wife-to-be. And then I remember he is not really an adult either.

Across the compound Nibret's sisters prepare her for her nuptials. They flutter around her like doves, strangely silent, solemn little faces bent on performing their ritual tasks. One runs a wide-toothed wooden comb through Nibret's oiled, perfumed hair. Another drapes her in heavy, silver necklaces. A third applies black to her lower eyelids, using spit and a rag to spread the kohl evenly. Nibret accepts all this quietly.

She sits expressionless as her dress is tugged into shape around her, earrings attached, bangles forced onto childishly plump wrists. Then after much chirruping and scrabbling a hand mirror is produced from a box of family heirlooms. The mirror would not look out of place on a Louis XVI dressing table – long handled, gilded and vulgarly ornate. It glitters surreally in the shaft of sunlight which has pierced the sooty gloom.

Nibret turns slowly this way and that, inspecting her new bridal face. She composes her features into as womanly an expression as she knows how. Then she bites her nails. It is sad to think that in almost any other circumstances most eleven year olds would love all the attention and fuss, the jewellery, the dressing and making up.

The men and boys have started the wedding dance. The best man, now draped in an emerald green blanket to complement his purple hat, is blowing a horn to announce the nuptial proceedings are under way. The men wave long sticks and chant as they dance. The horn grows more insistent, the chanting swells and the dancing becomes frenzied.

The mediator mounts his mule, ready to take possession of the bride. The groom is still not allowed to see her. The sun is high in the sky and it is hot. Distracted by the waving sticks the mule is restless. The mediator tightens his grip on the reins and beats the mule to steady it. The boys surge round the hut and everyone is shouting. The noise is deafening. I am sweating and nauseous.

Nibret is thrown over the shoulder of a man. She is packaged up in white muslin like a parcel. The man slings her up to the mediator and he heaves her over the mule and grabs her round the neck. She slumps in front of the saddle, trembling. The boys surround the mule, waving their sticks, chanting and stamping. The muslin is tight round Nibret's head and she looks like a cheese wrapped in cloth. It is difficult to believe that this bundle is really a person.

The mediator does not smile. His stern face is impassive under the scarlet umbrella he has raised against the sun. They set off, the umbrella visible for miles as the mule winds its way up the dirt track towards the road and Nibret's new life.

Our jeep arrives at the groom's home ahead of Nibret, to find the wedding party already in full swing. The groom's father is a handsome man of about thirty-five. He welcomes us courteously. He looks anxious – like his son, he has not yet set eyes on Nibret. The groom's mother is entertaining the women. They sit with the children round big tin trays of *njira*.

A leathery old man with a milky-eyed squint and wearing a grubby turban, scrapes an insistent jarring tune on his one-stringed wooden instrument. Young men are thumping a hectic rhythm on the drums and the old musician, egged on no doubt by the idea of untold riches, glues himself to Bill and me. He plays away enthusiastically, threatening our sound track, and we have to use energetic sign language to get him to back off.

A small boy scampers into the clearing to say that Nibret is close. We hear a shout and through the trees a flash of red announces the mediator's umbrella. Their journey has taken about four hours. Nibret's sagging posture beneath the muslin suggests exhaustion and defeat. The crowd surges round and leads the mule to the hut which is to be Nibret's home with her new husband. The groom waits inside.

An old priest emerges from the hut carrying a splendid Ethiopian cross, which he waves while mumbling various incantations. He presses it to the forehead of the bored-looking mediator and against the white bundle, which flinches. Through his zoom lens Bill can just make out Nibret trembling under the muslin.

Then the best man, his purple hat now dusty and awry after his journey, steps forward and hauls Nibret off the mule. There is shouting and tussling as he carries her through the crowd. The sacking in the hut's entrance is drawn back to let through the best man and his fragile burden. He stumbles slightly at the threshold as he stoops to enter. When the sacking falls back into place there is silence.

I am desperate to know what is going on inside that hut. I have been told that this ceremony is only a ritual betrothal and the marriage will not be consummated till the bride is fifteen. But I have seen the glint in the best man's eye, and watched him snigger and plot with the groom. These are reckless teenage boys bursting with hormones. There is no way Nibret will be safe with them.

Culturally it is a very bad idea for me to enter the hut.

'You can't,' says my alarmed local researcher Tesfay when I suggest it. 'They won't let you.'

The family and guests have been doing some serious drinking and the atmosphere is charged. If we push too far we risk being thrown out altogether, or worse. But I have to find out what is going on in that hut. Whatever the consequences, it is more important to know the truth.

Once Tesfay knows there is no stopping me he goes to work and eventually, somehow, we argue our way in. In a close contest the modern and near-universal desire for publicity wins out over anger and respect for ancient tradition.

Inside it is very dark. Tiny shafts of sunlight penetrate the dimness through slits. The groom and his best man sit together looking like cats about to consume large quantities of cream. Next to the groom sits Nibret with one of her sisters. Nibret is obscured by a thick sheet. In the murk I mistake her for a sack of grain propped up against the wall. There is a thick, rather sweet stench of sweat, goat and myrrh.

Then, determined as ever to pursue us, the old musician bursts in. He begins playing in front of Nibret. He thrusts his hips at her and sings in a high, hypnotic voice, miming a grotesque sexual ritual. Nibret shrinks against the wall and pulls the sheet more closely round her. Her sister surreptitiously clasps her hand.

After the musician has gone – only after much remonstrating from Tesfay, who shoos him out – there is a moment of silence. The bundle stirs. Bill quickly raises the camera. Through a narrow slit in the sheet, one dark, sad eye looks out at us before disappearing like a startled animal. Nibret's look is neither accusatory nor pleading. This is a child resigned to her fate, numb, voiceless, hopeless.

I tell Tesfay to ask the groom where he plans to sleep that night. Tesfay hestitates; he does not want to pose such a sensitive question.

'Go on,' I urge.

Tesfay speaks for what seems to be about five minutes. The groom says something short and grins wickedly. The best man snickers. Tesfay sighs.

'What did he say?' I ask.

Tesfay angrily swats at a fly which has settled on his ankle. He is ashamed to translate.

'He's going to sleep right here,' he says, eventually.

'With her?' I ask.

'I can't ask that,' Tesfay says.

'Please. It's important we know the truth.'

Tesfay uncrosses his bony legs and shuffles around. Reluctantly he puts the question.

'Yes,' says the groom, 'and I'm impatient to get started.' The best man smothers a snort of laughter.

'Is it your first time with a girl?' asks Tesfay at my insistence.

There is more giggling.

'Yes. It's my first time.'

I look at Nibret. Her head, still hidden in the sheet, is turned away but her hand has crept out from under the cloth and she is kneading her sister's fingers frantically.

My professional detachment has long since been in shreds. All I want to do is to pick up that little girl and carry her off to the safety of my hotel room. It seems inconceivable that we will walk out of that hut into the sunlight and then climb into a jeep and drive away. We are her only hope.

I know I must try to be realistic. I have no business intervening. It would be foolish and risky to do so, also cruel.

So even if I could spare Nibret today's ordeal, what then? She has to continue to live in her own community. I am in no position to adopt her and take her back to England. But the whole situation has got to me, and I go on fretting. Back in my hotel room I imagine her fear as the groom starts to grope at those layers of cloth. If not me, surely someone somewhere can do something?

There are people out there trying to do something for girls like Nibret, but they are a plane ride away in Addis Ababa. We fly to the capital to see a group of women lawyers who banded together in 1995 because they saw a growing need for girls and women to be protected against harmful traditional practices.

As soon as I meet Original Georgis I think that if anyone can make inroads into centuries of ingrained tradition and culture, she can. Beautiful, fierce eyes shine from an otherwise ordinary, pudgy, pock-marked face. She looks like a tired, middle-aged matron, sallow and slack. Then she starts talking about the abuse of Ethiopian women's rights and she blazes.

She marches us up to a big noticeboard on which she has pinned photographs, mainly of little girls.

'It is a myth that girls don't have sex with their husbands till they're fifteen,' she says contemptuously. She points at a photograph of a child smiling at the camera.

'This girl is just twelve years old. She's already divorced and selling liquor for a living. And look at this one.' She indicates a gazelle of a girl in flip flops looking warily at the camera.

'This one is ten and when she came to us she'd been repeatedly raped. We were so shocked we didn't know what to do. It made us realise just how much we have to do to tackle this problem.'

She sits us down.

'Let me tell you the case of the nine year old bride,' she goes on. 'She was betrothed to a twelve year old boy. On the night of the wedding, because they were both so young, the boy was unable to break her hymen. So the elders who surrounded them gave him an iron to use. Well, he poked her with the iron and you can imagine the rest. She's still in hospital and that was four months ago. I think the physical injuries may heal but as for the psychological scars, who knows?'

Bill and I are silent..

'Sometimes I wake up in the night and just burn inside with rage,' she says.

Apart from the psychological impact of early marriage, there are also potentially appalling physical consequences, especially those associated with pregnancy. When girls' sexual organs are not fully developed, repeated penetration or trying to give birth can rupture the vaginal walls and cause a 'fistula', literally a tear. This results in severe incontinence. Both faeces and urine leak into the vagina. Because the girl smells and can no longer have sex her husband normally throws her out. She has no choice but to return home, an outcast. Often her relatives refuse to take her back, because her condition is seen as a curse that brings bad luck to the entire family.

There is only one hospital in Ethiopia that can mend fistulae and it is in Addis, a long way from Bahir Dar. Most girls have to make do with basic surgery locally.

We are refused permission to film in the fistula hospital in Addis on the grounds that the hospital does not want to be associated with any 'negative image' of Ethiopian reproductive health care. So we visit Bahir Dar's only hospital instead, but the doctor we have arranged to interview has gone home and no-one else has the authority to speak. We are due to fly back to Addis the next day and this is our last chance to find out the real story from a medical expert.

Just as we have given up and are about to leave, an intense young man in a white coat steps forward.

'I am the midwife Dr. Said Fante and I will talk,' he says. Only last week he watched a thirteen year old girl die on the hospital doorstep before he could help her. She had been in labour for four days. The baby died too, trying to battle its way out of its mother's undersized body.

The hospital is under-resourced and does not have basic medicines or necessities like anaesthetic. Time and time again Dr. Fante witnesses the wreckage of early marriages but the problem continues to be ignored.

'I'm not sure I can cope any more,' he says. He has a thick film of sweat on his upper lip.

'So what keeps you going?' I ask.

'I have to go on,' he says. 'I can't just abandon these girls. They've nowhere else to go.'

Sewarag is one of Dr. Fante's assistants. She is a plump teenager in a lurid green sweatshirt emblazoned with an American cartoon character. She was married so young she can't remember how old she was. Her husband, a teacher, threw her out when she developed a fistula. Dr. Fante sent her to Addis for an operation. Now Sewarag is recovering but her future is bleak. Her parents are dead and her husband will not take her back. Dr. Fante has given her a job comforting and helping other fistula patients.

'I loathe my life,' Sewarag says matter-of-factly, 'but when I see how much pain and suffering other girls in the same situation are going through, it doesn't seem that bad.'

I ask her if she'd ever consider trying to go back to her husband. The efficient hospital assistant's mask drops.

'No. I don't want to,' she whispers.

She blinks hard so that we will not see her cry. Then she picks up a red plastic bowl and a jug of water and marches purposefully off down the corridor, her flip flops slapping the worn linoleum as she goes.

We ask Original what the authorities are doing about the

situation. Despite numerous workshops, discussions, political policy, educational programmes and all the efforts of NGO's and the UN, on the ground little is changing.

'Ethiopia is a very traditional country,' she says. 'Women are voiceless, some kind of chattel to be owned and possessed.'

In rural areas there are virtually no schools, so girls remain illiterate without any possible means of income.

Original's final rhetorical question sums it all up:

'How can we talk about development in this country when half the population are denied their basic rights?'

It was a sorry little tale, but one that captured the imagination of British audiences. The film was runner up for the UNICEF prize at the One World Media Awards and nominated for a Rory Peck Award for camerawork. An edited version was shown as the second lead item on Channel Four News. An additional bonus was that it was Original who found me my next and very important film.

211

15 SCHOOLGIRL KILLER
Ethiopia

I was in Addis Ababa interviewing Original about child brides. She was talking to me in front of a board on which were pinned photographs of little girls who had been forced into arranged marriages, but I was only half listening. I had been drawn to one photograph, of an extraordinarily beautiful face in which a pair of intense eyes stared back at me defiantly.

'Who's that?' I asked.

'That is Aberash Bekele – but it's a very different kind of case,' said Original. 'She's from Asela in the South.'

'What a face!' I said.

'Oh, if you knew her story,' sighed Original.

I had to know.

Fourteen-year-old Aberash Bekele is walking home from school one day when she is abducted by a group of armed horsemen. She is beaten, thrown across the back of a horse then taken to a hiding place and raped by one of her abductors. The next day she manages to steal a gun and escape. Her rapist gives chase. She fires warning shots into the air but he ignores her.

When he comes close enough to catch her she lowers the gun and shoots him. He dies. An angry mob, including members of her rapist's entourage, seethe round Aberash. They want to slit her throat on the spot. Luckily the police intervene, but then they arrest Aberash and charge her with murder. It is then that the Ethiopian Women Lawyers' Association becomes involved, and Aberash is now in a safe hiding place awaiting trial.

I turn again to the photograph on Original's board.

'I have to make this film,' I say, but it is easier said than done. It takes over a year for the BBC to commission the film. I keep in touch with Original, telephoning repeatedly and visiting her on my way through Addis to other assignments. I am determined not to let this powerful story slip through the net. Aberash's face continues to haunt me. I simply have to tell her story. It has begun to obsess me.

I try the idea out on several broadcasters. Channel Four are not interested. Various people at the BBC ponder and then decline. David Pearson, who edits the BBC's acclaimed series *Under the Sun*, thinks it would make an interesting film but is unsure how I can tell the story. At this stage, so am I. My confidence is based on a hunch.

Eventually the date is set for Aberash's trial. We either film now or miss a crucial part of the story. David turns up trumps – he commissions the film, and I set off for Ethiopia with a three-man crew and over twenty silvered boxes containing 16mm equipment, camera, lenses, tripod, lights, sound recording gear and stock. For once we have a big enough budget to justify shooting on film.

Aberash is now sixteen and luminously beautiful. She is slightly on the stocky side, which saves her from being entirely celestial, and moments of adolescent petulance tend to undermine her natural grace. She is shy but self-possessed. She occasionally hazards a little English, but generally listens with wide, brilliant eyes, speaking only when asked a direct question.

Aberash grew up on a farm in Asela, a remote, mountainous region towards the south of Ethiopia. Here the land is rocky and rugged and men ride around on horseback carrying whips, sticks and lassos. They wear chaps and Stetson hats that say on them things like 'Marlborough' or 'Cowboy'. Here in the wild South if a man wants a wife he goes out and grabs one. This practice of abduction is so deep-rooted in the culture that no-one can remember how or when it began.

The farm Aberash grew up on is a long walk from Kersa, the nearest town. One hot afternoon the crew and I set out for the farm to interview Aberash's parents. Aberash's father rides with us to show us the way. He is a tall, elegant man, wearing a shabby trenchcoat. When we meet he shakes my hand warmly and doffs his baseball cap politely, revealing a bald head.

We leave the cars by the road and begin walking. I am wearing wellington boots because of the mud. We trudge into lush countryside, down the slopes of steep green valleys, along streams, up twisting paths through waist-high grass to narrow ridges, down again across great plains. My feet soon become slippery with sweat. We are carrying the equipment – the tripod, stock, the camera, various lenses, some lights. None of us has thought to bring enough water, imagining this to be a twenty minute trek at most. Everyone has assured us it is not far. After years in Africa I laugh at myself for not knowing better.

When we arrive at the farm three hours later my feet are blistered and swollen and I have a bruise across my shoulder where I have slung a rucksack full of small lights. The farm consists of a cluster of thatched huts built around a small compound. Beyond, the great valley spreads to the mountains on the far horizon. It is mid-afternoon and we do not have much time to film: the sun will drop like a stone at six.

Aberash's mother shares her daughter's sculpted beauty, but it is more pronounced in her lean, older face, and accentuated by the way she wears her hair tied up tightly in a black turban. When she smiles her skin is taut across high cheekbones and her thin lips peel back to reveal a large set of perfect white teeth.

Aberash's little sister Mulatu is a very different character from Aberash. Just two years younger she seems less spirited, more timid and passive. I cannot imagine her grabbing a gun and using it. She helps her mother make *njira*, squatting quietly by the fire, a small figure in the dark hut. As the thick woodsmoke fills the air she seems to shrink into the shadows.

Aberash's story really begins with her elder sister Mestawet. At school Mestawet was a superb runner, matched only by her contemporary Duratu. The two girls were friends and competed fiercely with each other, jostling for top position in the school team. Both girls were already tipped to run for their country at the Olympics. In fact, Duratu did go on to win the Olympic Gold

Medal for her country and I have since watched her win the London Marathon.

On the eve of being picked for the national team Mestawet was abducted. I ask her parents to tell me what happened. By now the sun is sinking and the farm glows in treacle-gold light as the shadows lengthen. A cock crows in the distance and a breeze rustles the long grass. It is a peaceful and beautiful setting for such a savage story. Mestawet's mother tells me how her husband tried to rescue their daughter.

'He took a knife and tried to save her. I followed because I was scared they'd kill him. Had he arrived on the scene he himself would have been killed,' she says. She makes a swooping movement with her arm to suggest a brutal stabbing. Then she shrugs.

'We left Mestawet to her abductors because we just didn't want to die.' She bites her lip and stares out at the darkness creeping up on the mountains in the distance. A goat bleats.

Her husband gently takes her hand, then leans towards me. His voice is hoarse.

'We didn't have any choice,' he says. 'We had to leave our daughter Mestawet to such a miserable life.' His face quivers with shame at his own helplessness.

Mestawet is not yet thirty but she looks much older. She is scrawny and her face is worn, with bruise-coloured circles under angry eyes. She wears a brown and white dress in a synthetic material that has once been shiny but is now threadbare. Over it she wears a shabby cardigan, and her hair is hidden beneath a filthy scarf. The laces are missing from her rubber shoes. She now lives with her husband and four children in Kersa.

Kersa is a grim, mean little town made up of delapidated shacks sagging into the mud. As we drive in men stop to stare while we pass. Horses are tethered along the main street, flicking their ill-kempt tails irritably. Women squat by the roadside their clothes trailing in the mud. They gaze after the car indifferently. Boys huddle round rickety table-football, and a man carrying a bench on his head crosses the road very slowly, picking his way over the potholes, puddles and ruts.

Mestawet and her family live in a one-roomed, thatched mud hovel that also serves as a bar. A horse is tied up outside and a man in black chaps and a Marlborough cowboy hat is squelching through the mud towards the front door as we arrive.

Inside it is dark and stinks of stale liquor. On rough benches along the walls of the smoky room men sit drinking *arake*, a fiercely potent, home-brewed spirit. Mestawet, baby on her hip, moves amongst them dispensing drink from a red plastic jug. The men are red-eyed and engaged in a shambolic, tuneless and rowdy sing-song. It is about eleven in the morning. The *arake* fumes are so strong I feel light-headed.

One of Mestawet's sons, aged about six, is carrying round a red hot coal in a spoon so that the men can light their cigarettes. Mestawet's little girl gazes wistfully at the scene from a window in the corner that leads into a boxroom where the family sleep. Mestawet's husband Negash is amongst the revellers. Under a bright green baseball cap he has a jolly face with a gap-toothed smile. He sways along to the singing and laughs throatily before banging his mug on the bench and shouting for more drink. Mestawet moves along the row of men pouring, and ignoring the lewd remarks and obscene gestures.

The men sneer and jeer at us as we film. An old man in white robes, steadying himself on a staff as he drinks, takes a dislike to me.

'You are going to say we are all poor and ignorant,' he slurs.

His eyes are milky under inflamed lids. When I turn to look at him he spits, wipes his mouth on the back of his hand, and he too bangs on the bench for more alcohol.

At the back of the shack is a fire where Mestawet cooks and brews coffee. Beyond that is the yard, a miserable patch of grey, gluey mud. This is where the cow and goat live, where the family bathe, wash clothes and defecate, and where the children play.

Mestawet is washing clothes in a tin tub while her mud-smeared children squat round foetid puddles and cowpats, playing a game with old batteries. They have built a tiny bar out of rusty scraps of metal and the batteries are the mugs from which their fantasy customers are to drink. They whisper amongst themselves as they make their preparations. Then the youngest child begins to cry. Mestawet lifts him up and holds him away from her as he urinates. She laughs, embarassed in front of the camera.

She splashes his legs with some water from the washing tub, and then she kneels down in the mud and pretends to be a guest at her children's bar. She sips from a battery and exclaims at the high quality of the *arake*. The children giggle delightedly. When Mestawet smiles she is beautiful. To me she represents an extraordinary triumph of hope over despair. I would not last a day in that god-forsaken dump.

Despite her fierce love for her children and her determination to bring them up as best she can, Mestawet has not accepted her fate happily. She talks to us as she breast-feeds her baby beneath a blue crocheted shawl.

'I dreamed of being a champion. I used to come first and win medals. I trained hard to improve my long-distance running. I loved sport, but when I was abducted I had to give everything up. I had no intention of getting married. I wanted to complete my education, help support my parents and go on running. Because he kidnapped me I had to give up everything.'

She speaks in her own language and Daniel, a young lawyer who works on a voluntary basis for the Ethiopian Women Lawyers' Association, is translating. Her anger gives her words a jagged sound, but it is this very lack of passivity which invests what she says with dignity. Though her situation is intolerable, she is not a victim. She continues:

'When I look at the men around here, most of them don't care about improving their lives. All that interests them is abducting someone's daughter to become their so-called 'wife'.' She practically spits out the last word.

She is passionate, articulate, intelligent and rebellious. Yet without money there is no escape for this gifted woman, and she has no way of exploiting her talent.

I am fascinated to hear her husband's side of the story. To my surprise Negash readily agrees to talk to us. He lopes happily out to the yard and sits down on a three-legged stool, next to a tethered goat. He wears a mud-spattered pin-striped suit tucked into wellington boots, topped by a green baseball cap which gives him a louche air. I am worried he has not understood what we want to talk to him about, so I ask Daniel, who is going to translate again, to reiterate our line of questioning. Negash looks up at me and winks then laughs.

'He's completely happy,' says Daniel.

'Men abduct when they fall in love,' he begins. 'I myself abducted Mestawet. For one thing I loved her, and second I got angry when she said she didn't want me. In the meantime, my family had arranged another wife for me. But I was so young I thought it was all right to abduct her. I decided to show her who was boss. Besides, I was scared someone else would grab her and I didn't want to miss out.'

Negash's amoral attitude to abduction fascinates and appalls me, even though he does seem to suggest that it was only as a younger man that he had thought it 'all right' to abduct. He carries on blithely:

'I kidnapped her and took her virginity. The next day money was sent to her family and mediators began arranging our wedding. In the meantime she got pregnant. Now we've got four children and we're doing fine.'

He grins and sweeps his arm around as if to show off his splendid kingdom. Behind him, as if in answer, the cow defecates noisily.

'Once a woman gets pregnant she is trapped. She can't escape. She is chained to her home and child. She won't put up a fight after she loses her virginity,' he says. For all his talk of love, Negash has carelessly thwarted Mestawet's dreams and ambitions, in the same casual way he might swat a fly.

'Ask him if he thinks Mestawet's happy,' I urge Daniel.

Daniel smiles at me conspiratorially and asks the question.

Negash pushes the baseball cap to the back of his head and chuckles.

'Let me tell you something,' he says to Daniel, as if letting him in on a priceless philosophical gem. What he says next translates literally as: 'You cannot collect water back up from the floor with your hands,' which is the equivalent to 'no point in crying over spilled milk.' Negash is still chortling as he says this.

Clearly in this far away land of mud, poverty and harshness, abduction and rape are considered a legitimate and normal way of marrying, and women's happiness is not even a consideration. Yet Negash is not a stupid man. He has an intelligent and quite viable theory about why men abduct.

'Parents are also to blame,' he says. 'I want my son to marry the girl I choose. I don't want him to go off with just anyone. But he might fancy a girl he sees and then ask to marry her. If I refuse and insist he marry the girl I've chosen, he'll say, "No, I want this girl!" So he will abduct. This is the kind of thing that pushes men into it, even if families don't approve.'

In a way it is absurd of me to stand there huffing and puffing and feeling outraged and insulted on the behalf of Ethiopian women. My Western feminism is entirely out of place here. This is a culture in which men's choices are also limited – though not to the same appalling extent. I remember that many of the bridegrooms I have seen in the North were as young as eight or nine.

All of them live their lives in a rigid, patriarchal social structure that demands obedience from children regardless of their sex. In such a climate Negash sees abduction in the same way as a Western woman like me might regard elopement: as an act of rebellion, a way of asserting one's choice against parental authority. It is all a matter of perception, and I am going to need to shift my focus enormously if I'm going to unravel the complexities of this culture. It will not help if I regard every man I meet as a potential rapist, and it will certainly not help me to make any sense of Aberash's story.

Staying in Kersa is an experience on a par with staying at the cockroach-infested Hotel Paradise in Kapchorwa, Uganda. We are a relatively large crew. Apart from Daniel, there are Peter the cameraman, Charles the camera assistant from London and Colin the sound recordist from California. Then there are two drivers, Sy and Dave, and our local production manager, Maji.

Maji's mother is a successful businesswoman who owns truck companies and supermarkets, so Maji is highly educated and well connected. She is a beautiful, confident extrovert for whom no problem is insuperable. She makes our job five times easier than it might have been and, more than that, I am grateful to her for teasing me and making me laugh at myself when I take life too seriously.

That night in Kersa I am feeling depressed. Our rooms are mosquito-infested, stifling, concrete boxes with bare bulbs drooping despondently from cobwebbed ceilings, and mattresses with stained, synthetic sheets. There is no running water or lavatory, merely a barn full of human excrement. We need to charge our camera batteries, but there is no electricity except in the bar, where there is a generator but it is being used to power a television. There is a football match on and virtually the entire population of Kersa has gathered to watch. There is no hope of turning off the television for our own needs.

Someone tells us there is a mission nearby with electric power, so Maji and I decide to go with the driver, Dave, to find it. Dave is handsome and, like most men who come within her orbit, rather in love with Maji. He has soulful eyes, drives too fast and has an eclectic collection of wonderful music in his car ranging from esoteric reggae to Eric Clapton singing the blues. I like Dave because nothing fazes him, so I find his presence very soothing.

As it happens, our expedition is a disaster. We struggle out of Kersa on rutted, narrow roads deep in mud and almost impassable. Inevitably we get lost, in an area in which armed robberies are common and night travel notoriously dangerous. And when by some miracle we eventually find the mission the gentle missionaries are far too suspicious and frightened to let us in, and virtually slam the door in our faces. In fairness to them we must look alarmingly scruffy standing there in the shadows.

So we battle our way back to Kersa, and find a little shack

where they agree to cook us scrambled eggs with green peppers. It is all we can find to eat but there is good, strong coffee and home-made ouzo which we drink eagerly, dreading the prospect of the night ahead in our sordid rooms. We huddle round a single oil-lamp and the ouzo is warm and oily in our stomachs.

There's a radio on and while we eat our eggs, our faces dirty and slack with lack of sleep, a solemn newscaster announces that the war with Eritrea is escalating. Rather than depress us, the news seems to enliven us. We begin discussing the war and by the time we make our way back to where we are sleeping it is nearly three in the morning.

We sing as we pick our way through the puddles to our rooms. After my foray into the stinking cowshed of a lavatory I do not want my wellingtons anywhere near my room. I leave them outside and, despite the whining of dive-bombing mosquitoes, fall into a deep sleep.

I sleep for less than three hours. When I wake I am itchy and hot and there is the sound of banging. It is Peter the cameraman knocking on my door to wake me. We are going to film market day in Kersa and need to make an early start. I look at my watch. It is 5.30. I stumble from bed and step outside into a drizzly, dank day. Grey clouds hang heavy, bulging sacks ready to burst under the weight of their watery load.

My wellingtons have of course disappeared, and I have no other footwear with which to negotiate the mud. The wellingtons are worth about five times as much as the price we paid for the rooms so I know there is no point making a fuss, but after so little sleep I am inclined to grumble. I am complaining to Peter when I see Sy, the driver, emerge from his room.

'You don't look so well,' he says.

This probably refers to a number of things – my mood, my dishevelled appearance, my bloodshot eyes, the mosquito bites on my arms.

'Some bastard's stolen my wellingtons,' I say gloomily.

Sy bursts into laughter.

'No, but nearly,' he says.

He darts back into his room and emerges holding them at arms' length. They stink. He saw them lying outside my door last night and rescued them. He knows what a valuable commodity they are in Kersa. The poor man slept with those excrement coated boots next to his bed. I feel humble, grateful, embarrassed and relieved all at the same time.

Market day in Kersa is a big event. Men ride into town from miles around, often in search of a wife. It is a disconcerting time for young women. We are to film Aberash's mother going to market with Aberash's little sister Mulatu.

Mulatu slips her hand into her mother's as they walk along the main street. Men size up Mulatu from wooden carts, or look down at her from their horses. As the crowd thickens Mulatu's mother grips her daughter's hand more tightly.

I have not anticipated the frenzied amount of attention we draw. I am used to crowds in Africa, but nothing has prepared me for this day in Kersa. It is unheard of for white people to visit Kersa, let alone a team of them with camera equipment. On top of that, the market day has its own festive atmosphere. People have gathered from far and wide to buy and sell, but also to be entertained.

The minute we walk into the market place they surge round us, jostling and nudging. I fear for the equipment as well as for our personal safety. We stop to try and film Mulatu's mother buying vegetables. Some tomatoes and roots are laid out on a sack on the ground and two girls who look no older than twelve are sitting holding their hands out for the money.

Peter is trying to find a place to kneel and film, and Colin is pushing in with the microphone. With the tiny digital video camera I am being squeezed on all sides. We are all sweating, hemmed in by cowboys and children.

The cowboys leer and make obscene remarks. A teenage boy pulls my pony tail. I turn on him fiercely but the boy just squeals with delight as the crowd roars with laughter. Then a fat girl leans round and grabs one of my breasts. She makes a remark and some of the crowd titter.

Peter is unable to stand up now because he is being pushed from behind. He cradles the camera and looks anxiously for his assistant Charles, who is trying to edge nearer through the crush. Mulatu is mute, though her mother is trying to carry on as if it is an everyday event to be followed around by a BBC film crew. She is loading vegetables into her bundle and trying to see a way out through the mob.

Just then I feel a sharp pain in my bottom. I turn round to see a small boy with a knife. He has stabbed me. He is gazing at me in wonder, as if astonished that I should be made of flesh and blood.

'Peter,' I hiss, 'We have to move. Now.'

He tries to stand up, but the crowd surges forward and he stumbles.

'Move away!' shouts Peter. In the second the crowd hesitate, we push and elbow our way out and decide to head for the police station.

From then on we are escorted by two policemen, in their big boots and (despite the heat) olive green woolly pullies. They are there to keep the crowds at bay, and we all go on to the butter market in procession. Nothing discreet about our filming.

I am still feeling quite shaken. In such an environment it is not surprising that girls are such easy prey. Young women and girls walk quickly and stealthily, trying to look invisible. A group of men gathers where a lot of horses stand tethered. They eye up the women from under their cowboy hats. Women sidestep wooden carts, and shrink away from gangs of men on horseback. I begin to see how and why Aberash was kidnapped.

We go to the great plain that Aberash had to cross on her way home from school. It is like a greener version of Bonanza country – miles of empty scrub and grass, dotted with occasional acacia thorns and giant anthills. At intervals horsemen gallop along in clouds of dust or trot gently towards town, their shadows long against the sun. This is the heart of the wild South. It would be impossible to hide anywhere in this vast open landscape.

One of the village Elders, who happens to be Negash's uncle, was riding over the plain at the time of Aberash's abduction. He points out the exact spot where Aberash was snatched.

Then he says:

'I myself heard the screams. If I had known she was a relative I might have done something.'

Abduction is such an ordinary, everyday occurrence that no-one takes the blindest bit of notice. The terrain takes on an almost allegorical aspect, like the Plain of Despair in some Ethiopian version of *The Pilgrim's Progress*, as I imagine how terrified I would be to walk across it day after day, anticipating the rumble of approaching hooves, the hiss and lash of lasso and whip.

Aberash herself is curiously calm as she describes her ordeal. She speaks in Amharic and Maji translates. Only a slight frown and a narrowing of the eyes betray her inner turmoil. She was hurled carelessly across a horse, and so fell off three times. Each time she was yanked up and dragged back on. When they finally arrived at a small, isolated farmhouse, she had broken her arm and was severely bruised.

'What happened next?' we prompt her.

She speaks quietly, as if hoping we might not hear:

'My abductor came towards me. He hit me about the face. I nearly lost consciousness. He was a huge man and I couldn't push him away. He beat me senseless and took my virginity.'

It is as simple as that. She lays out the bare facts without feeling the need to embellish them. Afterwards the other abductors come into the hut and see she is bleeding. They give her a chair to sit on. It is then she realises the grim truth.

'The man who raped me was to be my so-called husband,' she says. For the first time she looks angry.

Aberash's ordeal is not over. She has to spend the night there with no attention given to her injuries. By now she is in severe pain and very frightened. Yet she manages to appear composed. In the morning her abductors tease her about being a smart, educated girl from town, despite her farm upbringing, and put salt in her coffee to punish her. After that she is left alone in the hut while two of the men keep guard outside. As the day wears on the men become careless. One of them leaves his gun leaning up against the wall when he goes to eat. Aberash sees her chance and takes it.

She grabs the gun and begins to run. Blessed with swift feet like her sister Mestawet, she manages to flee into a cornfield where she hides. By now her 'husband' has joined the chase and her abductors are closing in on her. It is not long before they find her. Her 'husband' runs towards her, shouting. She fires three warning shots into the air but he comes closer, not believing she will dare turn the gun on him. Trapped, terrified and desperate, Aberash lowers the gun and fires. Her 'husband', twenty-eight year old Gemechu Kebede, falls and dies.

In an instant an angry mob, including members of Gemechu's family and her other abductors, surges round Aberash. They want immediate revenge and justice. She is dragged to the corpse while the crowd argue about what to do with her. They are baying for her blood. They agree her throat must be slit there and then, over the body of her victim, to atone for the murder. The police arrive in time to disperse the crowd, but they then arrest Aberash and take her to the police station, where she is formally charged with murder.

16 SCHOOLGIRL IN THE DOCK
Ethiopia

The police have saved Aberash's life but her victim, Gemechu Kebede, lies in a hillside graveyard, quiet in the shadow of an ancient yew. Ethiopian tombstones are decorative and colourful and his is no exception. It is painted scarlet and bears a portrait of Kebede and a drawing of a tractor to indicate his status as a farmer. We visit the grave with Kebede's brother. He steps up to the grave, removes his cowboy hat and bows his head. We stand quietly while he says a few prayers.

Afterwards his brother tells us Kebede was a well-liked and respected member of his community. I am intrigued to know what made him abduct and rape a fourteen-year-old schoolgirl he has never seen before. What if he decided he did not like Aberash, after he had raped her? Then what? I wonder if men are able to 'return' girls. His brother just shrugs.

He helps us to secure an interview with his parents. When we arrive at the parents' house a very angry younger brother confronts us. His eyes glitter as he points at me and threatens us. He wants us all out of there. We stand our ground. We are with the young lawyer Daniel, who again acts as a calm and professional intermediary. An hour passes. Not understanding what is being said all I can do is stand and wait. At one point Daniel tells us to go outside. Then we go back in again and with Daniel translating I explain why we are there. There is more arguing.

The sun has climbed the sky and we are hot and thirsty so our driver Dave drives off in search of water. Chickens scratch around our feet as the arguments continue. Eventually the younger son is sent away. He stalks off, glaring at us as he goes. His parents are ready to talk.

The family of the man Aberash killed lives in a thatched hut

227

in a meadow full of fruit trees. A horse stands outside, red and blue pom poms dangling from its bridle and tail, and a dog pants in the shade. Inside it is cool and dim. The walls are lined with newspaper, and clothes hang from a line strung amongst the beams.

Kebede's father wears an old raincoat. His wife has milky, near-blind eyes and just one yellow tooth. She is swathed in a white shawl, her hair wound into a tight black turban. Husband and wife sit together on a wooden bench, looking small and vulnerable under the high dome of thatch. He takes his wife's hand and strokes it with slender, trembling fingers.

'She stole our means of survival,' he says, pointing an accusing hand at an imaginary Aberash.

'Our son abducted her for marriage, not to be killed by her. She's given us grief forever.'

Then his wife begins to talk in a rasping, gravelly voice. She uses her hands to stress her points.

'My son did nothing unusual. Many people marry through abduction. There are a lot of women who have good lives, and who go on to have children after marriage through abduction.'

Her son had planned a three-oxen wedding and wanted to invite important people down from the capital, and she had envisaged a great future for him.

'He would have had a beautiful life,' she says, directing her clouded eyes angrily towards us,

'But his friends here misled him. I don't know if this girl wanted him or not – I certainly didn't want any of this to happen. It's ruined all our lives.'

She lets her hands fall into her lap and gazes about her. A buzzing fly settles on her face but she doesn't notice.

I ask them if they have a photograph of their son. The old man walks wearily over to a chest, rummages around and returns with an A4 sized black and white photograph, framed in gold. An elegant, handsome young man stares out, a neat moustache suggesting a sophisticated urbanite rather than a farmer. The parents of this man sit holding their son's photograph between them, facing us so we can take a shot of it.

I notice that the old man is feeling for his wife's hand again, round the edge of the photograph. Both of them hold the frame delicately and carefully, with quivering fingers as though afraid to drop it or defile it. When the old man finds his wife's fingertips he holds them so tight that their hands are clasped together around the last existing image of their beloved son.

'She could have been my daughter-in-law or the mother of my grandchildren,' says the old man, referring to Aberash.

'Now she's just my son's murderer.' They clasp the photograph closer to them.

'We're lost without our son,' says the old man, finally succumbing to tears.

After Aberash is arrested the village Elders gather. Traditionally it is they who act as judges. They are wizened old men swathed in white shawls. They carry long, sturdy staffs and sport a variety of headdresses – one a baseball cap, one a bright green floppy sunhat and the third a towel wrapped around the head turban-style. They sit in a row looking like the three wise men in a mythical tableau.

On Aberash's case they make up their minds quickly and decide that, since there was a loss of life, Aberash's family should pay blood compensation to the victim's family. And Aberash must go into exile, never to return.

Aberash's parents have to sell all their cattle and borrow money from relatives to pay the compensation, but they accept their daughter's fate stoically. Her father tells me:

'In our country, when a woman kills a man she has to go across the river and live far away. Let her live as the Elders decree. It saddens us but we're glad she is alive.'

So Aberash leaves her home and goes to live with a relative in Asela, the regional capital. Here she waits to be charged.

The story is such a scandal that it is not long before the Ethiopian Women Lawyers' Association hears about it. Meaza Ashenafi, one of EWLA's co-founders, travels down to Asela to meet Aberash. Meaza is a tall, beautiful woman who would not look out of place in a Parisian drawing room. Her long, auburn hair is sleek around her face and she wears scarlet lipstick and jewel-coloured silk shirts. She also speaks flawless English.

'This is no ordinary rural girl,' says Meaza, describing the first time she sees Aberash in court.

'We decided to represent Aberash because the case is very symbolic, in that it is almost a revolution against the culture. Abduction is considered as one of the accepted ways of marriage and Aberash is the first woman to challenge and resist it.'

Relatives of Aberash's victim resent the publicity which surrounds her case, and the fact that she has smart lawyers from Addis to defend her. Meanwhile, the Elders feel their authority is being undermined and are furious. They regard the intervention of the lawyers as audacious and unnecessary. As far as they are concerned, the case is closed, finished.

Meaza decides that Aberash is not safe where she is, so as soon as EWLA begins planning the defence Meaza moves Aberash to the relative safety of an obscure orphanage in Addis where we go to visit her.

It is an eerie place on a hill high above the city. We drive through heavy iron gates and up a long drive. Tall trees close out the light with long branches and compound the dismal atmosphere. The orphanage itself is housed in a big, grey building. Weeds sprout round the steps leading up to the front door and a teddy bear peeks forlornly from an upstairs window.

We are not alone for long. News of our arrival spreads fast and within minutes we are surrounded by excitable girls. Colin, our sound-recordist, wears his hair in a pony-tail. That, combined with a scarlet baseball cap and a pair of purple wraparound sunglasses, gives him instant heart-throb status amongst the girls. They are confused about his surname, which is Belton, and think he is related in some way to the popstar Michael Bolton. When we come on a second visit the love letters start arriving. Girls throw them into the car windows. Others just droop around, leaning on the bonnet, sighing and gazing lovingly.

The girls are typical lovelorn teenagers, but they are also kind and sensitive to people's feelings. Aware that Peter and Charles are not receiving the same amount of attention as Colin, they politely pretend to be equally susceptible to all three.

'You are handsome too,' they say to Charles, with shining, merry eyes.

'Oh, and you too, Peter.' They are adorable.

Inside the dormitories are crammed with two-tiered bunkbeds decked out in cheerful striped counterpanes. Aberash has a top bunk near a window which looks onto the lugubrious cypress trees. Here she keeps her most treasured possessions – a couple of books and a bottle of metallic green nail varnish.

Here, too, Aberash talks of how homesick she feels. She says she cannot go back home even for a visit, for fear that someone in Kebede's family will see her.

'My abductor's family sees me getting all this publicity. They think I'm doing very well out of it. They don't want me to win. They want me to pay for the death of their son. They want to shorten my life.'

Aberash does not exaggerate. Daniel communicates his anxiety to Meaza:

'The parents of the dead man say they want to see justice done. They don't want to see the eyes of their son's killer. They say they want her dead. I'm not sure if they will wait for the court's verdict, or if they will take matters into their own hands.'

All the weight of the law cannot protect Aberash against this local vigilante-style justice.

Meaza has acted as a surrogate mother to Aberash since she has been living in Addis. She lives up many flights of stairs in a big airy flat overlooking the city. Somewhat grudgingly Meaza agrees to let us film Aberash visiting her. The minute Aberash arrives Meaza hugs and kisses her, plies her with tea and cookies and listens to all her worries with concern. I find Meaza's manner a little bit artificial but little Aberash cannot stop smiling. She is much in awe of her glamorous patron.

But as cosmopolitan Addis replaces her life on the remote farmstead, Aberash is beginning to change. In French cafés

231

women wearing suede and gold sit at tables laid with gingham cloths and sip espresso from tiny cups. Men in designer sunglasses read European broadsheets as they pick at croissants or *pains au chocolat*. Teenage girls wearing Hilfiger and Lauren chatter in French over their capuccinos.

At the newer American-style diners boys in box-fresh trainers queue for cheeseburgers, and teenagers sit around big tables and flirt as they sip coke and feed each other French fries. This is a metropolitan élite, a long, long way from Aberash's rural roots. Yet she seems quite at home browsing through a boutique or eating ice-cream in a shopping mall.

Sometimes I feel Aberash has deliberately stowed her emotions away where they cannot pierce her polished surface. She is coolly dismissive about boys, in particular shrugging off the idea of having a boyfriend. But there is one way to puncture her façade. Just to mention her little sister brings out in Aberash the frightened, guilty, helpless little girl:

'My little sister Mulatu wouldn't be stuck at home if I could do anything about it. The same fate as mine will happen to her. There's nothing I can do about it,' she says.

To avoid the terrifying walk home across the open plain where Aberash was abducted, Mulatu is staying with a relative in Kersa itself. Even so, she never walks to school on her own.

'I think what happened to Aberash will happen to me soon,' she says. 'I've been terrified ever since Aberash was abducted. I can't even go home to the countryside on my own. I'm always scared to go to school or market.'

The boys in Mulatu's class do appear to be much older than her, many like grown men. It is hard to remember they are schoolboys and not potential kidnappers and rapists, especially in the light of Mulatu's fear.

'Ever since Aberash's abduction I've been terrified of the boys at school. They keep saying they will abduct me too,' stammers Mulatu.

'Even when I'm surrounded by friends at breaktime, they come up to me and tease and threaten me. They say: "Where will you find a gun to kill us like your sister did?" '.

Almost more poignant than Mulatu's fear and Aberash's dismay is their parents' sense of utter helplessness.

'How can we protect our children from these kidnaps?' asks her father.

He is on the verge of tears yet controls them – crying does no good. Nothing does.

'Abductors are always following girls around,' he goes on, 'They don't care whether the girls finish their schooling or not. If only we could, we'd move them away from here.'

Homesick, miserable, in exile and facing an official trial for murder, Aberash is paradoxically far safer than her little sister living in the bosom of her loving family.

Eventually a date is set for the trial. A stern-looking woman lawyer accompanies Aberash from Addis back to Asela, the regional capital. Aberash shrinks back in the car, clutching a teddy bear. She wears a scarf round her hair and an American sweat-shirt. The court is housed in an ugly, squat, concrete building. Crowds have gathered.

Inside Aberash stands in the dock, nervously picking at her bangles. The courtroom is full. People crane their necks from the public benches to look at the outrageous young woman who has killed her husband.

The three judges walk in and take their seats at high backed chairs behind a big, plain table. The chairs screech as they scrape on the floor. As they whisper amongst themselves Aberash's eyes widen in alarm. The only hope now is that her lawyer can persuade the judges she has acted in self-defence. This plea will depend on how well her lawyer interrogates the witnesses. These sit on a simple wooden chair in the middle of the room, facing the judge with their backs to Aberash and her lawyer.

One of the witnesses, a middle-aged man with bright blue eyes, was at the police station when Aberash was brought in. He testifies to the fact that she was beaten so badly she couldn't walk. He says he thought her arm was broken, and lifts his own to show how it hung limply.

This seems to be the evidence so desperately needed to prove Aberash's life was endangered. Most witnesses claim to have been in the vicinity, to have heard the shots and seen the mob gathering, but none can say exactly what happened.

The judges adjourn, and when they reconvene the atmosphere is tense. People in the crowd stare at Aberash and listen to the judges, brows furrowed and mouths slack with the effort of concentrating. The presiding judge sums up. He speaks in a low monotone, reading from his notes. Aberash's lawyer frowns and leans forward to hear him.

'He took her virginity by force,' the judge is saying. He rumbles on:

'The deceased used force to harm the defendant. His action violates the law. The court understands the defendant has been deprived of the right she has been given by law to defend herself. The action she took was the only course she had to defend herself.'

Aberash's lawyer is motionless, holding her breath. The judge is quoting various Articles of Law. Aberash's eyes have never looked so wide. Then, just as suddenly and in the same monotone, the judge says:

'This court sets you free.'

Aberash buckles. In the film, she disappears from the frame as she reacts to the news she has hardly dared hope for. The courtroom remains silent. No-one reacts straight away. Aberash's lawyer bows stiffly to the judge. It is only when she catches her lawyer's eye that Aberash allows herself to smile. Once she starts, she cannot stop.

The family comes together to celebrate in a small bar, where a musician has been laid on for dancing. Aberash dances with her brother and then with Mulatu, radiant tonight, her worries forgotten. The sisters dance together, wriggling their shoulders in the traditional way.

Their father claps along, his face glowing with happiness. He leans over and kisses his delighted wife on the cheek. Then he stands up to dance with his daughter. Unable to restrain himself he hugs her to him, whooping with delight as the family clap and cheer them on. In the affray his hat falls off and he laughs and holds his daughter closer.

Yet Aberash's freedom is illusory. She is still unable to return home. As far as the Elders are concerned the judgement of the court is meaningless. Whether or not she killed in self-defence and is not guilty is irrelevant. She has killed a man and tradition dictates that she remain in exile. The following morning her parents have no choice but to leave without her.

Aberash's older sister Mestawet was unable to leave her children to travel to the trial, so we persuade Aberash to travel safely and secretly with us to visit her. It is the first time she has returned to her home since her exile began. Daniel comes with us to look after Aberash and as we drive into Kersa he tries to convince her she will be safe. The cowboys stop to stare. Any one of them could be related to her abductor.

'I'm scared,' she says in a tiny voice. Daniel puts his arm round her to comfort her but she is rigid with fear.

Mestawet rushes out of her hovel to greet her sister. In the mud, they embrace for a full two minutes, kissing each other time and time again on each cheek and then on the mouth. Mestawet draws Aberash inside, where the children cluster round very much in awe of their aunt in her jeans and sweat shirt.

Mestawet makes coffee. She has a hacking cough bubbling away in her throat. The smoke from the fire exacerbates it but she is so excited to see Aberash she does not care. She begs Aberash to stay the night but Aberash says it is far, far too dangerous. It will not take long for the word to spread that she is in town and there are plenty of people still baying for her blood.

While the sisters talk Daniel allows himself to accept a tiny glass of *arake* from Negash. Daniel's eyes water as he sips,

'It's strong stuff,' he says.

'It keeps you warm in the winter,' says Negash, chuckling.

'Ah, so you wear your coat on the inside,' says Daniel.

I think it is rather ironic that Aberash's great supporter, and a lawyer who defends women's rights so vigorously, can end up drinking with a self-confessed abductor, and we say so in the film. It makes Daniel absolutely furious.

Mestawet is fiercely proud of her sister and I am impressed by her ability to admire Aberash without envy.

'When I heard that Aberash had killed her abductor I was overcome with joy,' she says.

'I can't say there won't be any more abduction, but men are a little bit more afraid to abduct girls now. I think men will only change if the law on abduction is strictly enforced. If the law continues to be lax men will be out of control forever.'

Sadly, Mestawet's faith in the impact of Aberash's actions is unfounded. The result of Aberash's trial has done nothing to alleviate Mulatu's fears. We visit Mulatu at her relative's house and find her in a back room squatting over a charcoal brazier brewing coffee.

'I have no hope,' she says without self-pity. 'All I can do is hide at home and I won't be able to finish school. I think about living with Aberash but it's impossible. I have nowhere else to go. All I can do is wait to be abducted.' She turns back to the coffee with a shrug.

We return to Addis Ababa with Aberash. She has been set free but none of her abductor's accomplices have been brought to justice, and she is furious.

'No action has been taken against these criminals; they can commit the same crime again. Nothing's been done to stop them so they're encouraged to go on abducting,' she says, thinking about Mulatu. I can see real anger in her eyes.

'I don't think of myself as having murdered anyone,' she says.

'When I think of all my suffering, the way I see it I just killed my enemy. I don't feel sorry for him as I would for anyone else. I could have been killed myself.'

Aberash's life has changed irrevocably. She cannot return to her old life even if she wants to.

For us, it is time to leave. We buy Aberash some clothes and shoes and go to Meaza's flat to say goodbye. I go to a bedroom to thank Aberash privately, and to give her some money for the next few months. She is distraught.

'You have to take me with you,' she says, shrilly. 'I cannot stay here. I will die.'

I try to explain that it is impossible for her to come with us, and that we are leaving to-morrow.

'I can stay with you,' she says. 'You can find me work.'

I tell her I wish life was that simple, but she has neither passport nor visa and it is impractical for her to become my dependant.

'The best thing you can do is finish your education,' I say, aware that I am sounding both pompous and heartless.

She begins to plead. All she wants to do is leave Ethiopia. She holds on to me, begging.

'I'm sorry Aberash, I can't,' I say, and then I begin to cry myself.

Saying goodbye to Mestawet is just as hard. I have so much admiration for her courage and defiance and when I leave we hug for five minutes, holding tight as if to imbue one other with our different strengths.

'You are an amazingly strong woman,' I say to her. I hate leaving her, imprisoned in her squalid life with nothing to look forward to but toil and poverty and mud.

Later I hear that Mestawet has actually made a brave and determined bid for freedom. She left her husband and children and disappeared. I rejoice for her, and hope desperately that her intelligence and determination will enable her to survive in what amounts to an alien environment. A short while later I hear that she has returned, unable to abandon her children. As far as I know she is still in Kersa.

Later still there was happier news for Aberash and Mulatu. When the film was finally broadcast there was an extraordinary reaction. The story captured the public's imagination and I was inundated with letters and offers of help. Some people sent cheques, others asked what they could do. Aberash and Mulatu were found places in a secure, safe boarding school and with the support of a wonderfully selfless couple called Peter and Jenny

Metaxa-Barham we set up a trust to pay their school fees.

Part of me felt happy with what we had achieved. Professionally, too, the film was an unqualified success. It attracted a great deal of warming praise from people who really know Ethiopia well, and whose good opinion I value greatly. It also went on to win several awards, and was short-listed for the One World Media Award for Best Documentary. As a maker of documentary films I had, if you like, arrived.

But another part of me was uncomfortable with how little I had been able to do for so many people in deep distress: Aberash, Mestawet, Nibret the little child bride, and all the others. I come, I see, I weep. I film, I hug, I weep again, and then I go. The best part of the job is when you feel you may have made a difference. The hardest part is when you have to walk away.

EPILOGUE

I have come a long way since my first trip to Africa nearly twenty years ago. Back then I was by no means sure I wanted to work in film, and I had no conception of what this vast continent had to offer beyond exotic holidays. Certainly I had no idea it would change me irrevocably, and that as part of that process I would learn my trade.

The films I made in Africa launched my directing career. Yet more than any skill of mine it was the Africans who took part that made some of my best films compelling; characters like Aberash, Dr. Piri, Wingstone, Professor Makumbe, Irene and Amina. Their presence breathed warmth and life into my serious, issue-driven and often potentially chilling documentaries. Uncomfortable subjects which at first glance had no apparent relevance to our own lives – child marriage, polygamy, cholera, albinism or female genital mutilation – became the stories of people we liked and cared about.

After much early doubt and disappointment I am gradually recovering my belief that the right films, properly used, can be of value. They can challenge prejudice, educate, inform, inspire, surprise and even entertain along the way. They can help raise funds. They can also be used to lobby agencies and even governments, and thus lead to reform and change. My films have been seen in the House of Commons and at UN conferences round the world, as well as on television and in classrooms, both African and European.

But that growing confidence leaves no room for complacency. I am not an aid worker, I am a film-maker and my usefulness can legitimately be questioned. Sometimes I am accused of 'interfering' in other people's ways of life, and of 'judging' them. I have to be reminded that, seen through African eyes, mine is the alien culture.

Of course my Western liberal values have occasionally coloured my views. Sometimes too when presenting an upsetting situation I have been unable to resist milking it a bit, to tweak the audience's heartstrings. Similarly I have discreetly assisted some self-serving politicians, fundamentalist sheiks and women wielding circumcision blades to reveal themselves in their least appealing light. Everyone knows films are made in the cutting room and that people's words and actions are edited.

So no film can truthfully claim to be entirely objective, and nor can this book. My films and this book alike may reveal nearly as much about me as they do about the people and the cultures they portray. What I have tried to do is to be as honest as possible about my reactions, prejudices and motivations, accepting that in the process I may sometimes be doing myself no favours.

Much about Africa continues to confuse and shock me, but I am learning all the time how much and in what specific ways it has changed me. Both my parents became fatally ill with cancer while I was filming in Africa. From Africans I learned how to cope with illness and death with far more dignity and acceptance than I imagined possible. African women in particular have taught me to be deeply grateful for my education, and to value the freedom to choose whether or not to marry, or to have children. Above all, their ability to sustain optimism in the face of dire poverty, disease, drought, cruelty, pain and war has been a lasting inspiration.

It is Africa's biggest tragedy that it is fast losing its most precious resource – its best people. Aberash is typical: she will not rest until she is out of Ethiopia for good. She has no intention of using her precious education to benefit her own country. To this day I receive letters from her begging me to find her a home in London.

Worse, when Africans do plough their talent and education back into their own countries they are often thwarted, pushed aside or prevented from helping – just as Dr. Manasseh Piri was removed from his post by the Zambian president, and KSM was deprived of his radio frequency in Ghana.

As I write I have not been back to Africa for four years. I have been making films in other parts of the world: Britain, the Middle East and America. A chapter of my life has closed, and a new one opened. But I still crave Africa. I miss the smell of it, the heat, the bustle, the beauty, the chaos.

Most of all I miss Africans. It is a devastated continent yet everywhere I went I found people with the strength to endure unspeakable hardship, the energy to challenge complacency, the courage to speak out against corruption, and the determination to educate their children and give them better lives. These are men and women who passionately believe that eventually the twenty-first century will belong to Africa. Perhaps it will. I would love to believe so.

ABOUT EYE BOOKS

Eye Books is a young, dynamic publishing company that likes to break the rules. Our independence allows us to publish books which challenge the way people see things. It also means that we can offer new authors a platform from which they can shine their light and encourage others to do the same.

To date we have published 30 books that cover a number of genres including Travel, Biography, Adventure and History. Many of our books are experience driven. All of them are inspirational and life-affirming.

Frigid Women, for example, tells the story of the world-record making first all female expedition to the North Pole. A fifty-year-old mother of three who had recently recovered from a mastectomy, and her daughter are the authors – neither had ever written a book before. Sue Riches is now both author and highly sought after motivational speaker.

We also publish thematic anthologies, such as The Tales from Heaven and Hell series, for those who prefer the short-story format. Here everyone has the chance to get their stories published and win prizes such as flights to any destination in the world.

And here's what makes us really different: As well as publishing books, Eye Books has set up a club for like-minded people and is in the process of developing a number of initiatives and services for its community of members. After all, the more you put into life, the more you get out of it.

Please visit www.eye-books.com for further information.

NEW TITLES BY EYE BOOKS

Jasmine and Arnica

– Nicola Naylor

Nicola Naylor experienced India in a way that few others will, as a sightless European woman alone – and in so doing learnt more than she had expected. She came home with an enhanced understanding of aromatic oils, but also of her own inner strength and resilience. Jasmine and Arnica is a powerful and evocative celebration of her remarkable journey.

ISBN: 1 903070 171. Price £9.99. April 2003

Touching Tibet

Niema Ash

Touching Tibet takes the reader on a unique journey into the heart of this intriguing forbidden kingdom. Niema reveals some of the country's most fascinating secrets; unveiling the truth behind the mystery and painting a picture of places which few will ever see.

ISBN: 1 903070 18X. Price £9.99. August 2003

Behind the Veil

Lydia Laube

Behind the Veil is the honest and sometimes shocking account of an Australian woman's resolve to survive in the hostile environment of a Saudi Arabian hospital. Wearing head-to-toe coverings in stifling heat, and battling against unfathomable bureaucracy, Lydia managed to maintain her sanity whilst struggling to carry out her work.

ISBN: 1 903070 198. Price £9.99. September 2003

Riding the Outlaw Trail

Simon Casson

A true story of an epic horseback journey by two Englishmen from Mexico to Canada, across 2,000 miles of some of America's most difficult terrain. The objective? To retrace the footsteps of those legendary real life bandits Butch Cassidy and the Sundance Kid, by riding the outlaw trails they rode more than a century ago.

ISBN: 1 903070 228. Price £9.99. January 2004

First Contact

Mark Anstice

This is a true story of modern day exploration by two young adventurers and the discovery of cannibal tribes in the 21st century. An expedition far more extraordinary than they had ever imagined, one that would stretch them, their friendship and their equipment to the limits.

ISBN: 1 903070 260. Price £9.99. March 2004